KITCHEN ANTIQUES

HARPER COLOPHON BOOKS
Harper & Row, Publishers
New York, Cambridge, Hagerstown, Philadelphia
San Francisco, London, Mexico City, São Paulo, Sydney

Acknowledgements
Mr. & Mrs. David Malkins
Nancy & Don E. Bailey
Michael Parten, Interior Designer, Richard Parten
Bonnie Grossman of Ames Gallery, Berkeley, California
Kim & Kirk Craig
Bernice Pereboom and Erwin Pereboom owners of Crescent Cottage
Jerry Stamps, Marcia Yearsley, Decorator
Jeffrey Mayfield
Gloria M. Follett, Geraldine Townsend, Eureka Springs, Arkansas
Crystal Gardens Antiques, 190 Spring Street, Eureka Springs, Arkansas 72632
Louise S. Young, NYC
Carol Zimmerman, Interior Designer
Babs Watkins, Design Accessories

Special thanks to Hugh Van Dusen, Cynthia Merman, Karen Graul, Elaine Greene, Barbara Bucholz

For Libby

Produced by Jeffrey Weiss

Text by Susan Osborn
Design by R.J. Luzzi
Production: Color Book Design , Walter Berkower, Richard & Dan Sirota, Barbara Frontera
Photography by David Leach
Additional Photography: Michael Kanouff, Jon Elliot, Jeffrey Weiss , Nick Gunderson

 For information address Harper & Row, Publishers, Inc., 10 East 53rd Street, New York, N.Y. 10022. Published simultaneously in Canada by Fitzhenry & Whiteside Limited, Toronto.

FIRST EDITION

LIBRARY OF CONGRESS CATALOG CARD NUMBER: 80–7831

ISBN: 0–06–090813–0

80 81 82 83 10 9 8 7 6 5 4 3 2 1

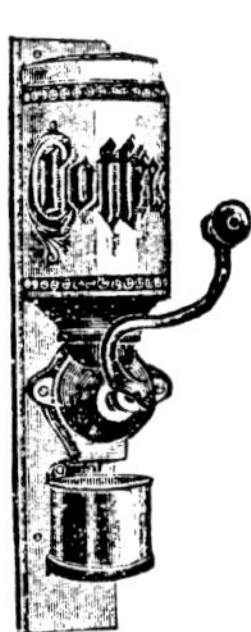

The simple functional beauty and ingenious design of kitchen antiques make them appealing to everyone. Kitchen utensils are straightforward, honest and utilitarian. They are rarely made of precious metals and they seldom bear the maker's name. Every kitchen utensil has a unique personality; people are attracted by their pleasing shapes, their weight and feel, the smooth wooden knobs and handles, the neatly-fitting gears and the gleam and shine of polished metals. Some old kitchen implements were crafted by experienced artisans; others were crudely forged by unskilled householders who devised their own tools out of necessity. Kitchen antiques form an invaluable record of our social history. We can see how the fully automatic kitchen of the 20th century evolved from the wood and iron utensils used by the first American settlers. By looking at kitchen antiques, we can trace changes in fashion and our economy, and we can detect the influence of the city on the country and of the country on the city. Historians and hoarders alike are discovering that there is intrigue and art to be found in the old kitchen.

When the first settlement of Jamestown was established in 1607, the Colonists lived in crude, one-room shelters, often a thatched-roof hut or a hovel dug into the side of a hill. The single room served as kitchen, bedroom and living room. It had a minimum of furniture, few windows and a dirt floor.

As houses were enlarged, the kitchen, or common room, remained the home's center of activity. All cooking was done over the fire. The fireplace was made of stone or brick. Some of the earliest fireplaces were eight to ten feet wide, large enough to roast a whole animal. Some had a small window in the back and benches inside where one could sit for warmth. The chimney was made of wood, daubed on the inside with clay. A wooden lug pole hung inside the chimney and cooking pots were suspended by hooks over the fire. A housewife could cook a whole meal in one pot by putting various foods in a jar or linen bag and placing the bag into a cauldron filled with boiling water. By the early 18th century, the wooden lug pole was replaced by a wrought-iron chimney crane, or reckon. This crane consisted of a horizontal bar forged to an iron hinge which was secured to the back of the hearth. The crane could be swung out into the room, making it easier to remove kettles.

The housewife of the 17th and 18th centuries was occupied with chores unknown to many 20th-century homemakers. Every bit of food was precious, and grain and flesh had to be kept from autumn to spring. The housewife preserved as much food as she could. She made her own sauces, pickles and jams. She ground spices and prepared setting agents from animal bones. She made rising agents from ale and polishes and washing compounds from beeswax and ashes. The coldest side of the kitchen was fitted with shelves and stands where the housewife stored her preserved foods and utensils not in daily use. Dried fruits and herbs were stored in homemade paper bags. Butter was salted and packed into stone jars or oak firkins. Lard was kept in pigs' bladders and sausages in intestines. Cheese was stored in a dark cool place, turned each day and rubbed with fat fired out of salt pork. Salt-glazed stoneware crocks were used for keeping jam, preserved fruits, salted foods, cider and vinegar. Jars were kept airtight by stretching a bladder or cloth dipped in wax or mutton fat over the opening. Salt, the most precious preservative, was stored in a box or jar by the fire to keep it dry.

For the most part, the earliest kitchen utensils were crafted by the members of the family. Brooms, brushes, cheese hoops, butter paddles and bread troughs were all made at home. Most of the homemade implements were made of wood. The householder made his own mortars and pestles, bowls, plates, spoons, noggins and peels, long-handled unpierced flat blades used to turn baked goods. As villages developed, craft shops were established and kitchen utensils were made by professional artisans according to the needs of the community.

Simplicity, a lack of ornamentation and a direct relationship between form and function characterize 17th- and early 18th-century utensils. Potters made storage jars, jugs, pitchers, bowls, mugs and milk pans. Wet or "tight" coopers made kegs and casks for liquids; dry or "slack" coopers made barrels for bulk commodities like flour and sugar. The coppersmith made pots, pans and skillets. The blacksmith was of greatest importance to the community. (Indeed, because the blacksmith also forged weapons and ammunition, he was the most carefully guarded member of a town during a war.) The blacksmith forged cauldrons, grills, trivets, gridirons, skillets, spits, pierced spoons for skimming and skewers. The skewer was an indispensable utensil for cooking meat in the 17th- and 18th-century kitchen. Meat was fastened to the iron pin, usually six to eight inches long, and roasted over the fire. Every tool used in the preparation of food had a long (up to five feet) handle, to keep the cook from burning her hands.

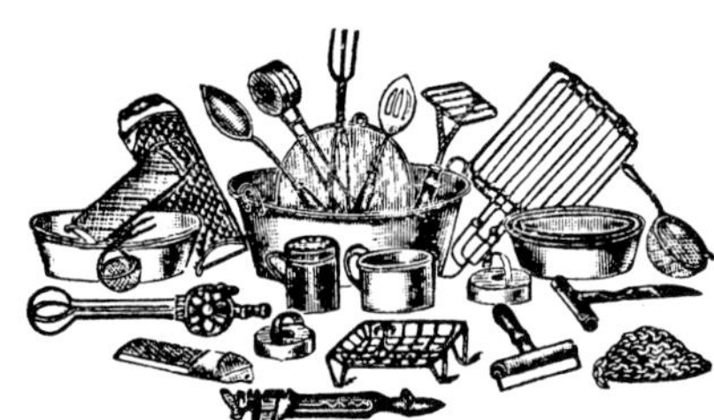

The first pewtersmith is listed as working in 1635, but until after the Revolutionary War, the pewtersmith struggled to earn a living. No tin deposits had been discovered in North America and tin was imported from England. (Pewter is basically tin with a percentage of copper added.) Because the British levied high duties on block tin and no duties on finished pewter, British pewter poured in to the Colonies while the local smiths were limited to repairing or reworking old pieces. Naturally, early marked examples of American pewter are now highly prized. The early pewtersmith was influenced by the work of the silversmith, but pewter forms show a much greater simplicity of design and decoration. At the time, pewter was known as "poor man's silver" for only the wealthy and the Church owned silver. The variety of pewter goods was limited to porringers, tankards, plates, tea and coffee pots and pitchers.

During the late 18th century, the kitchen was further expanded. Chimneys now included an oven and and an adjustable pot hook, or trammel, which was used to raise or lower pots over the fire. Utensils showed a subtle refinement. There were more sizes to choose from and some were ornamented simply. More varied metals were used to make utensils. Pewter rather than wood was the common material used for tableware. Copper and brass were more frequently used to make molds and other utensils. Although these metals were more expensive than iron, their lighter weight offered greater convenience and made them more attractive to the housewife.

Craftsmen formed a greater variety of tin utensils. They made tin candlesticks, lanterns, graters, coffee roasters and even a special oven for roasting meat. Many products formerly made only of iron could be made of tin and carried by itinerant peddlers to isolated communities. Although ninety percent of these products were undecorated (since tin is fragile and ages quickly, neither the craftsman nor the consumer was interested in "fancying up" a piece of tin), some housewives did decorate their tinware by painting, punching, wriggling or japanning. Japanning is the application of a varnish-like coating that imitated the look of Oriental lacquer. Potters made colanders, bowls, crocks and jugs. Wood was still used for mortars and pestles, grinders, storage boxes and rolling pins.

By the end of the 18th century, there were more utensils suited for a particular job. A housewife baked in a Dutch oven, a covered pot which stood on its legs in the embers. The top of the lid was covered with coals, producing enough heat to bake bread. A kettle-tilter was used to pour soups or other liquids from a kettle without lifting it. The tilter, also known as a lazy-back or idle-back, was an adjustable handle which allowed the housewife to tip the suspended kettle without the risk of burning her hands. A flip dog or toddy dog was used to heat drinks. The long-handled implement had either a tear-shaped or pointed end and was placed directly into the fire and then into a drink, adding a pleasant smoky flavor.

Industrialization brought remarkable advances in the way Americans lived. The kitchen of the 19th century bore the mark of the machine age. Until the 1850s and 1860s, utensils were basically handcrafted by the blacksmith, the cooper, the tinsmith, the itinerant craftsman and the householder. But after the Civil War, labor-saving devices were mass produced in factories in New York, Boston, Philadelphia and St. Louis and were made widely available to the public. Thousands of people patented tens of thousands of inventions, some practical and some inept, in an attempt to make housework easier. In fact, there were so many inventions patented in the early part of the century that in 1833 the head of the Patent Office wanted to retire because, he said, everything "seems to be done."

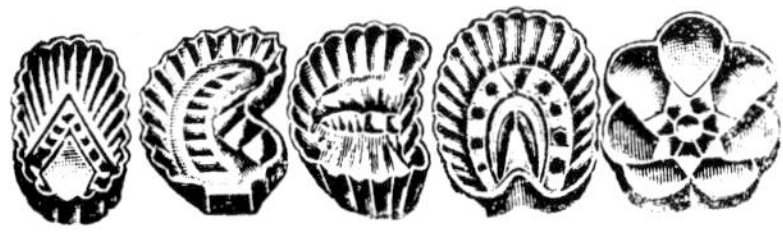

In the early part of the 19th century, the stove replaced the fireplace. Although iron cooking stoves were available at the end of the 18th century, they were not standard kitchen equipment until the middle of the 19th century. New, lighter, smaller pots and pans, made to fit the lid openings of the stove tops, replaced fireplace utensils. The development of Sheffield plate and electroplated silver, both stronger and more resilient than silver, permitted the manufacture of cheaper, sturdier cookware. Pewter bowls were replaced by ceramic ones, especially those made of yellowware. By the 1830s, yellowware was made in molds which allowed the potter to make bowls with embossed patterns. By the late 19th century and early 20th century, yellowware was offered in three- or five-piece sets through mail-order catalogues. Steam power made cooking much quicker. The "digester," the forerunner of the 20th-century pressure cooker, softened bones to make soup or broth. Crank-operated devices pared fruit, seeded raisins, ground meat and cracked nuts. One of the first wooden iceboxes was patented in 1803. Before the 19th century, the only way to keep food from spoiling was to dry it or preserve it with salt. There was some confusion over the purpose of the early icebox though. Most people thought it was important to save the ice, so they wrapped the ice in a blanket which preserved the ice but not the food. By 1840, tin- and zinc-lined iceboxes were patented. Ice cut from a lake or delivered by the iceman was placed in the botton of the box and food was placed on top of it. Not until the 1850s did people discover that the ice should be at the top of the unit with air circulating around it. By 1860, a "refrigerator" was marketed, which consisted of a top capinet filled with pieces of crushed ice and a drain for carrying off melted ice. The late 19th-century icebox provided a much greater variety of foods for the average American.

There was a dramatic upheaval in the way people lived after World War I. Family life had changed, few people had kitchen staffs, and 19th-century inventions had radically altered the nature of housework. Convenience and practicality were the watchwords of the new century. Kitchens looked clean, white and antiseptic. Floors were covered with washable, waxable tiles or lineoleum, and a glossy, easy-to-clean enamel was painted on the walls and ceiling. Sinks, stoves and refrigerators were covered with white porcelain. The geometric Machine Art style of the 1920s imposed pure forms on most household objects. Following the lead of the artists of the time, designers saw purity of form as the only eternal, valid design solution. During the '30s, designers formed more organic shapes by making greater use of compound curves and sculptural space, but the design remained basically geometric. Even tableware took on the geometric shapes of the '20s with finely finished surfaces as their only decoration.

New gadgets were invented to take advantage of lightweight, easy-to-clean materials like aluminum, stainless steel and Bakelite. For the first time, a housewife could give up her heavy cast-iron and hard-to-clean copper and brass utensils.

Electricity revolutionized the kitchen in the 20th century and freed housewives from many laborious, time-consuming tasks. For the first time, electricity was the source of heat for cooking foods. Westinghouse marketed the first electric frying pan in 1911. The electric egg beater was another welcome invention. Before the prepackaged mixes of the 20th century, the housewife prepared her cakes and puddings from basic ingredients. Although hand-operated egg beaters were developed as early as 1869, and lightweight beaters with tin or stainless steel blades and gears and wooden or Bakelite handles had been manufactured in the early part of the century, the introduction of General Electric's portable, electric "Handy Ann" in 1926 was a great success. But perhaps the most significant development of the early 20th century came in 1914 with the introduction of an electric refrigerator that could make artificial ice. This new machine made the iceman—with his picks, chisels and tongs—obsolete. The refrigerator eliminated the need for large storage containers for perishables. Manufacturers designed lightweight glass containers suitable for the smaller quantities of food kept in a refrigerator. In fact, many refrigerator manufacturers used glass as a promotion and sold refrigerators fully equipped with various-sized glass containers. During the Depression, inexpensive glass containers, made predominantly in green, blue and amber and occasionally embossed, were used as refrigerator containers. By the 1930s, electric appliances like waffle irons were designed with automatically controlled heating systems. An electric toaster with a timer mechanism was developed in the 1920s, but the toaster only had coils on one side so when the timer indicated that the heat was off, the cook had to turn the bread around to brown the other side. By the middle of the 1930s, a fully automatic pop-up toaster was developed.

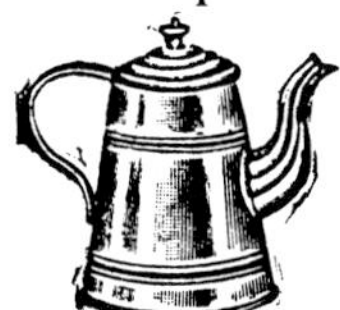

Many utensils used during the 17th and 18th centuries were still used in the 20th century, but they were made of plastic and other synthetic materials instead of wood and metal. Trivets were no longer needed after the stove replaced the fireplace, but they were still used on the dinner table. Tin and twisted wire, silver, nickel-plate, china, crystal and tile trivets replaced the hand-forged, cast-iron trivet used on the early American hearth.

Individuals, decorators and professional collectors are discovering the fascination of kitchen antiques. Except for those made in the 17th and early 18th centuries, there is a wide variety still available. A restoration or historical society can provide information on utensils you can expect to find in your area. Kitchen antiques can be found at thrift shops, flea markets, garage sales, house auctions and antique shops. For a few dollars, a collection can be started at a used-merchandise store like Goodwill or the Salvation Army. Take time to look carefully through all the boxes. Most of the merchandise will be 20th-century, but you may find a real, old jewel. Check newspapers for garage sales, church bazaars, rummage sales and street fairs. If you go to an auction, arrive early and inspect the merchandise for its character and condition. Large, well-established flea markets are probably the best place to find a variety of utensils made of different materials. Antique shops are good places to find old kitchen utensils, but they are usually the most expensive place to buy. Beware of artificially distressed surfaces; some antique shops are notorious for painting a new patina on an old piece of iron or wood.

The value of a kitchen antique is determined by its condition, quality, workmanship, scarcity, beauty, historical interest and collectibility. Although rusted, worn or damaged merchandise is never as valuable or desirable as merchandise in good condition, kitchenware is utilitarian, not decorative, and any utensil will show signs of age and use. Prices vary from month to month and city to city. The demand for an item may be high now, but not a year from now. Because kitchen antiques have only recently been considered collectible, most are still reasonably priced. But their value is increasing as more people discover their allure. The more you look, the more you will be able to form your own price guide. Although 17th- and 18th-century utensils have been collected for years, making their prices immoderate, there is still an illimitable and affordable variety of 19th- and 20th-century antiques. Just a few of the less expensive items include biscuit cutters, corkscrews, beetles, molds, sifters, juice extractors, knives, raisin seeders, whisks, pot hooks, funnels, baking pans, fish scalers, meat frets and pastry forks.

Because many professional collectors avoided handcrafted items, wood utensils, when you can find them, are still considered a good value. As wood ages, it shrinks across the grain. Because of this, a truly old bowl will appear oval, not round. Old wood grows lighter and takes on a smooth quality difficult to duplicate by other means. A handmade piece always shows signs of the tool that formed it. Wooden utensils were too important to discard if broken, and many old pieces will show signs of repair. Because wood is porous, old pieces will show signs of their former use: Spice boxes should smell, grease bowls will be stained, milk bowls will be bleached white and butter bowls should show a distinct fat line. As with any kitchen antique, decoration enhances the value of woodenware. Maple butter molds which were used to stamp a decorative design on butter are occasionally available. Their value is determined by the design of the stamp. Common designs include shocks of wheat, flowers and geometric patterns. Rarer, more expensive designs include birds, animals and people. Potato mashers, spoons, butter workers and flour sifters are just a few of the other wooden utensils available to the collector.

Simple, unadorned iron pieces are also reasonably priced and are often found at yard sales, flea markets and auctions. Although wrought-iron utensils were forged as early as 1685, these pieces are rarely named or dated. Wrought-iron is distinguishable from cast-iron by the grainy appearance wrought-iron takes on when rusted. Cast-iron will rust to an even, orange-peel-like surface and will not show any discernable grain. Unlike cast-iron, wrought-iron pieces often show a series of coarse ridges running through them, indicating the direction in which the piece was drawn.

Copper and brass utensils are in great demand and are expensive to collect. Only smaller utensils, like molds, are accessible to most collectors. Painted tinware or "toleware" is also popular and expensive. Because there are many reproductions around, check to make sure you are buying an original. If there are scratches or signs of wear in the japanning, the piece is probably original. The paint that was used to decorate old pieces is softer than the more durable oil paint used on most reproductions and it should have abraded. Undecorated tin is more widely available and less expensive. Most silver utensils were acquired by museums and wealthy collectors long ago, and few pieces are offered today for public sale.

Many people collect only factory-made kitchen utensils. Even though most of these pieces are embossed with a name, date, place or patent number, it is difficult to determine precisely when a particular factory-made utensil came into widespread use. When the North was industrialized and factory-made merchandise was available to every household in the region,the West was still being settled and housewives there used handcrafted implements fifty years after they had been replaced in the North.

After years of wear, kitchen antiques require attention to restore them and insure their preservation. If you want to use the utensil, it must be clean and free of health hazards. When cleaning, avoid altering the patina of the piece. Surface marks are part of the character of an antique.

As noted, woodenware will be marked by the food it contained; removing the stains is a matter of personal preference. To remove excess dirt, scrub the piece with warm soapy water, rinse it and let it air dry in the sun. Sterilize an old piece before you use it to serve food by pouring boiling water over the inside, keeping the outside dry. Air dry it thoroughly and rub it lightly with salad oil. Pieces for display may be coated with beeswax to preserve the wood.

The early 19th-century housewife tried to prevent rust from forming on her iron utensils by applying a paste made of daffodil stalks dipped in red oxide of iron and sweet oil. Most old iron pieces will be somewhat rusted. Fine steel wool will remove most rust. If the piece is badly rusted, soak it in kerosene and then loosen the rust with naval jelly; the rust will come off with coarse steel wool. Rub the dry piece with salad oil and wax and repeat as necessary to keep the rust from reforming. Cast-iron should be seasoned before you cook with it.

Clean copper and brass with a commercial metal cleaner. (Or you can do it the old-fashioned way, by rubbing the piece with room-temperature buttermilk, whey or sour milk, every day.) Ornamental pieces can be coated with lacquer.

Treat old tinware gently. Old tin is simply plated iron and excessive cleaning will remove the tinplate and expose the iron. To remove grease or baked-on food, soak the piece in soapy water, but do not scour it. Let it air dry. Japanned tinware should be cleaned with a soft damp cloth and, according to the 19th-century housewife, polished with dry flour.

Boil peeled potatoes in enamelware to remove stains. Remove stains on pottery by soaking the piece in a solution of chlorine bleach and water. Clean aluminum with a special aluminum cleaner or, as some old household books recommend, by cooking tomatoes or rhubard in it.

Kitchenware lends itself to display. Small items like mashers, beaters, rolling pins or choppers can be hung on a large piece of pegboard and mounted on a wall. Pots, pans, trivets and other iron utensils can be arranged around the fireplace—on the walls, the hearth or the mantel. Woodenware may be displayed in cupboards or on shelves. Objects that can be washed may be displayed on the kitchen walls, but since grease and dirt is hard on some old surfaces, particularly japanned tinware, do not display anything in the kitchen that cannot survive a washing. Rotate your displays—that way they won't become "invisible." Add to your collection by collecting miniatures of the same kind of utensil. You may want to include engravings or woodcuts of kitchen scenes or pictures, prints or paintings of old utensils. Advertising or lithographed trade cards, aprons, mail-order catalogues, old stove parts and promotional giveaways can enhance your collection. The wonderful diversity, pleasing shapes and great functional beauty of kitchen antiques offer illimitable variety and endless fascination.

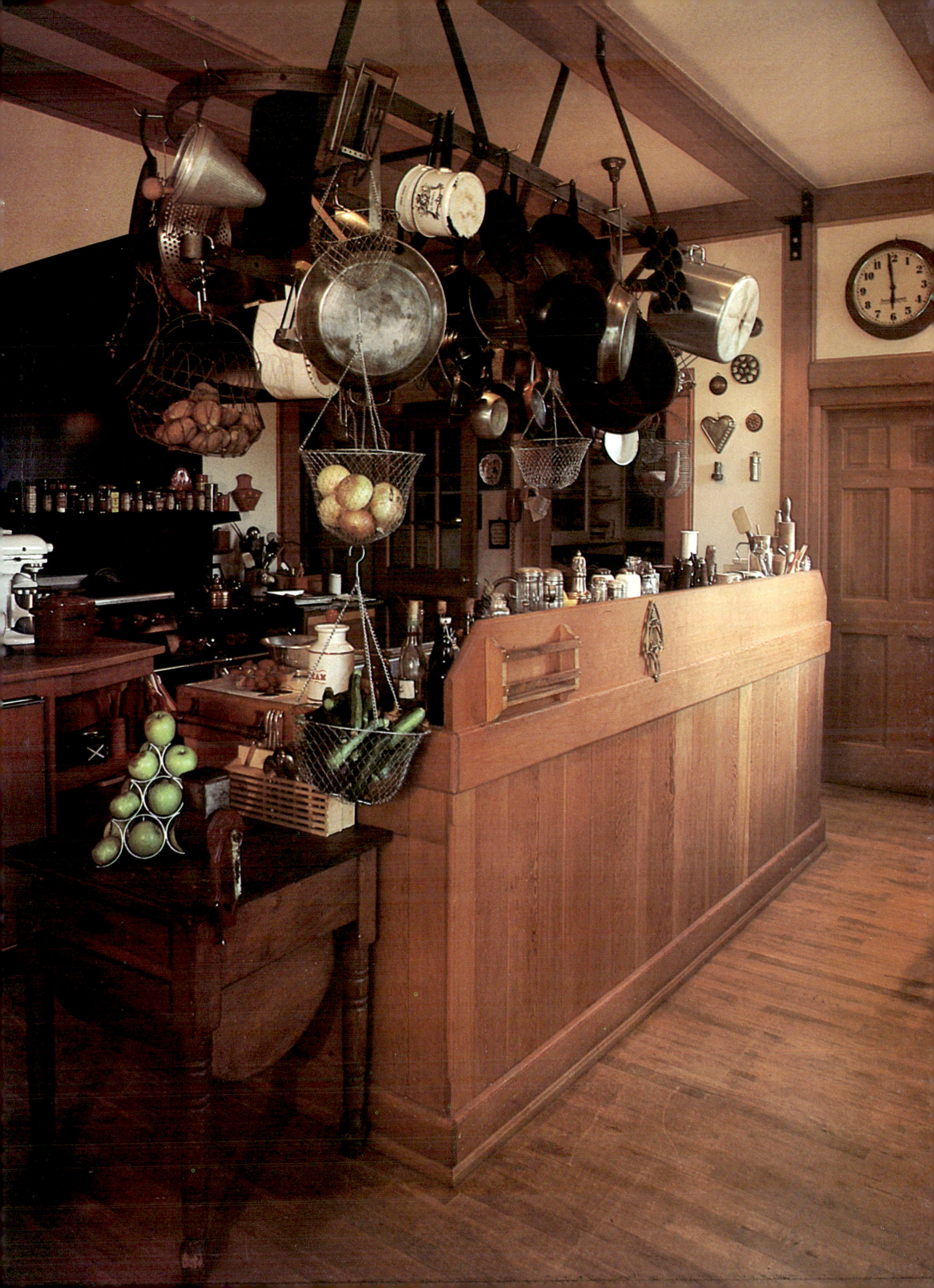

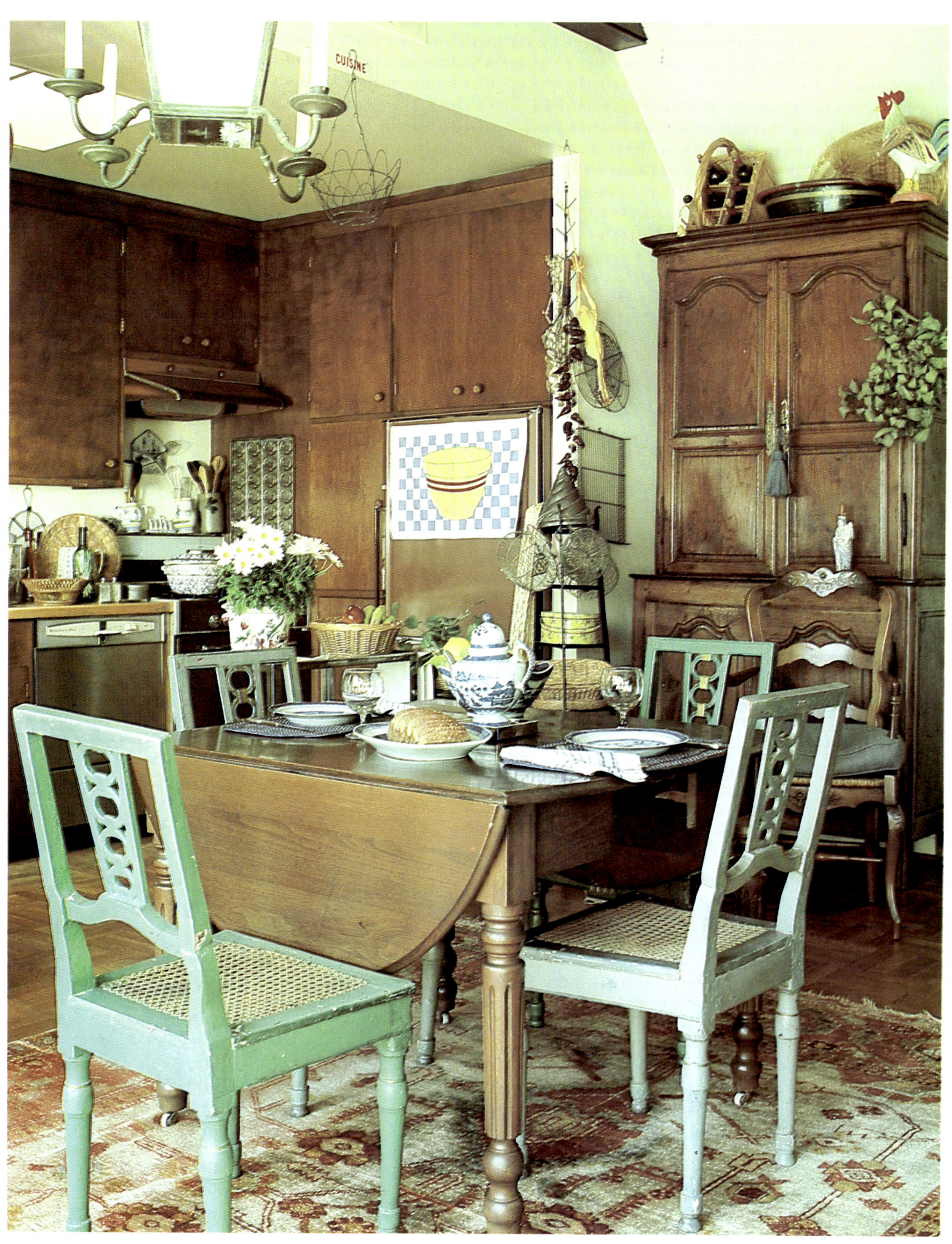
CUISINE

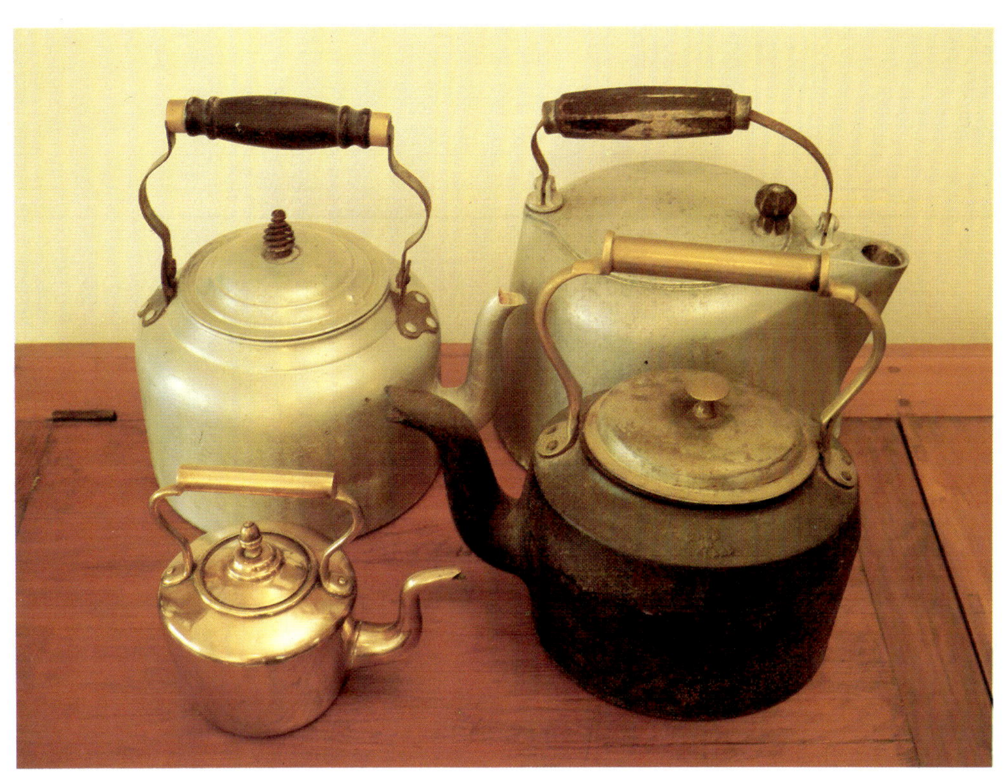

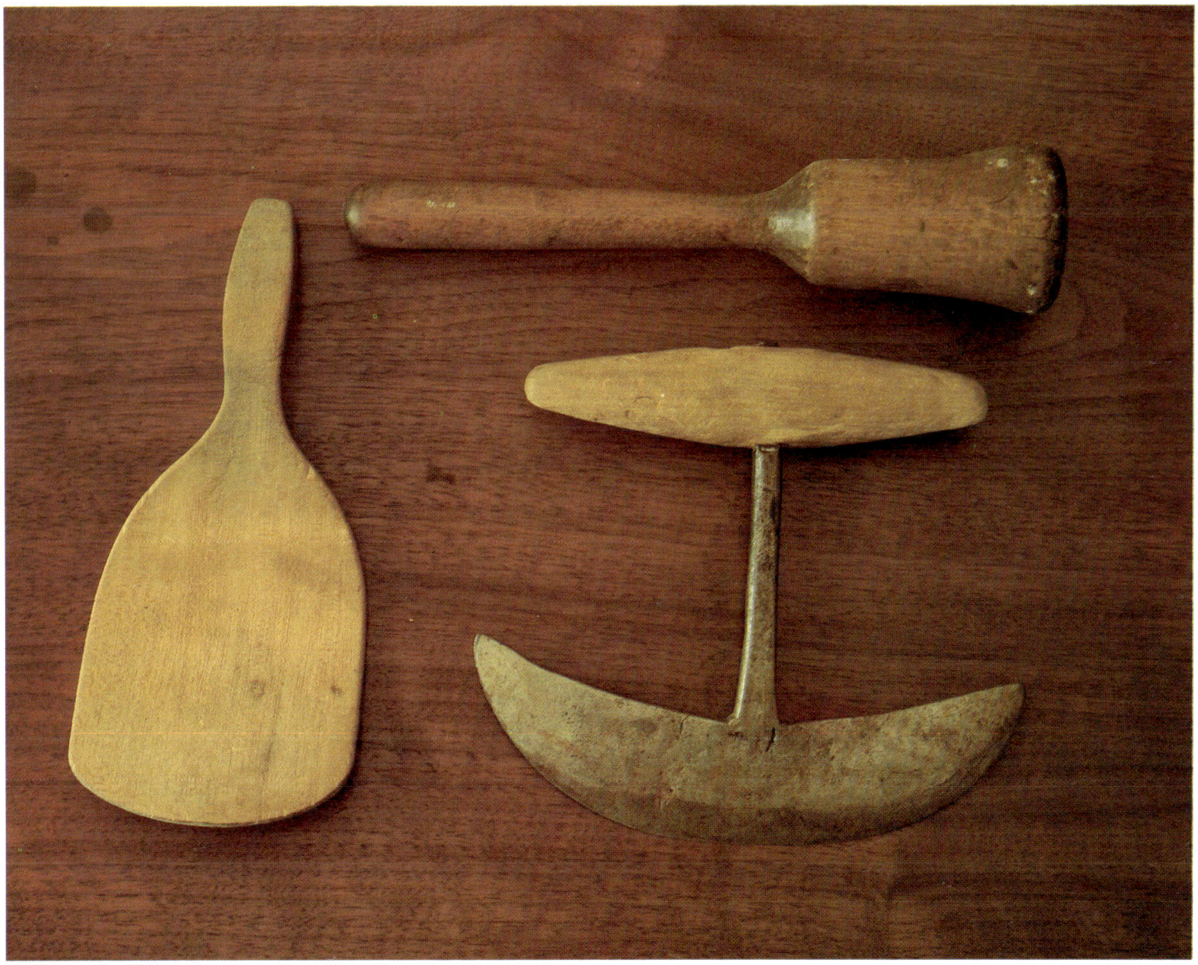

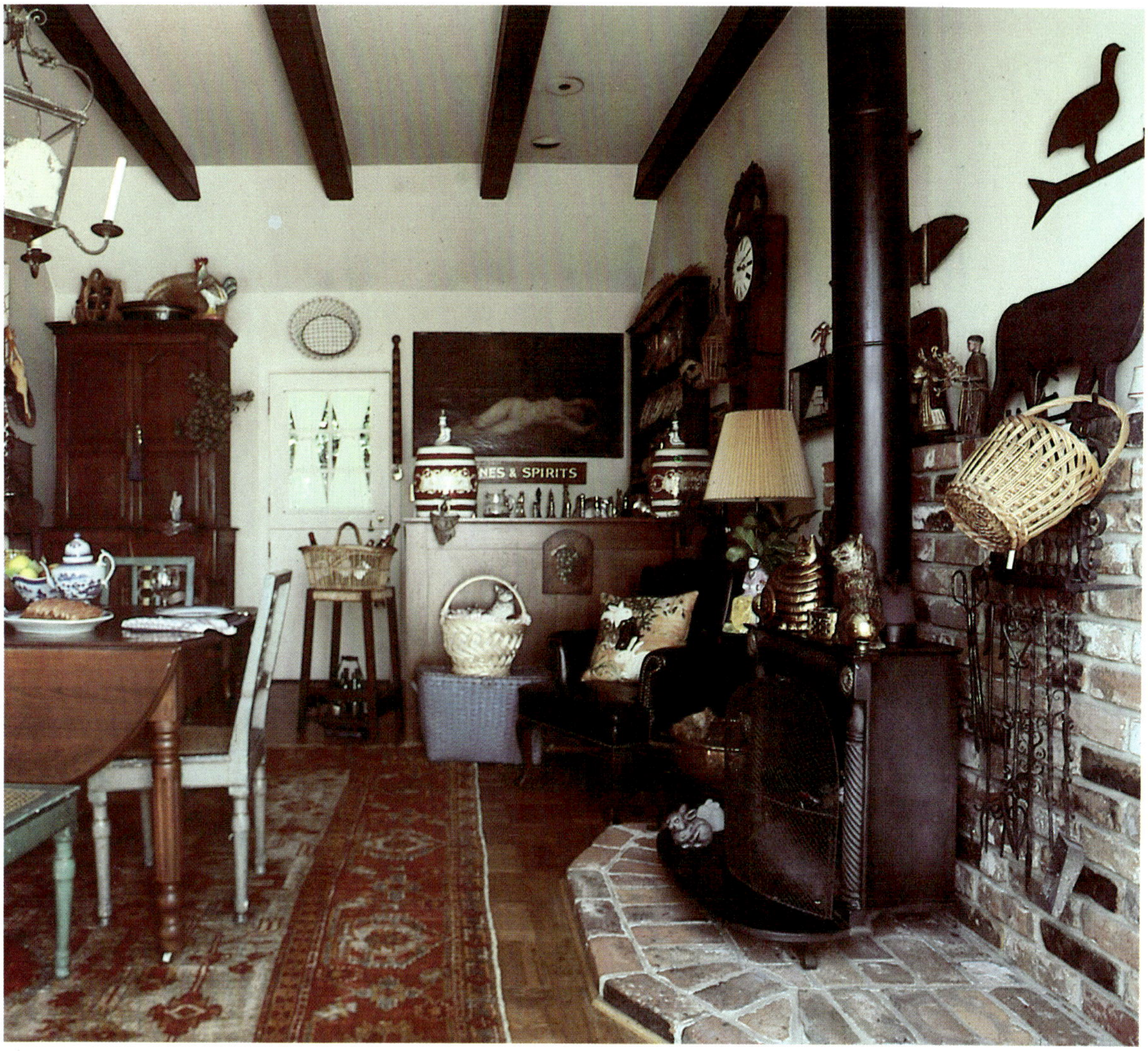

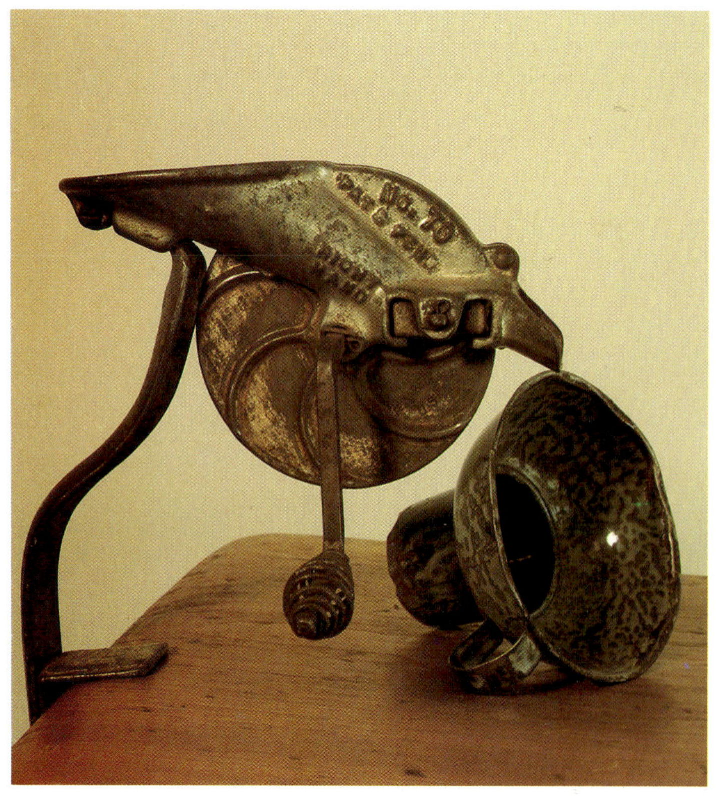
No. 70
PAT'S PEND

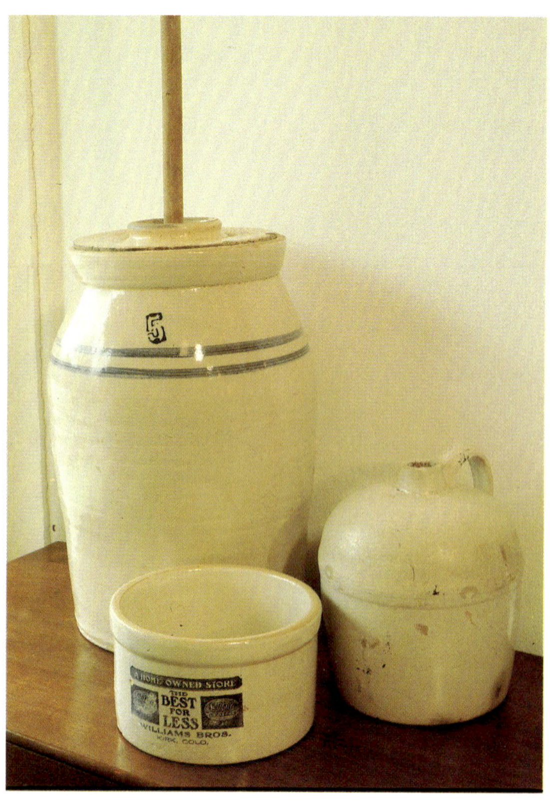
5
A HOME OWNED STORE
THE BEST FOR LESS
WILLIAMS BROS.
KIRK, COLO.

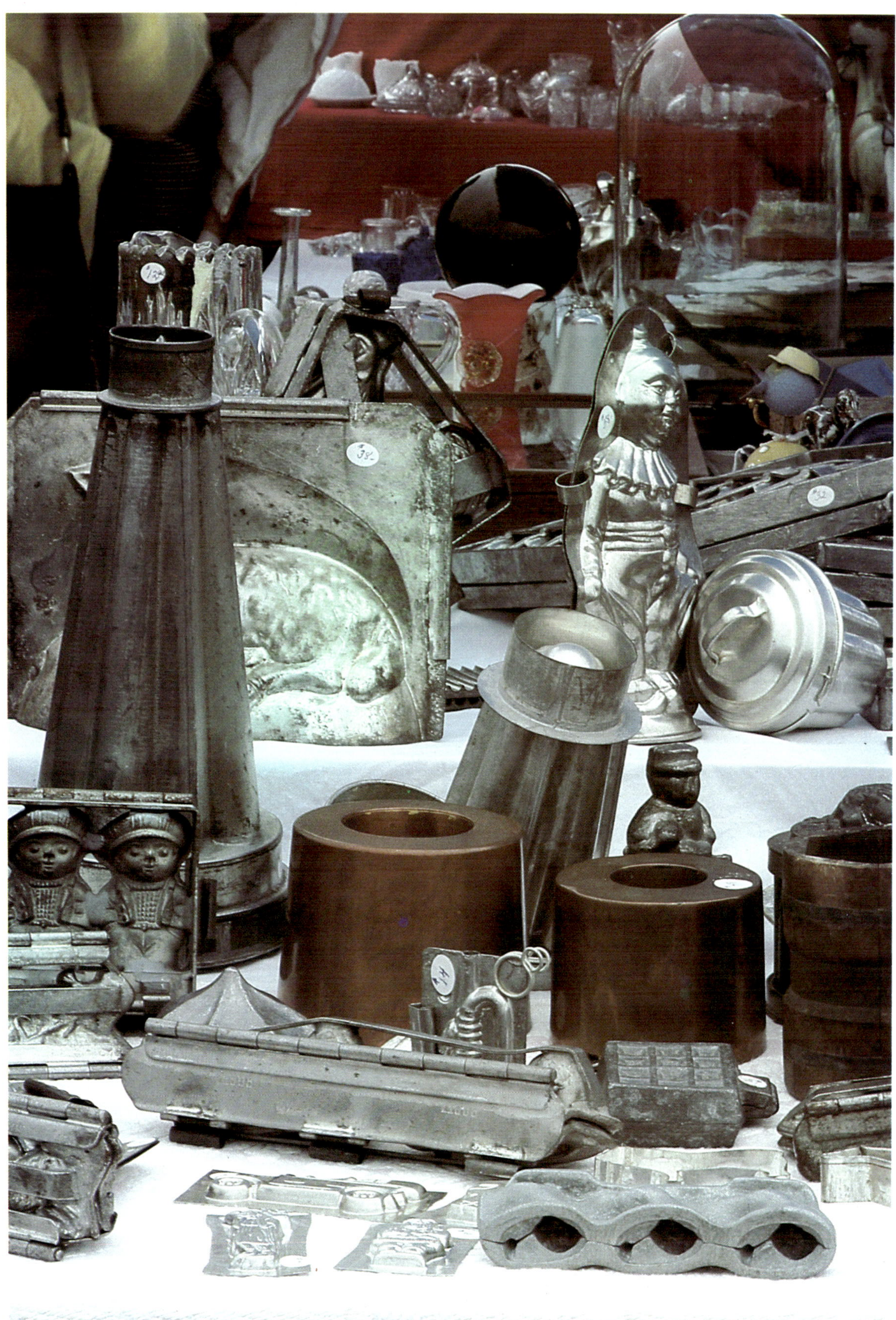

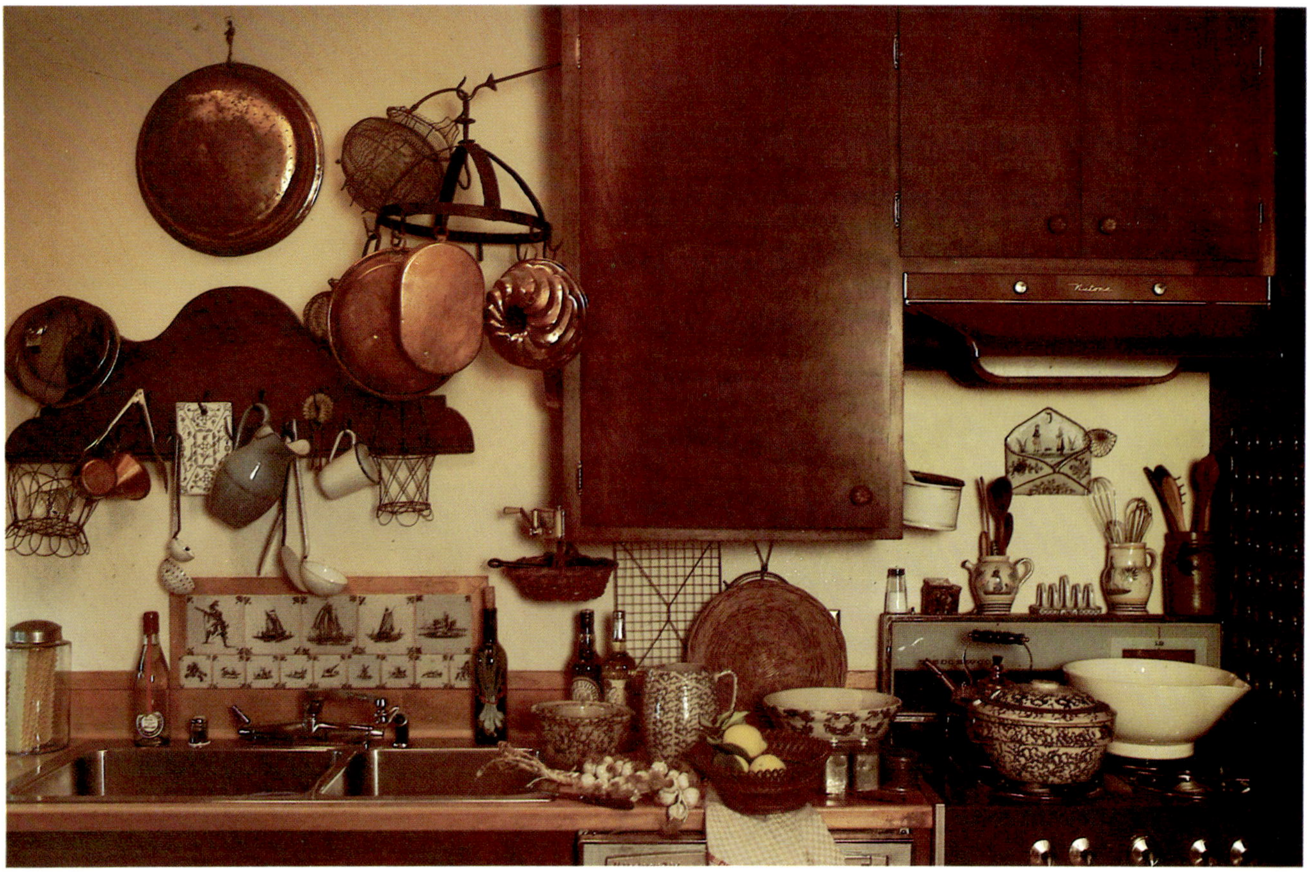

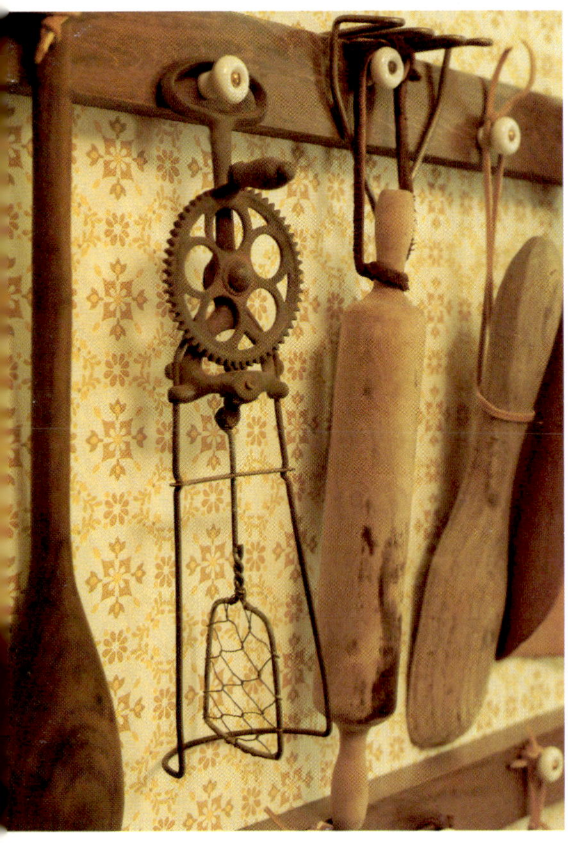

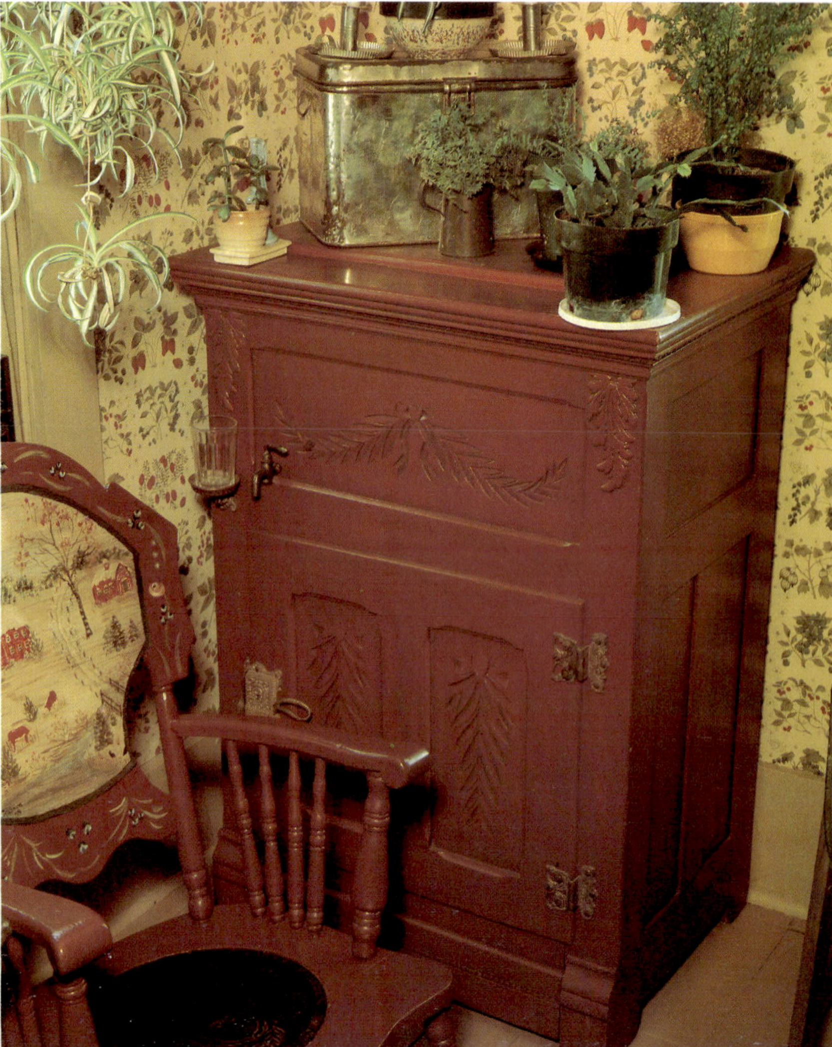

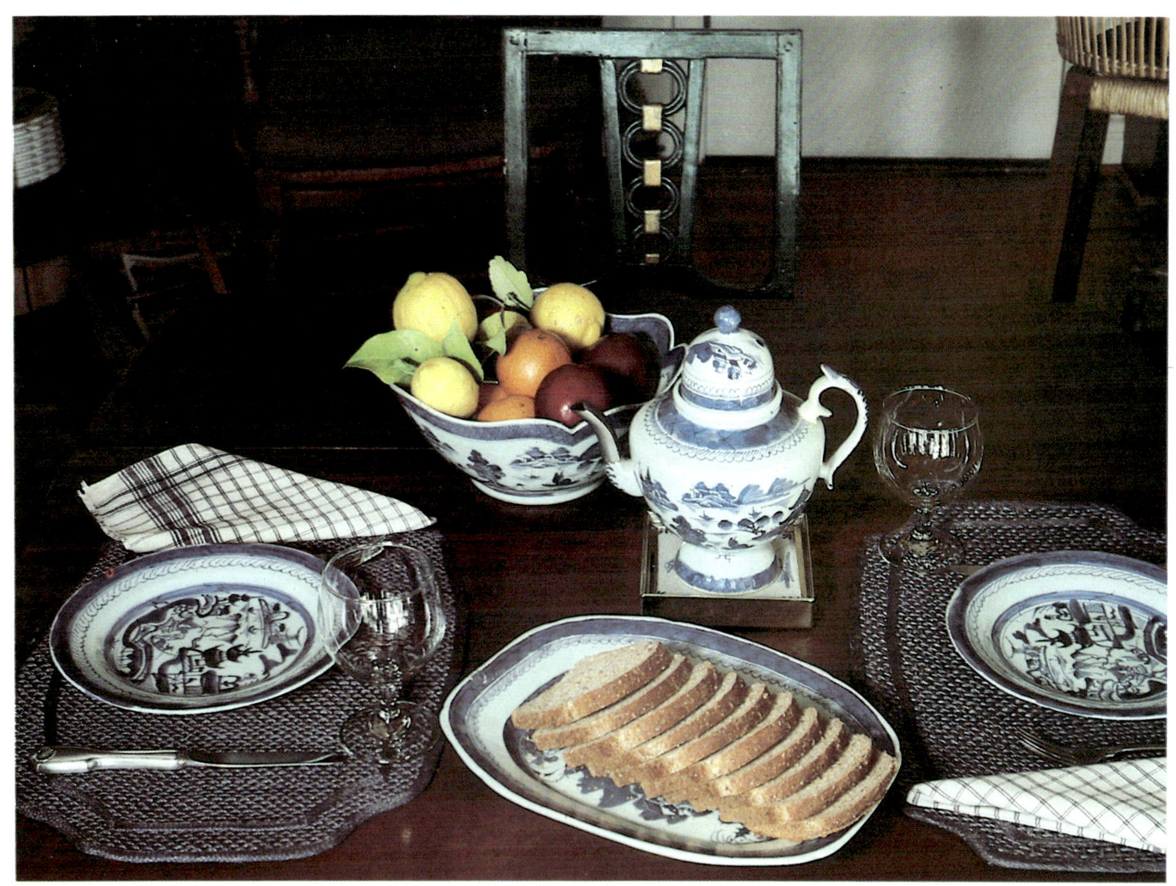

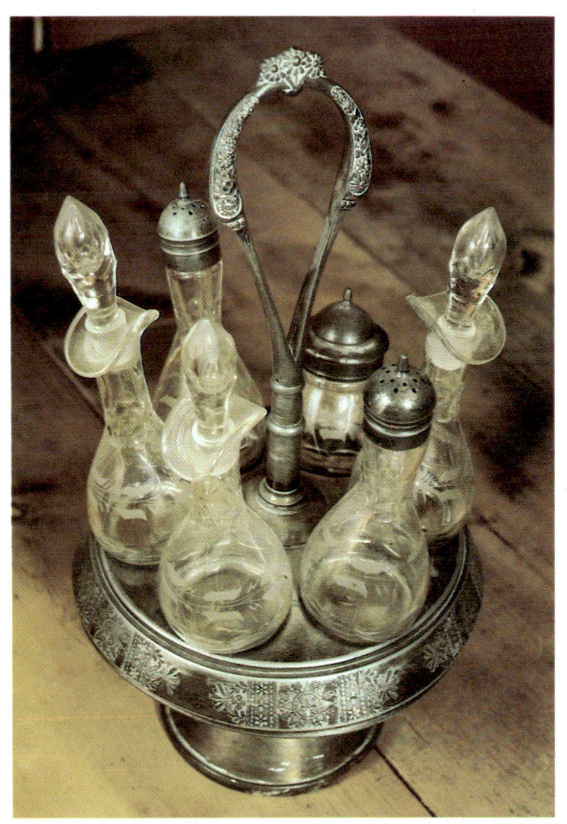

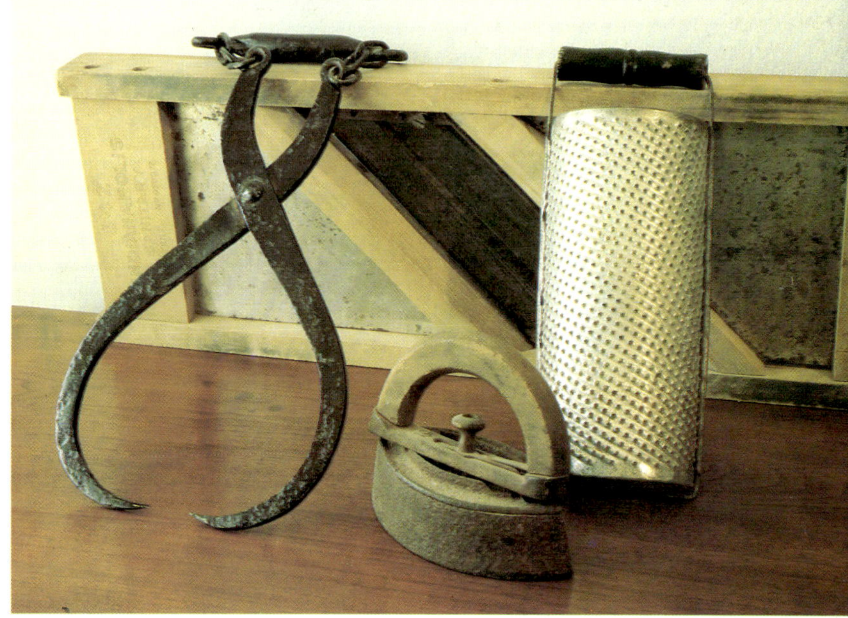

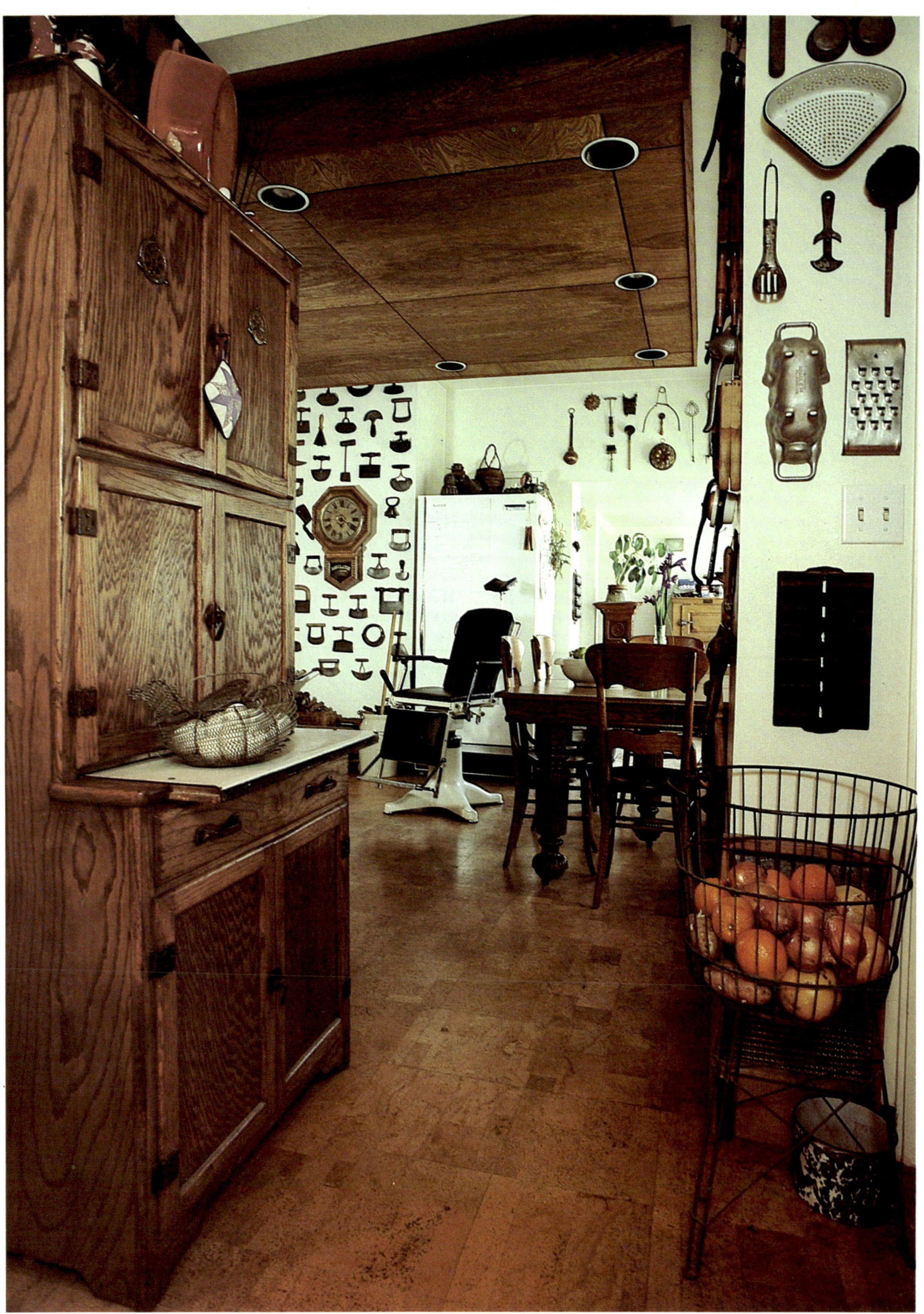

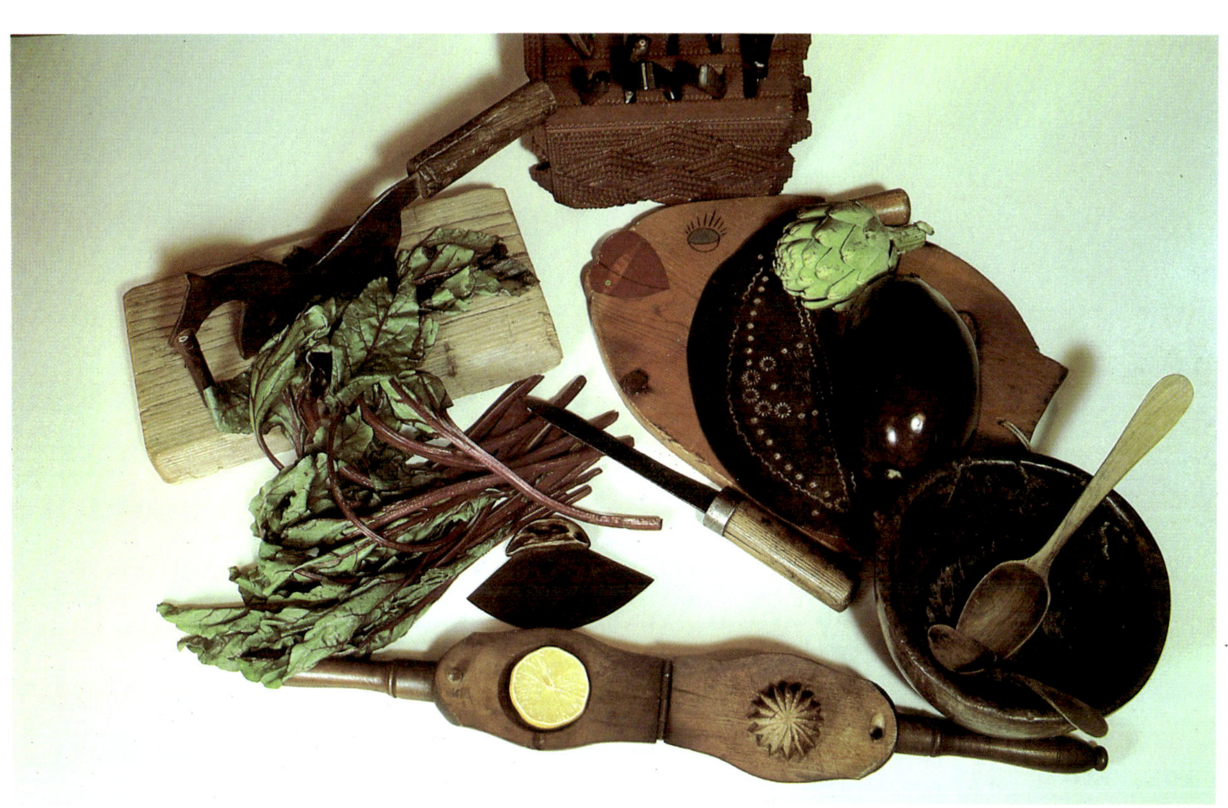

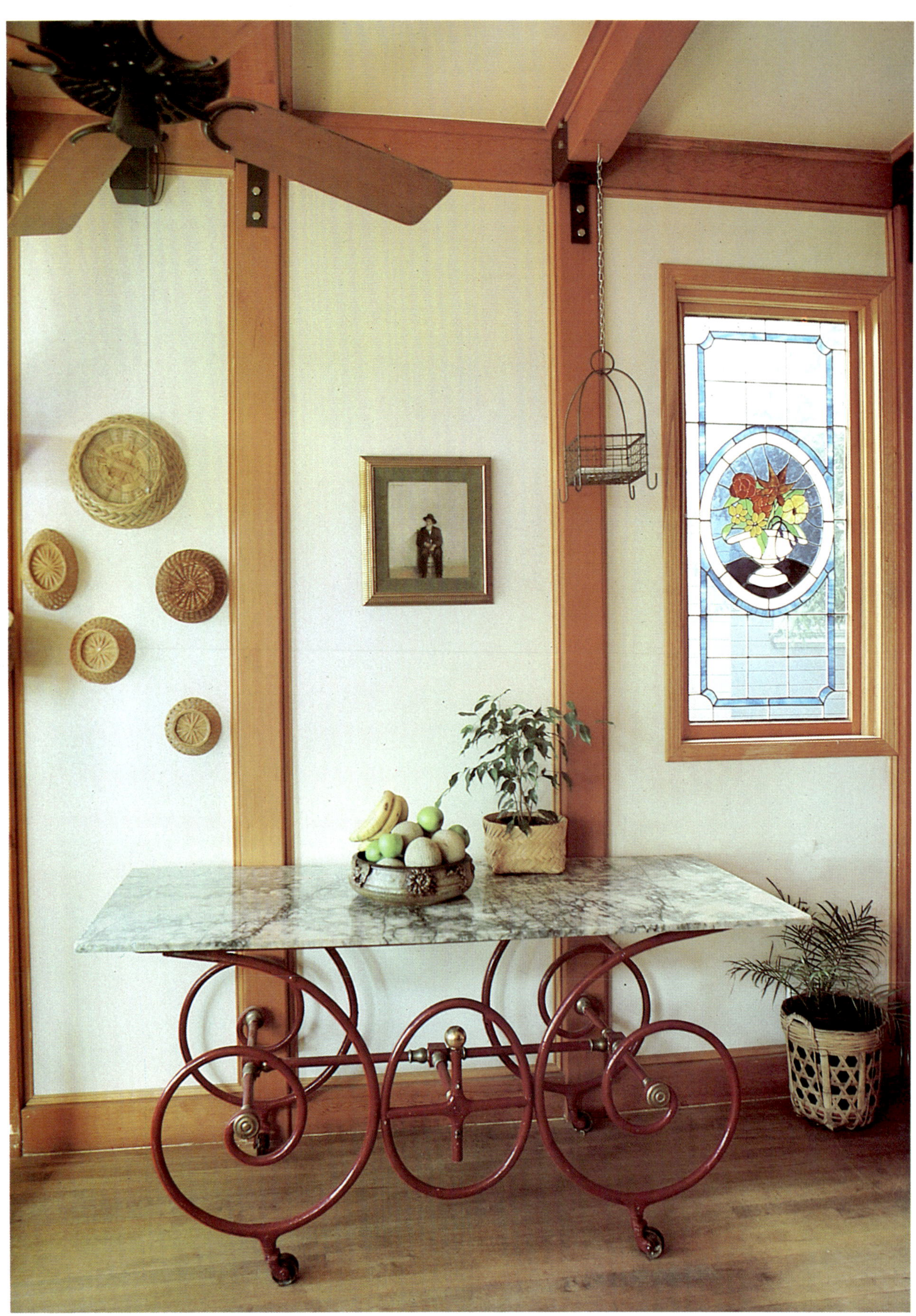

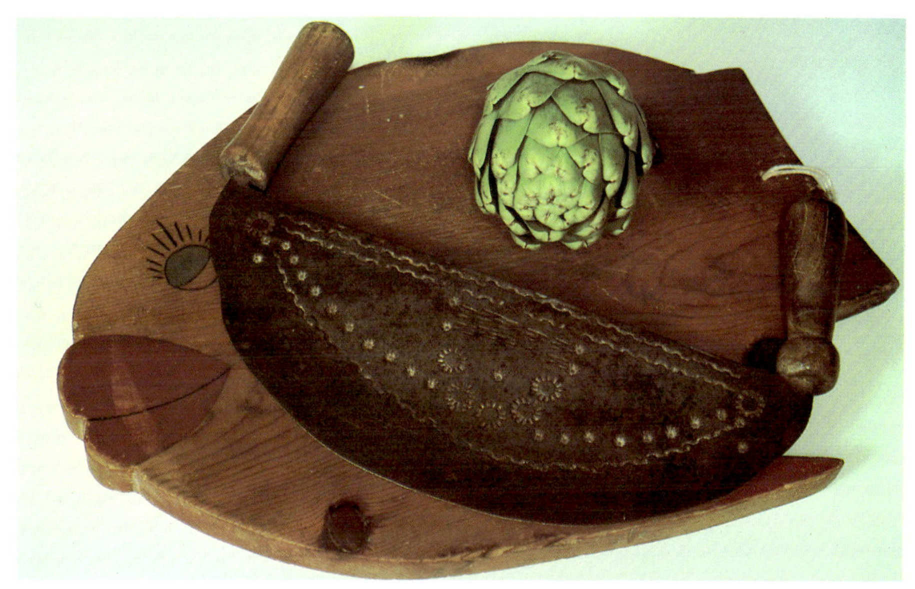

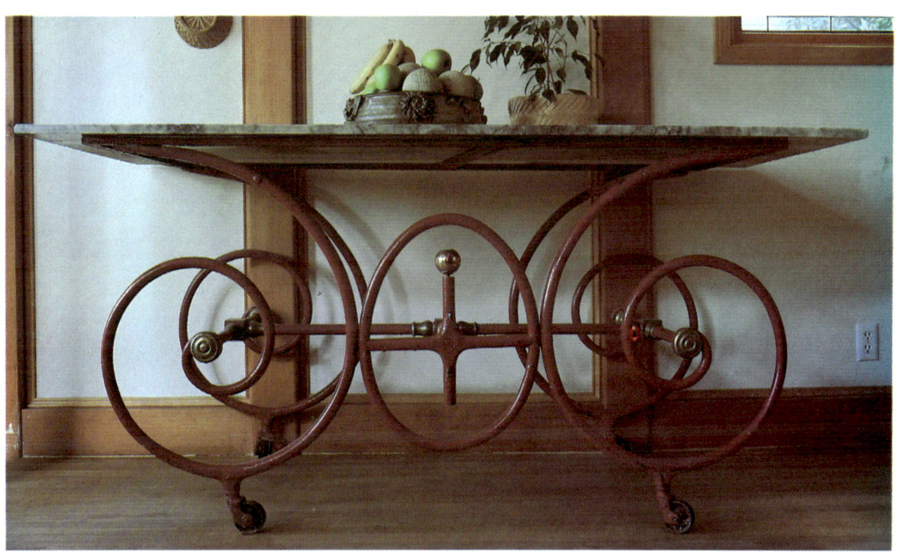

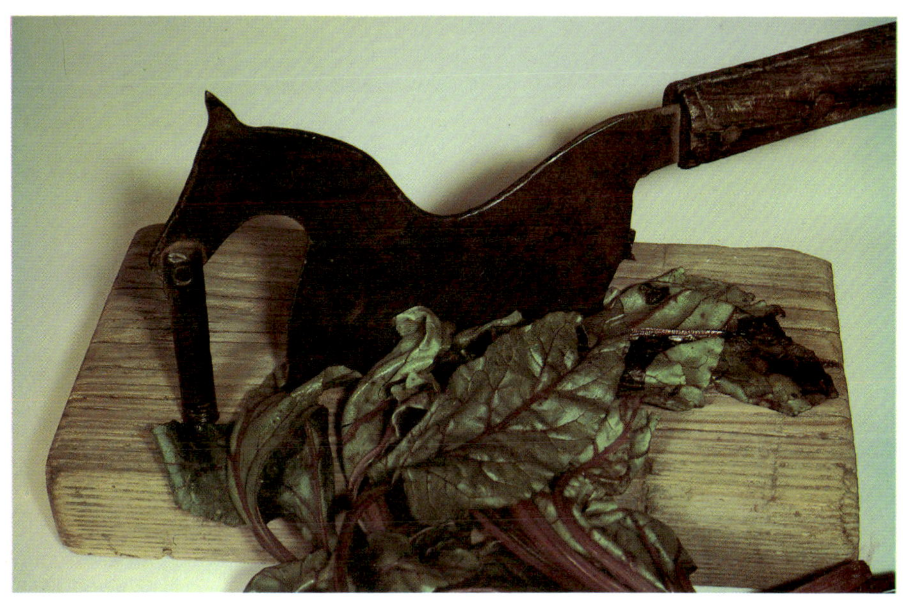

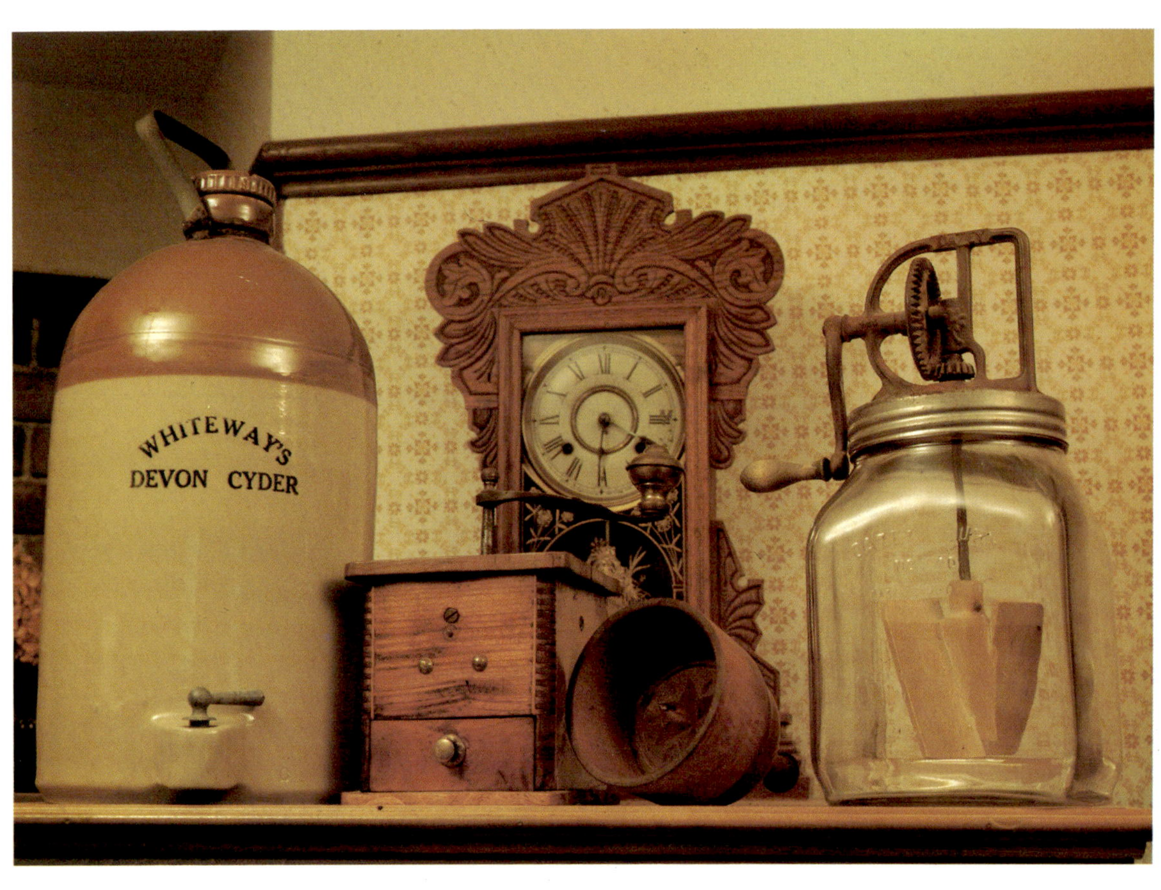
WHITEWAY'S
DEVON CYDER

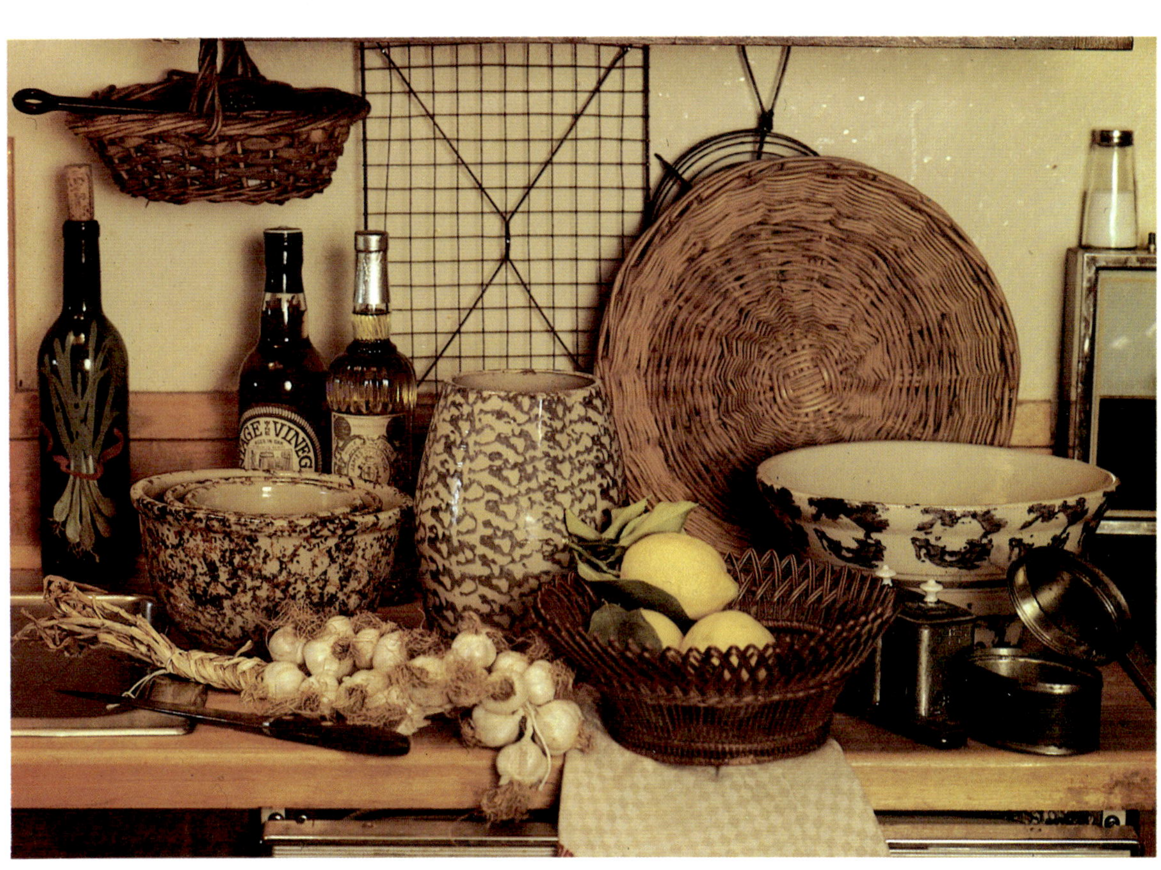

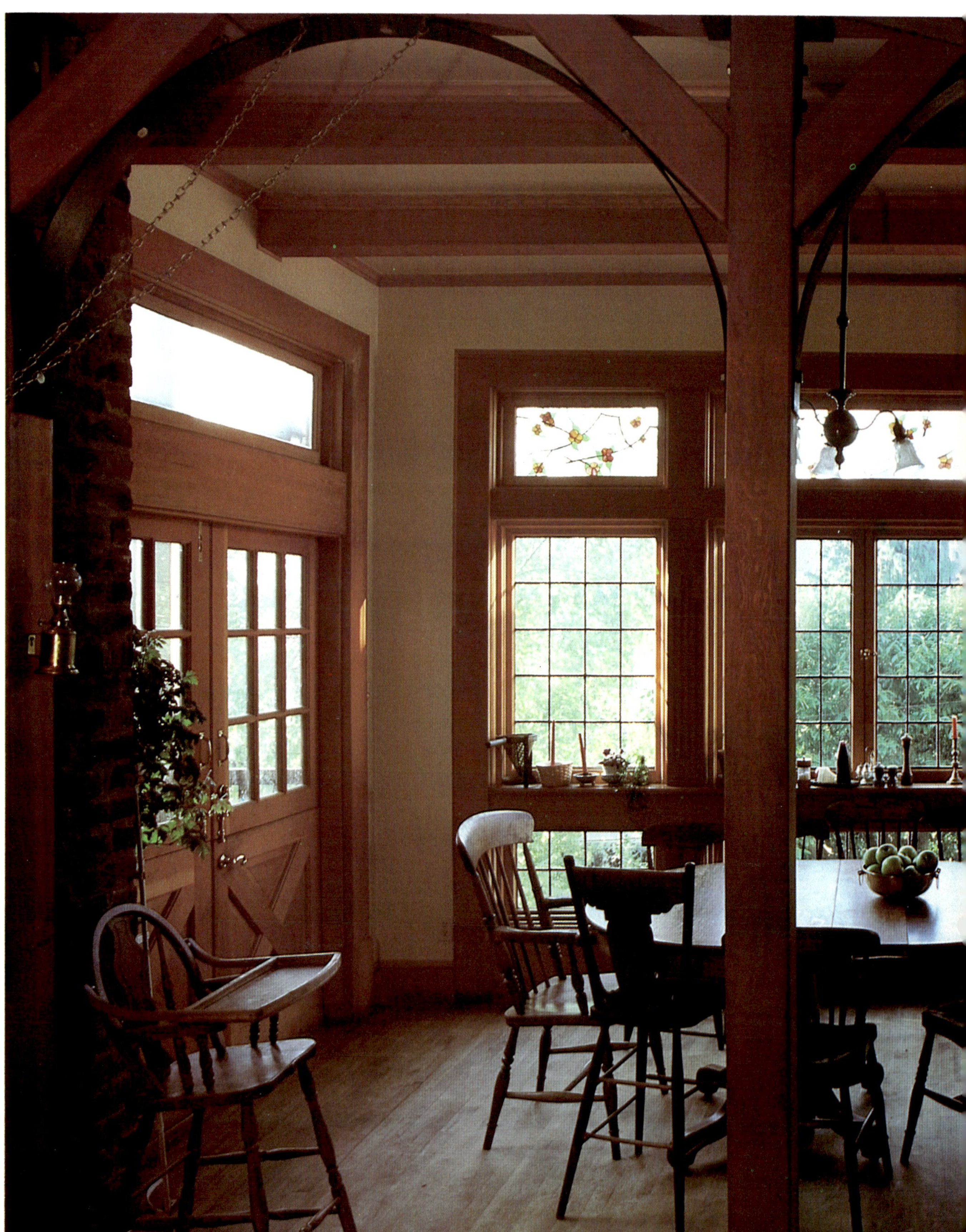

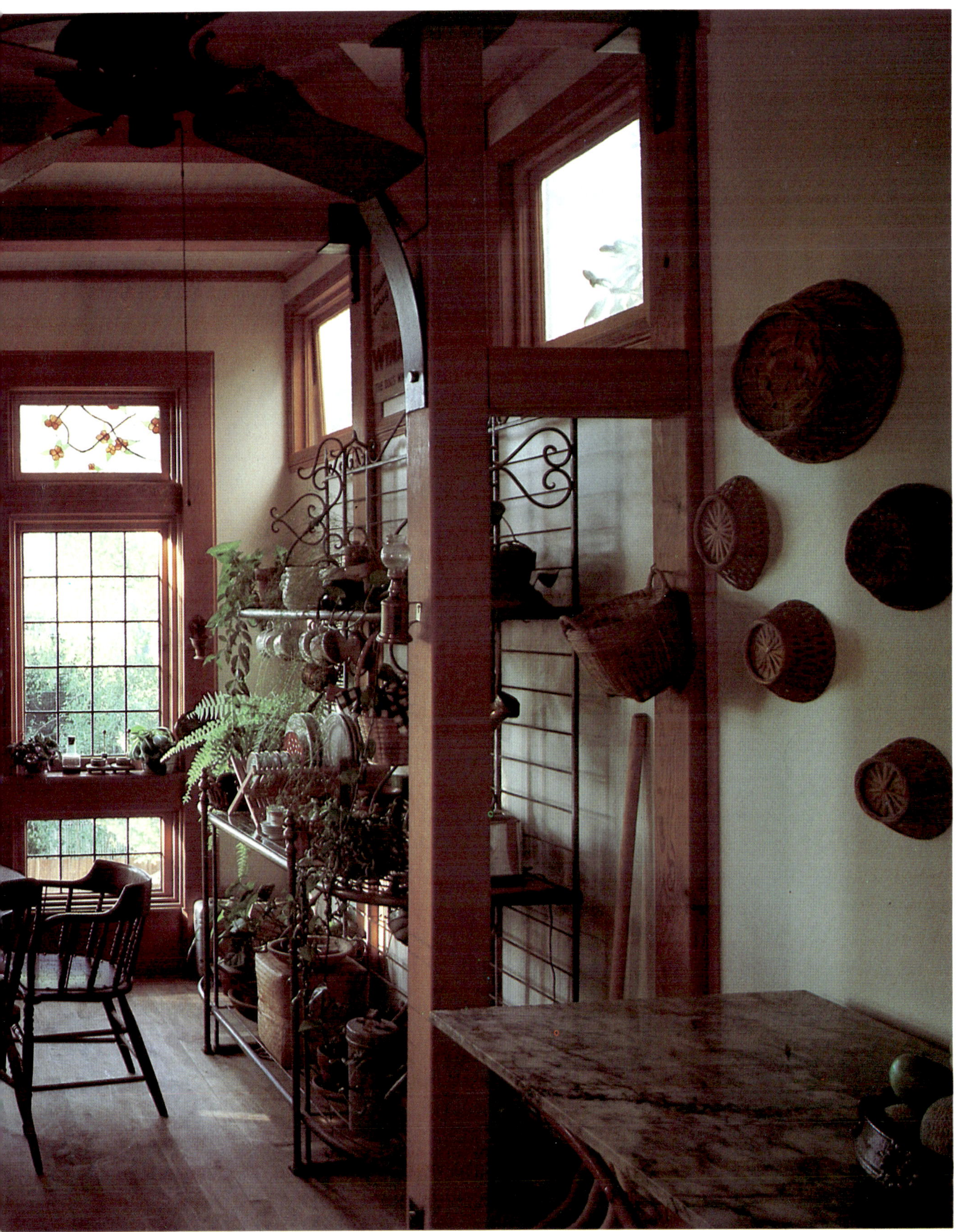

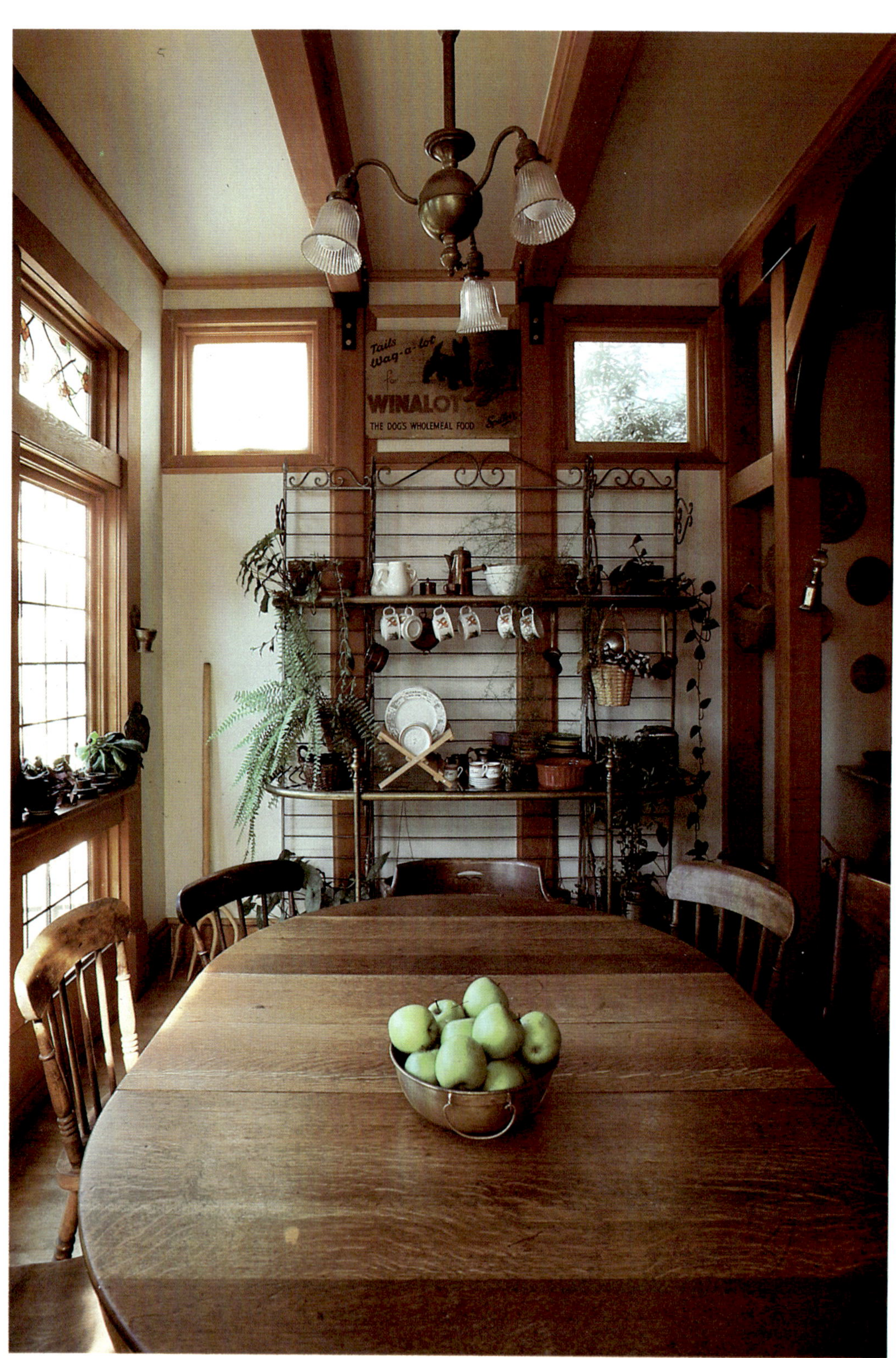
Tails
Wag-a-lot
WINALOT
THE DOG'S WHOLEMEAL FOOD

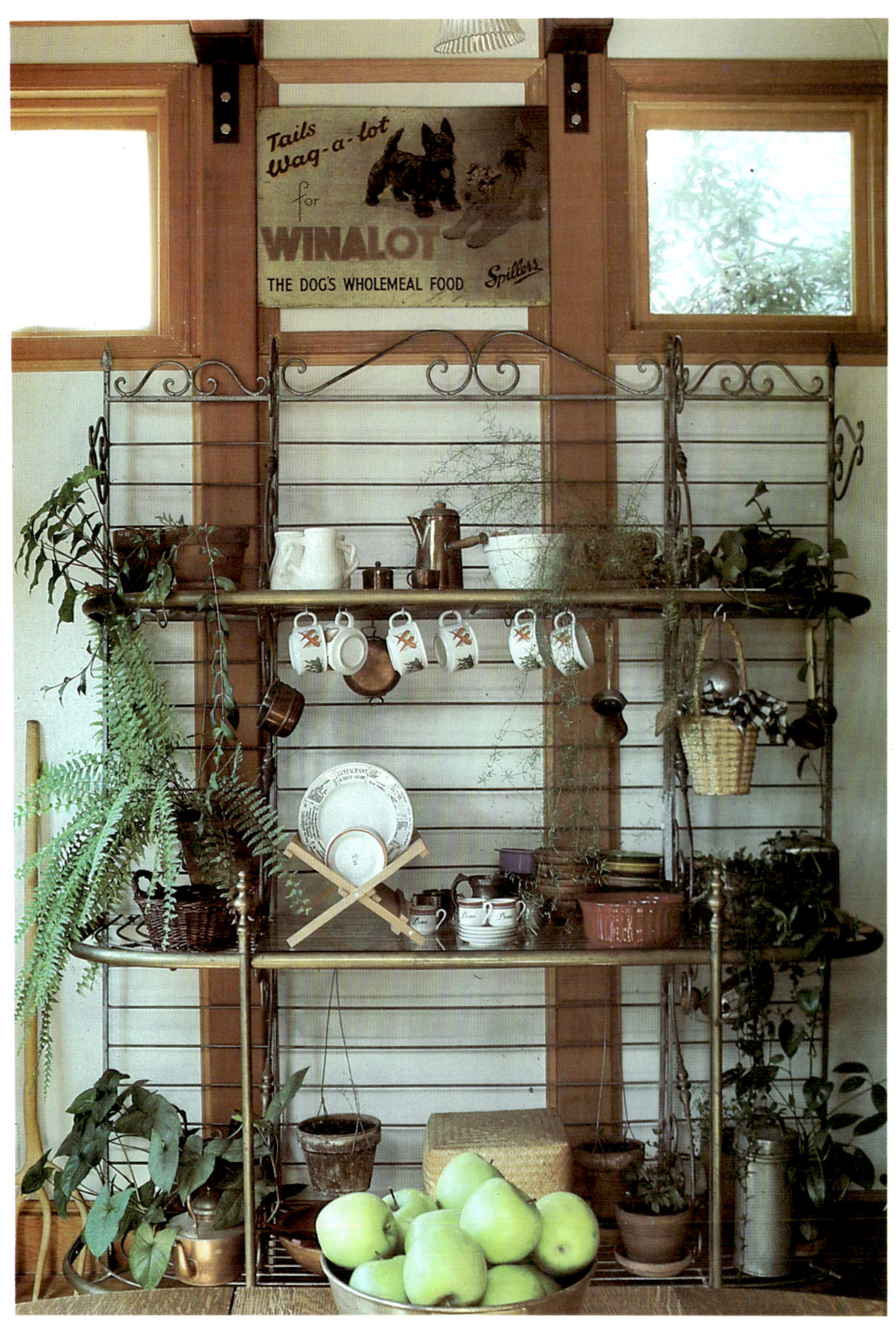
Tails Wag-a-lot
for
WINALOT
THE DOG'S WHOLEMEAL FOOD
Spillers

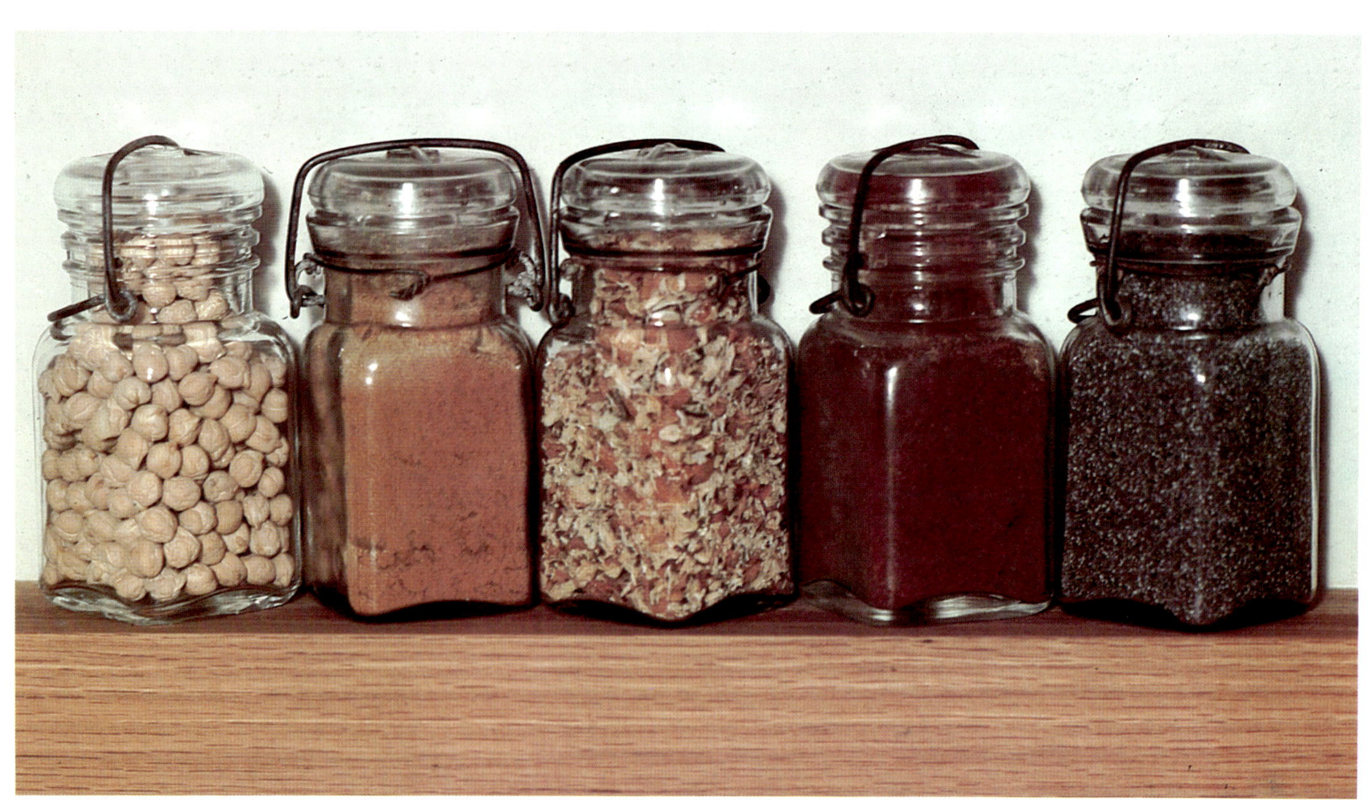

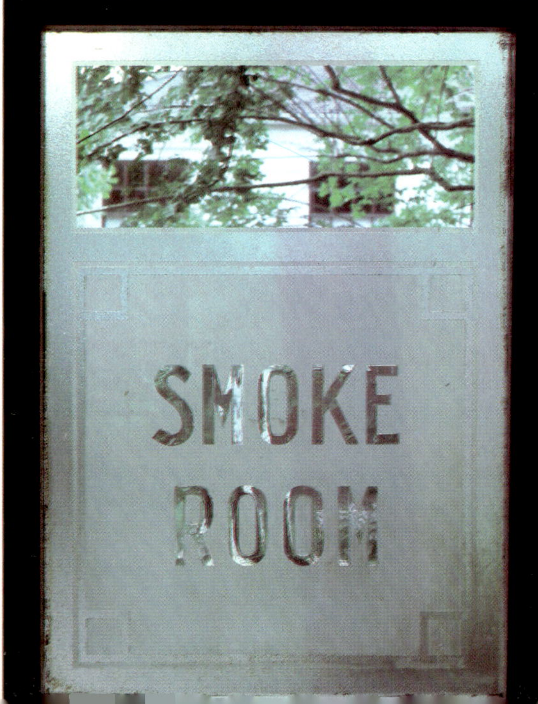
SMOKE
ROOM

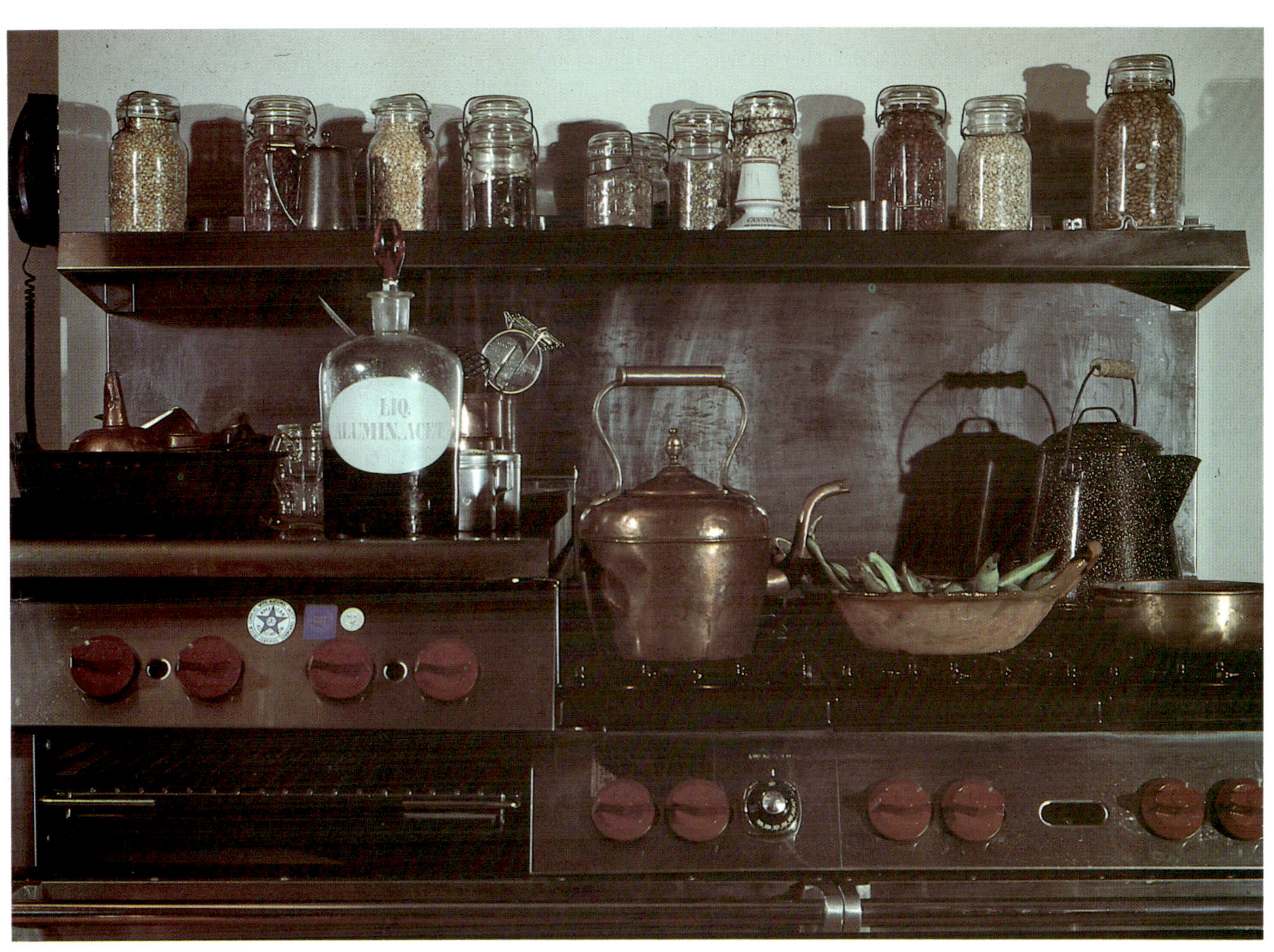
LIQ.

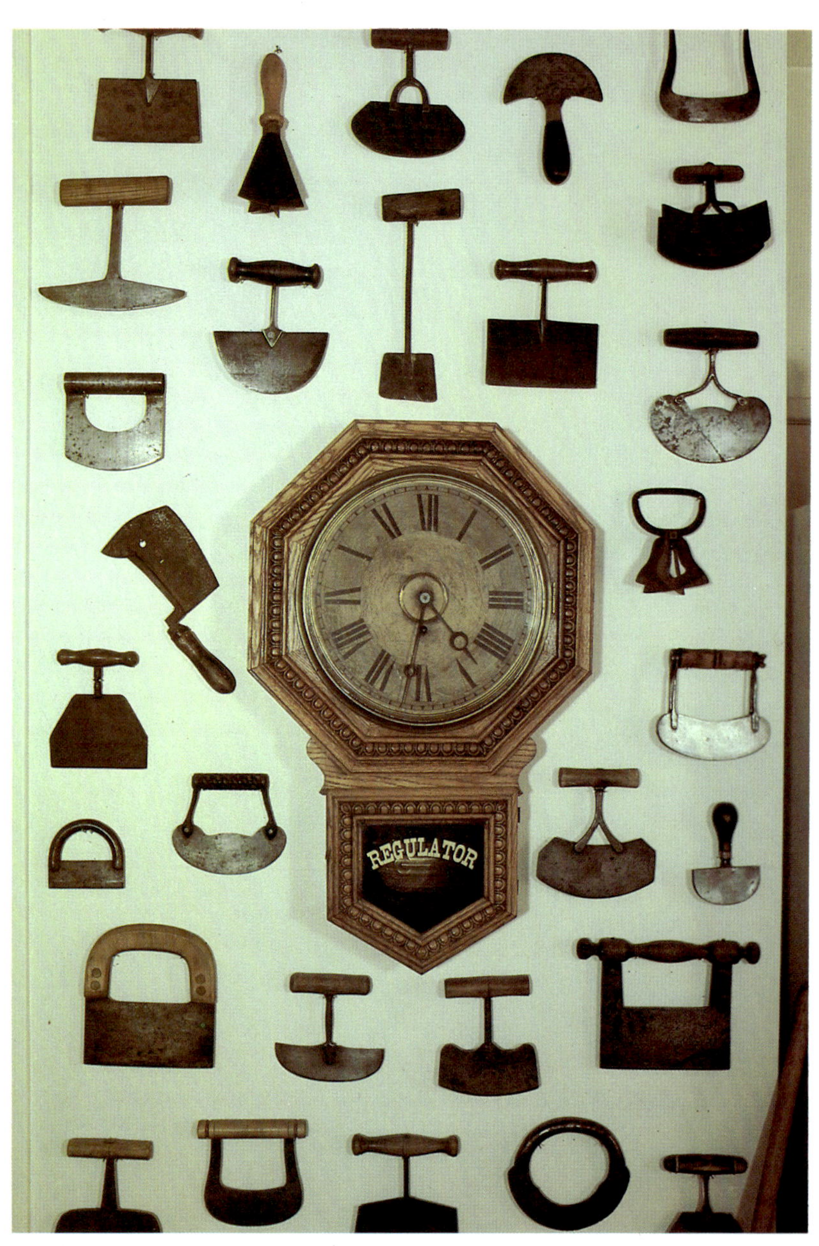
REGULATOR

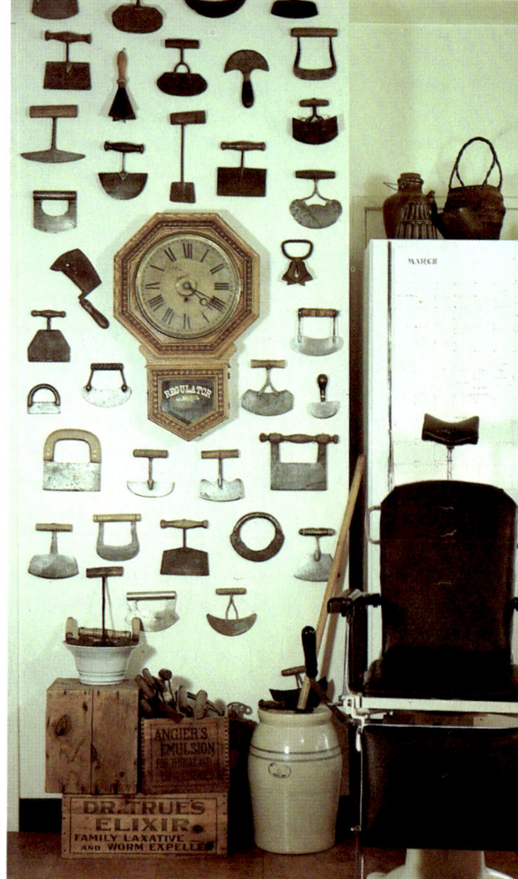
REGULATOR
ANGIER'S
EMULSION
DR. TRUE'S
ELIXIR
FAMILY LAXATIVE

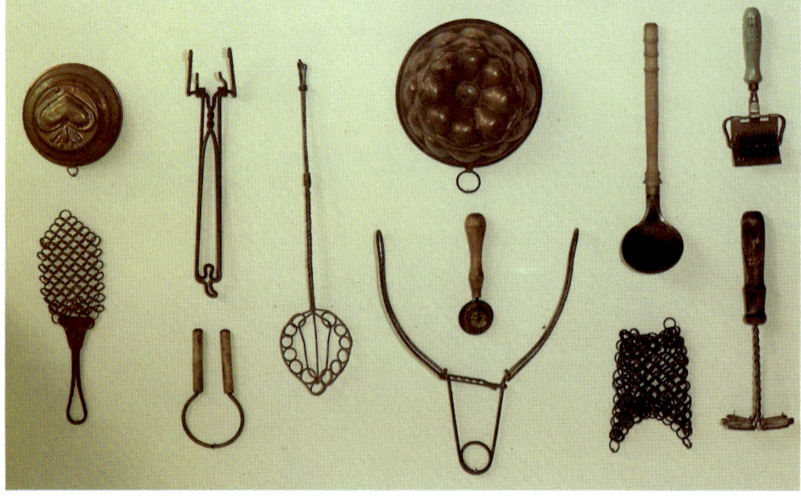

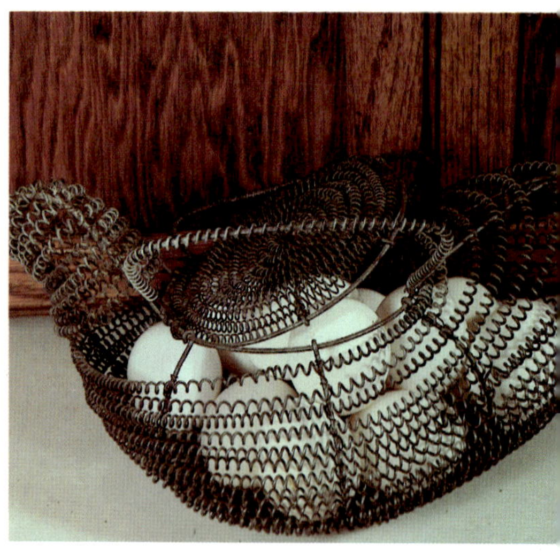

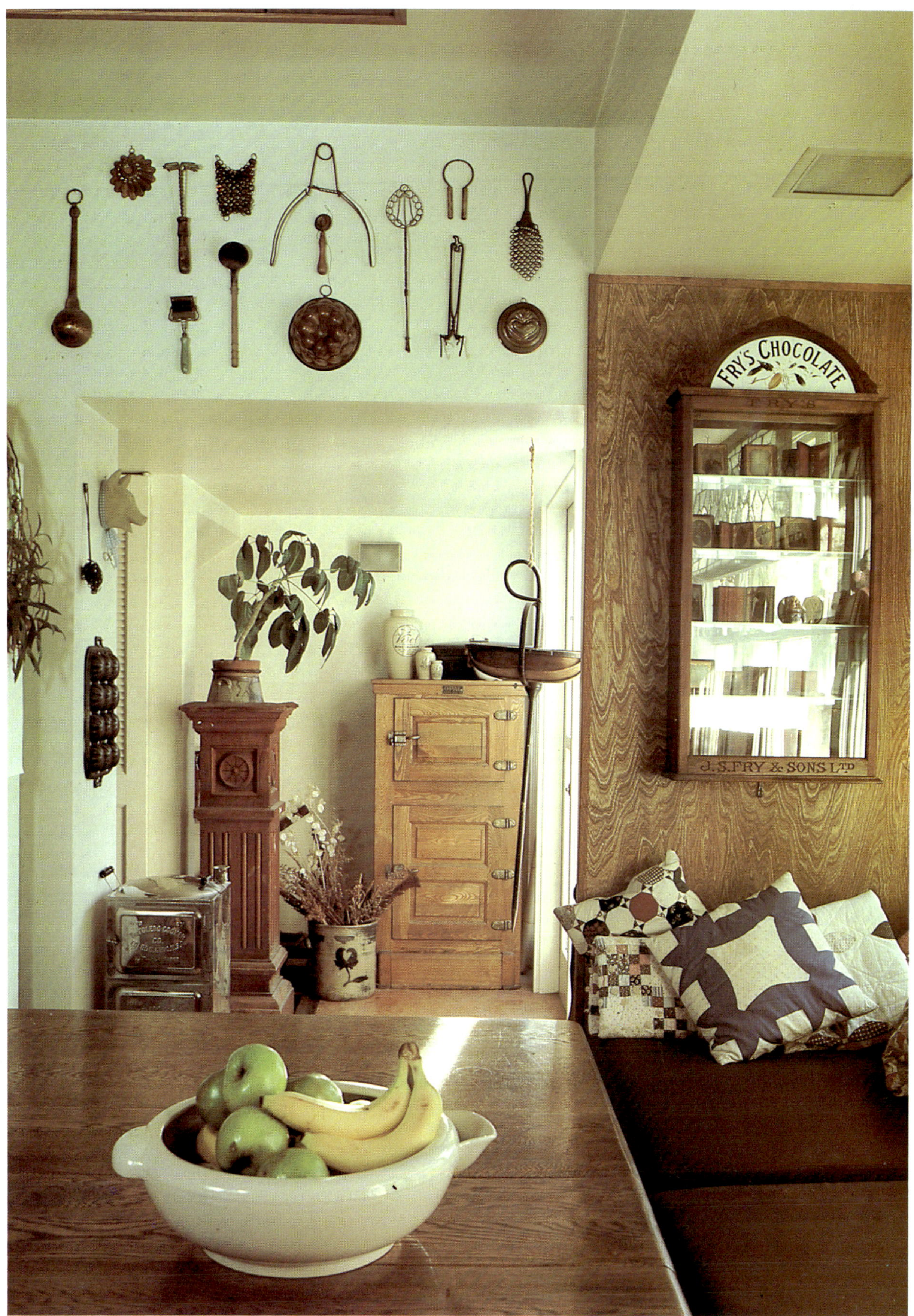
FRY'S CHOCOLATE
J.S.FRY & SONS LTD

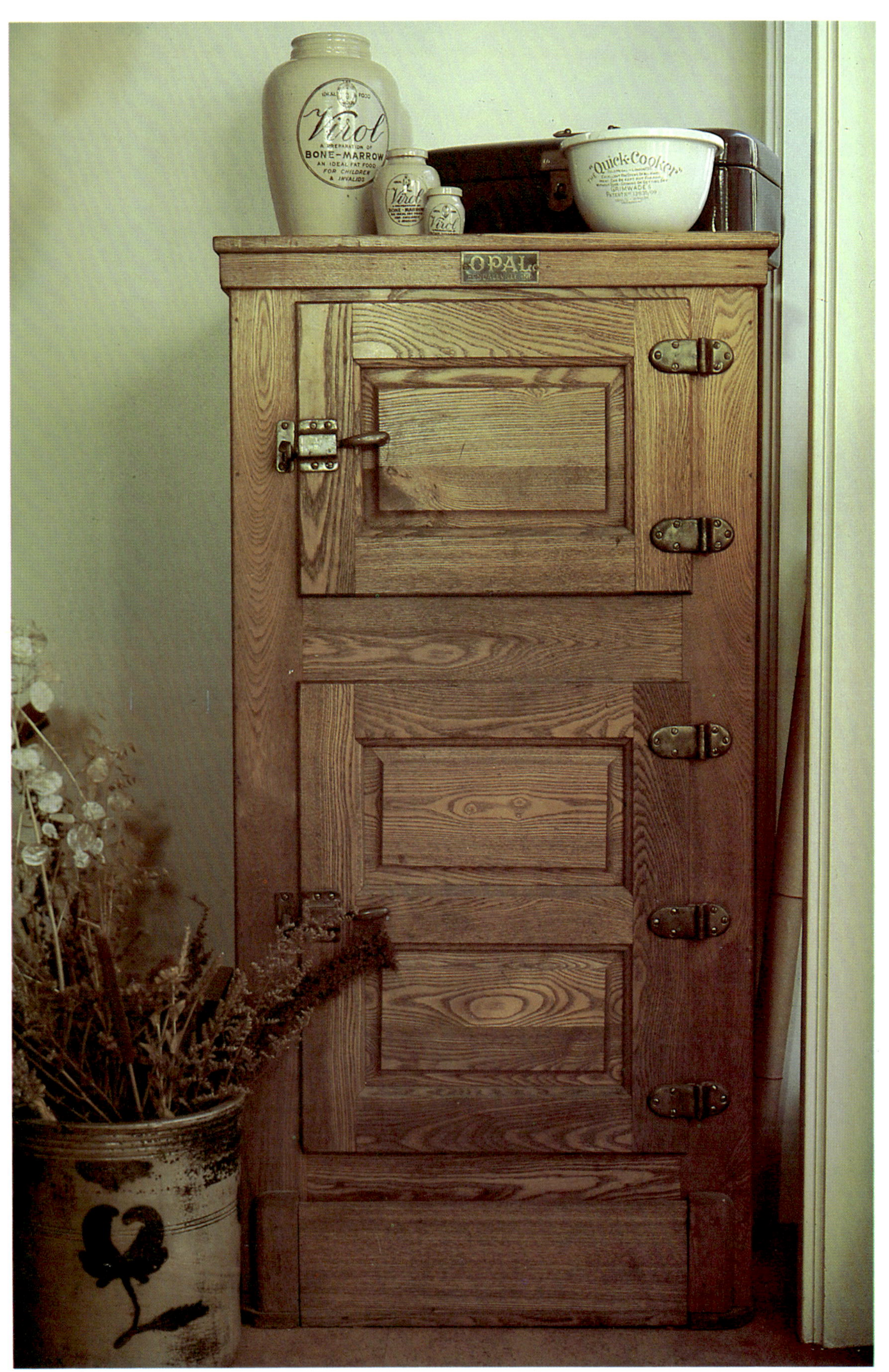
IDEAL FOOD
Virol
A PREPARATION OF
BONE-MARROW
AN IDEAL FAT FOOD
FOR CHILDREN
& INVALIDS
Virol
Virol
THE "Quick-Cooker"
GRIMWADE'S
OPAL

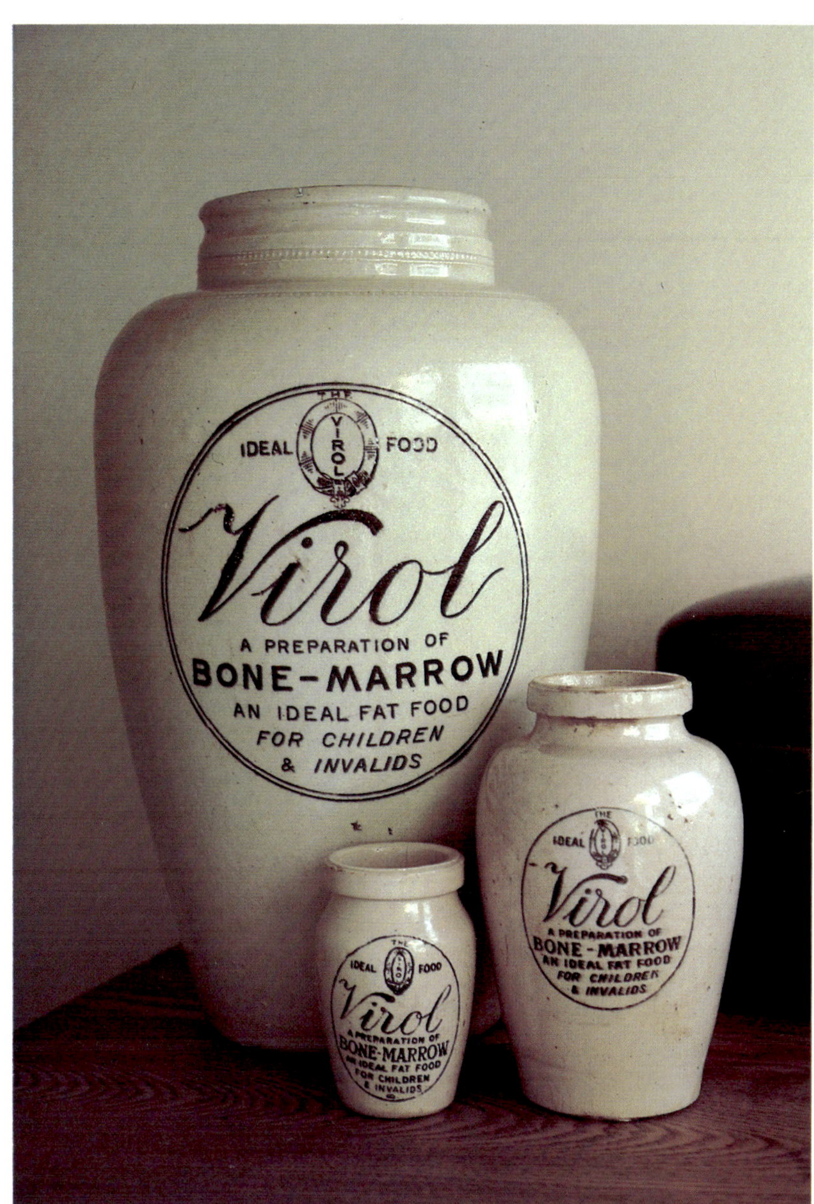
THE
VIROL
IDEAL FOOD
Virol
A PREPARATION OF
BONE-MARROW
AN IDEAL FAT FOOD
FOR CHILDREN
& INVALIDS

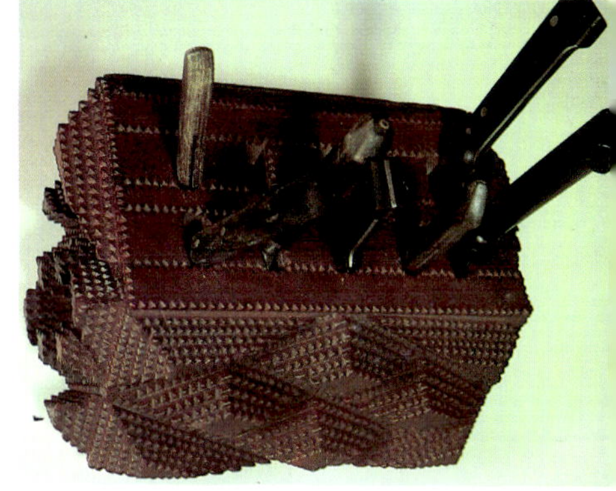

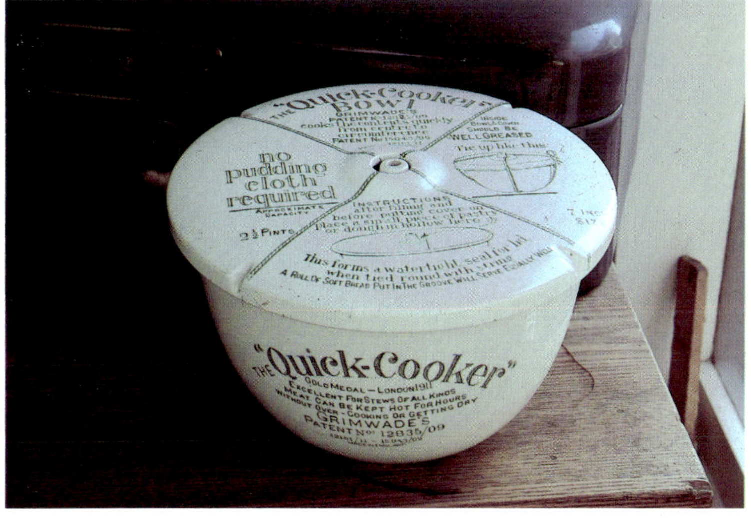
"THE Quick-Cooker" BOWL
GRIMWADE'S
cooks the contents quickly from centre to circumference
INSIDE BOWL & COVER SHOULD BE WELL GREASED
Tie up like this
no pudding cloth required
APPROXIMATE CAPACITY
2½ PINTS
INSTRUCTIONS after filling and before putting cover on place a small piece of pastry or dough in hollow here
This forms a watertight seal for lid when tied round with string
A ROLL OF SOFT BREAD PUT IN THE GROOVE WILL SERVE EQUALLY WELL
"THE Quick-Cooker"
GOLD MEDAL — LONDON 1911
EXCELLENT FOR STEWS OF ALL KINDS
MEAT CAN BE KEPT HOT FOR HOURS
WITHOUT OVER-COOKING OR GETTING DRY
GRIMWADE'S
PATENT No 12835/09

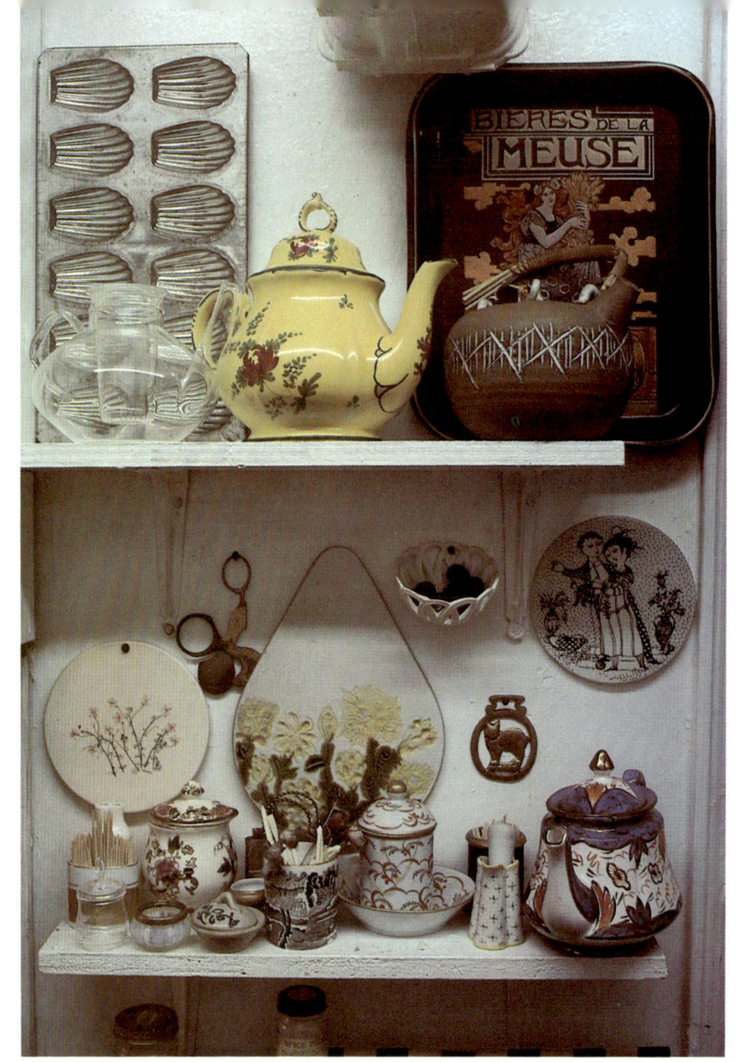
BIERES DE LA
MEUSE

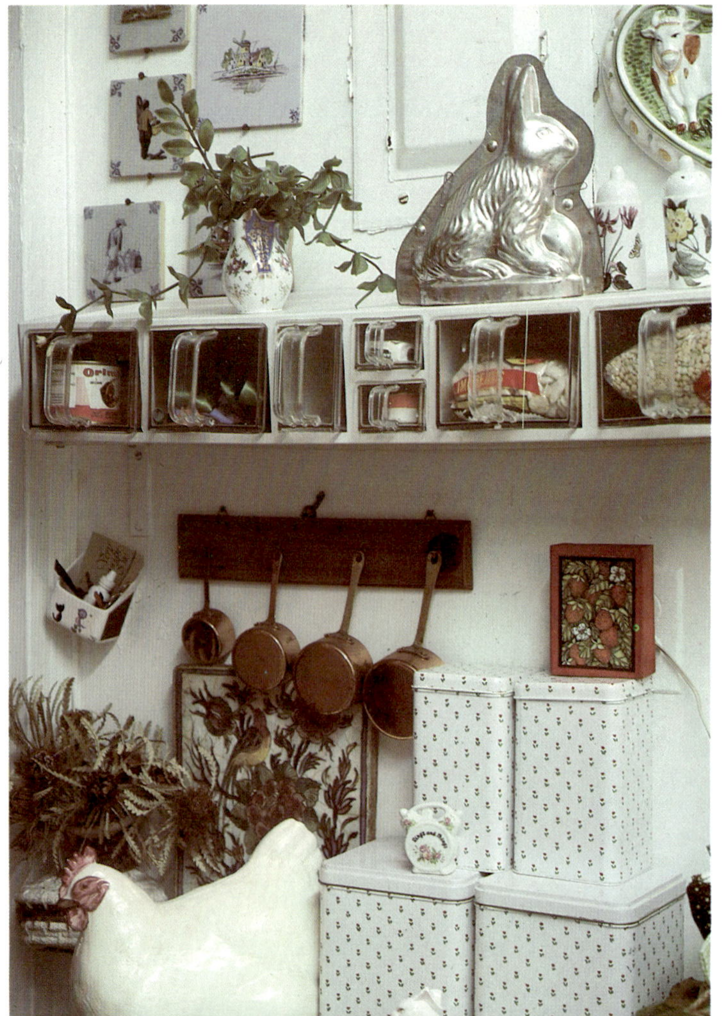

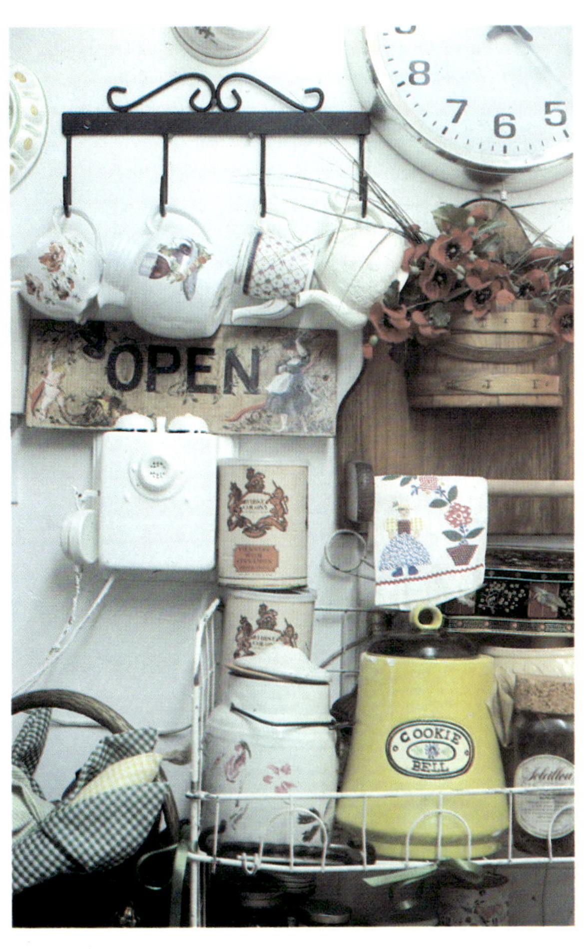
OPEN
COOKIE
BELL

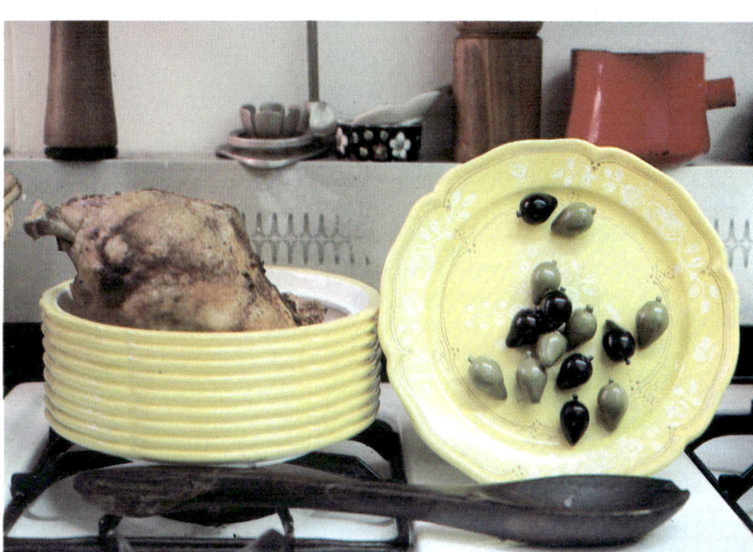

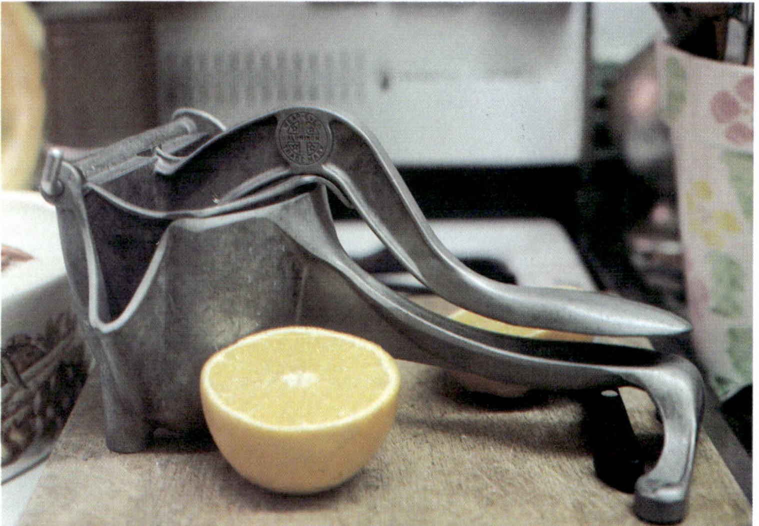

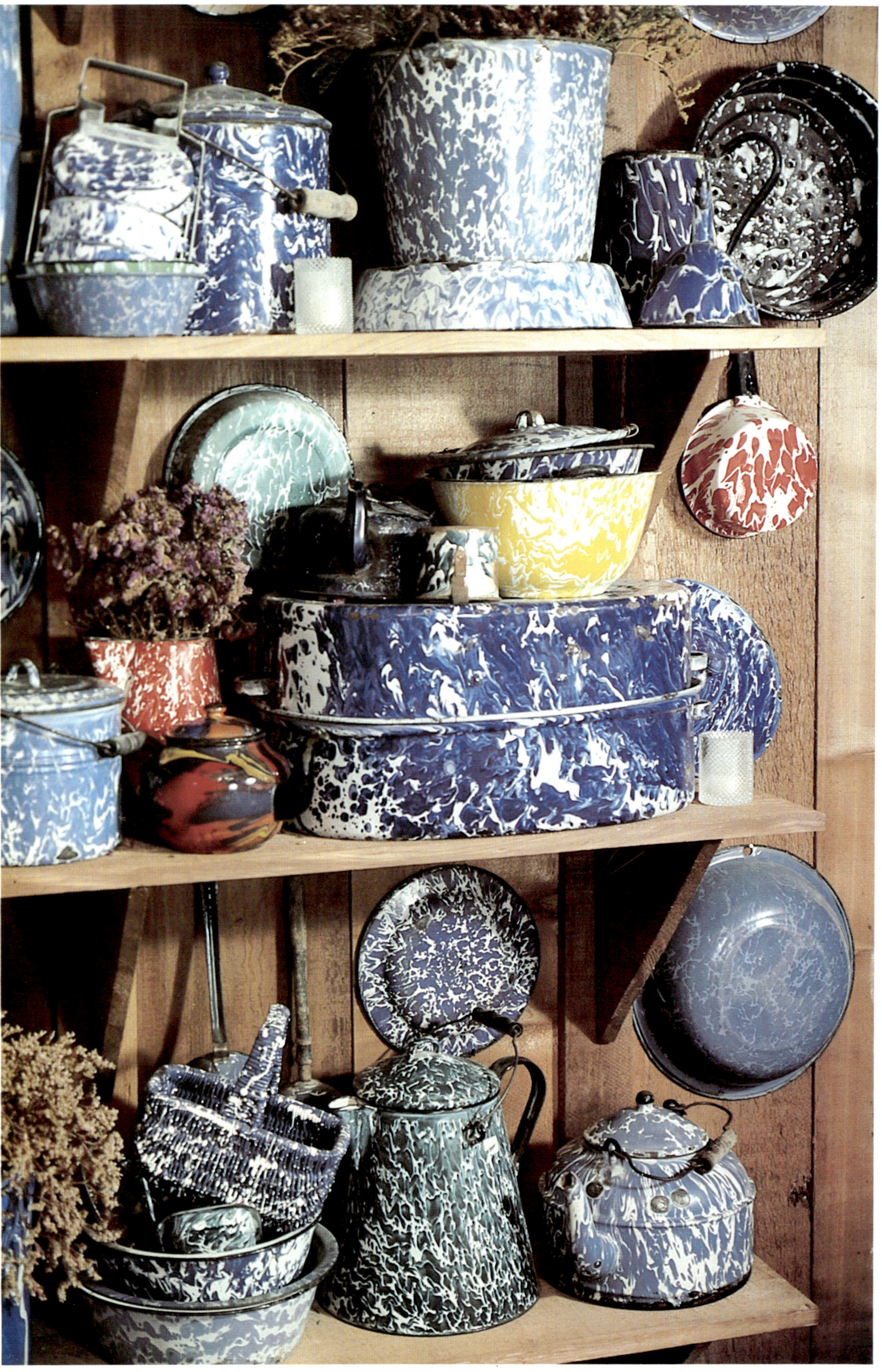

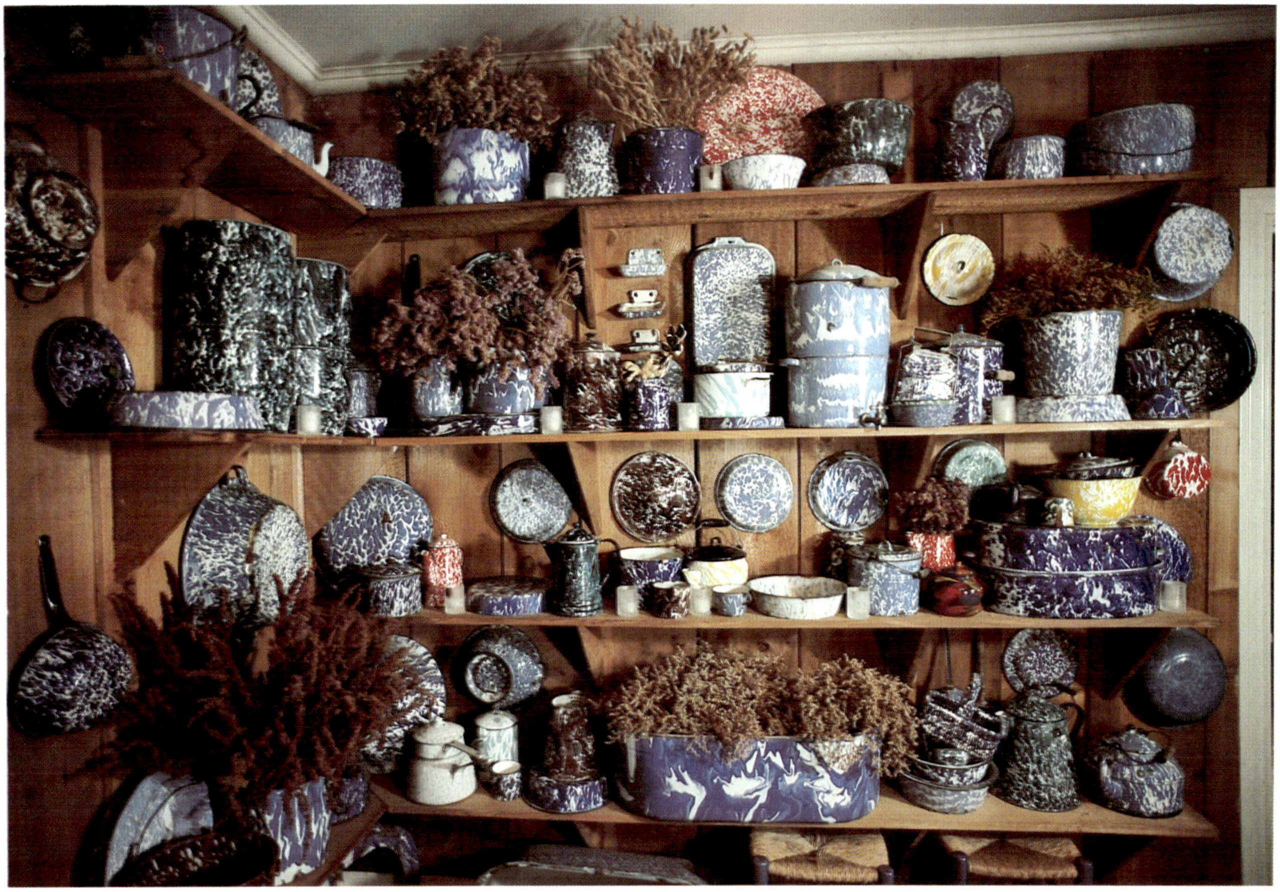

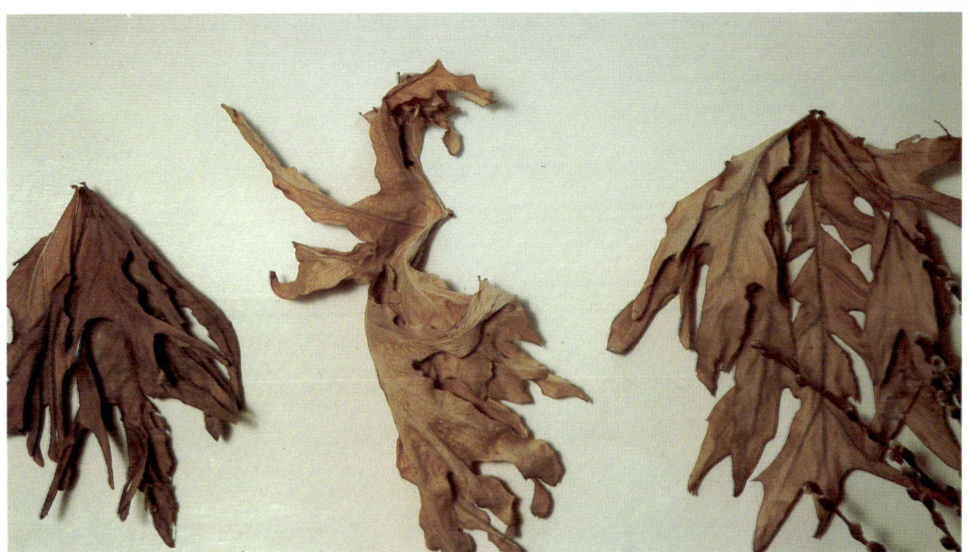

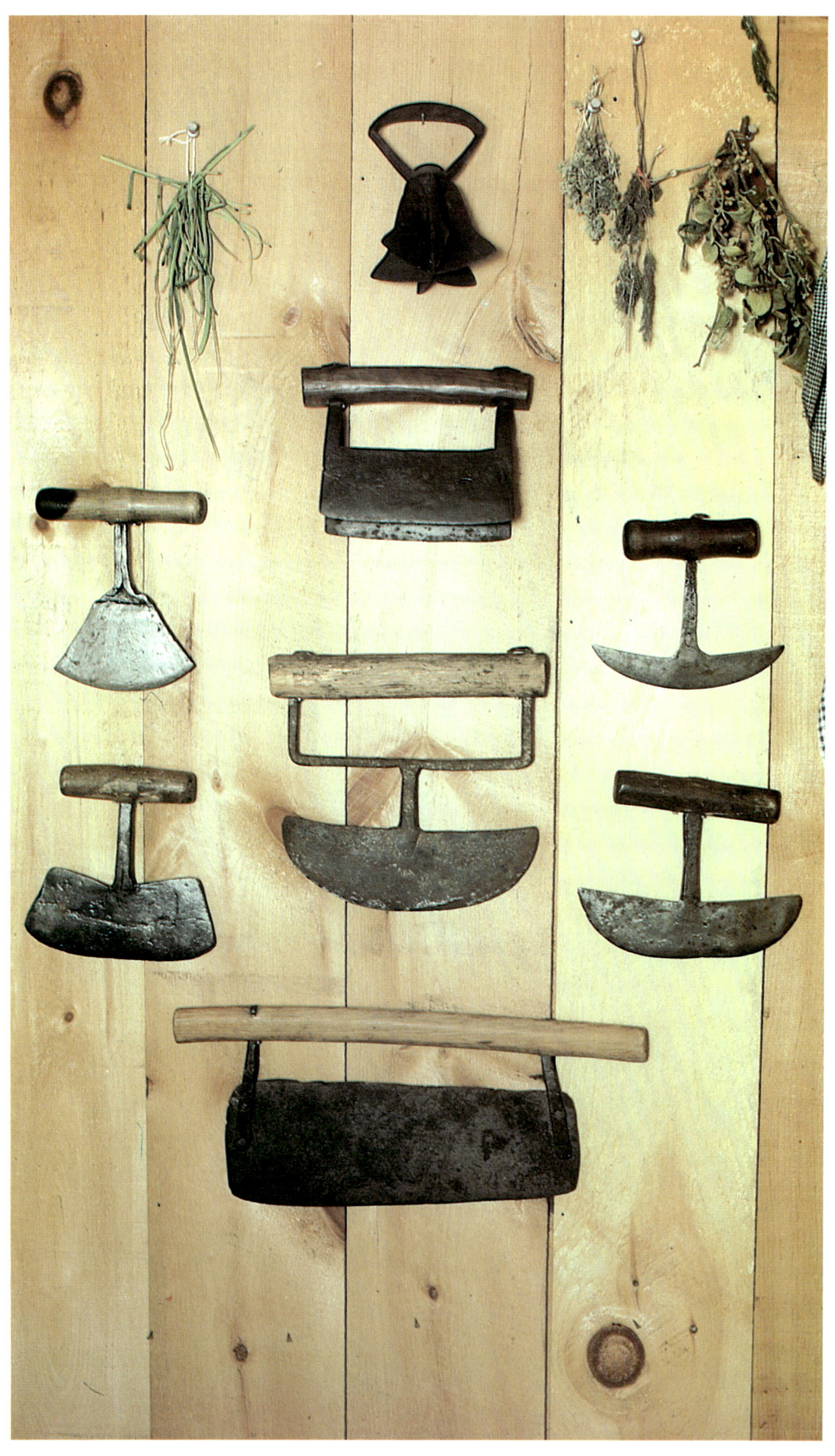

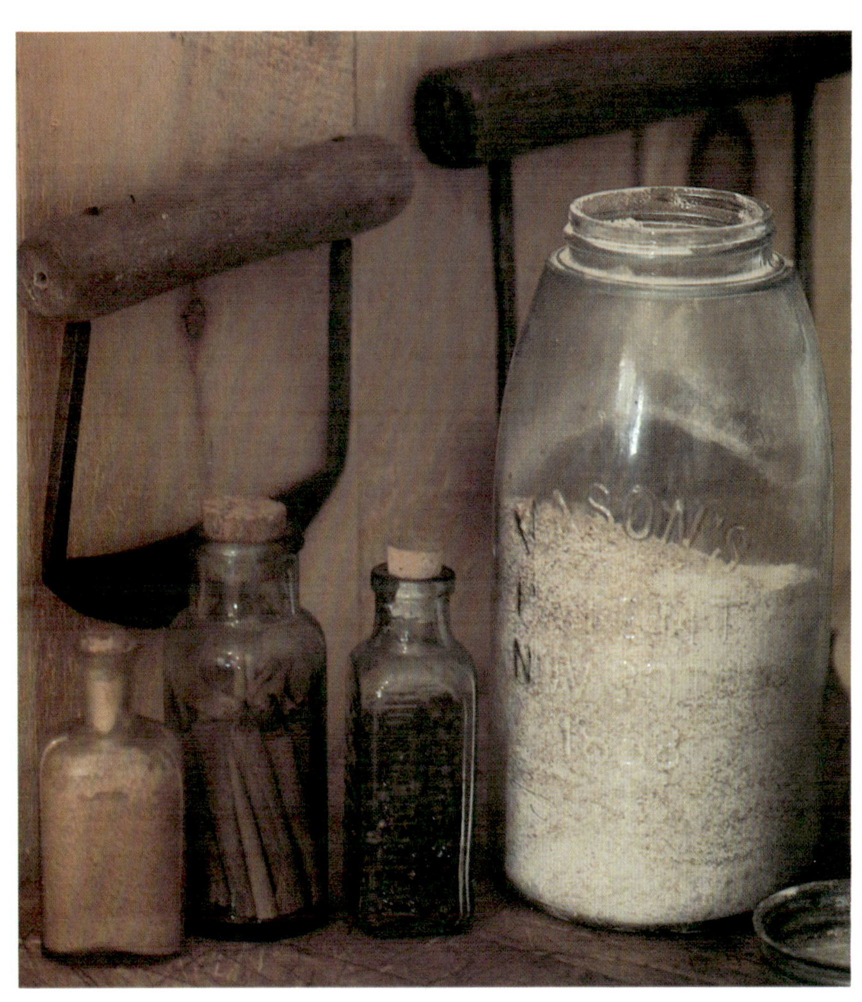

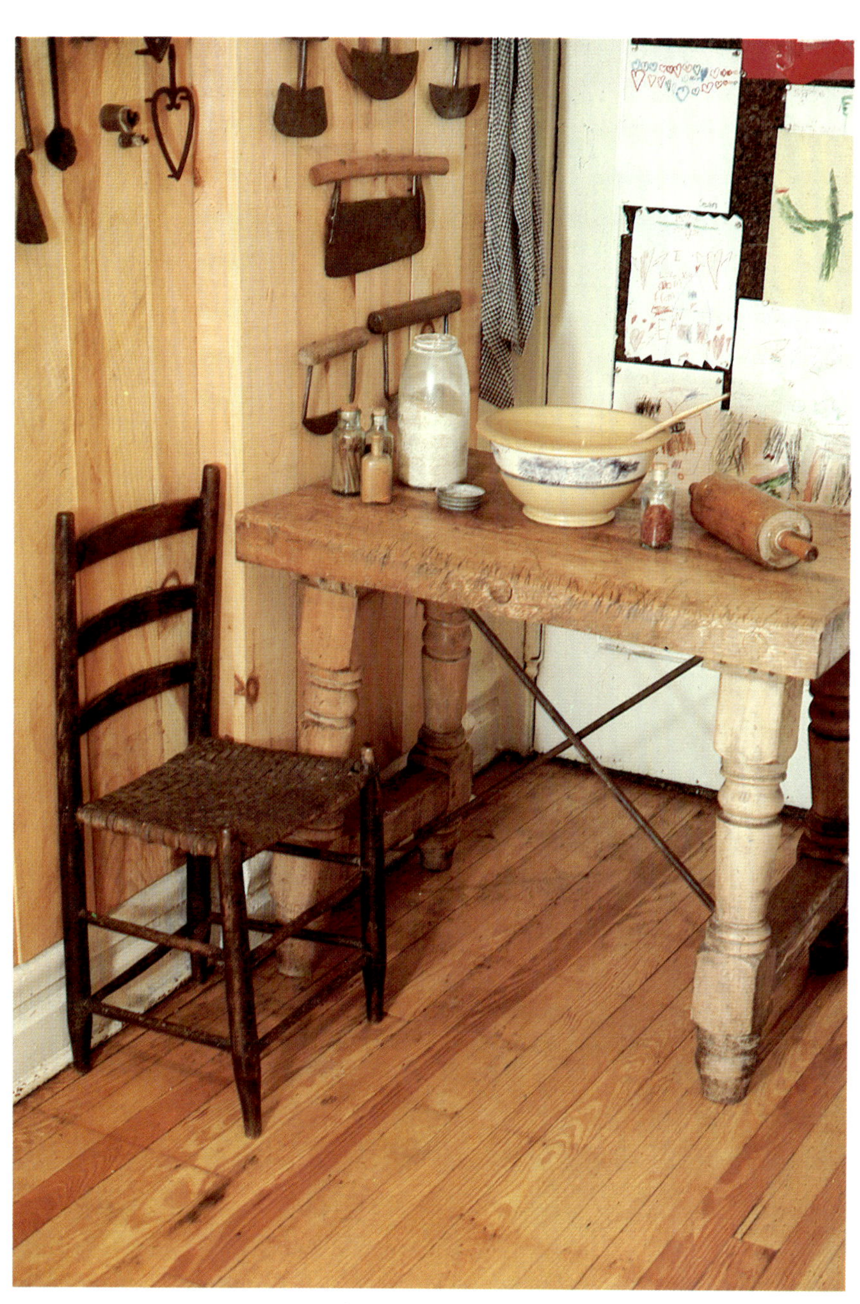

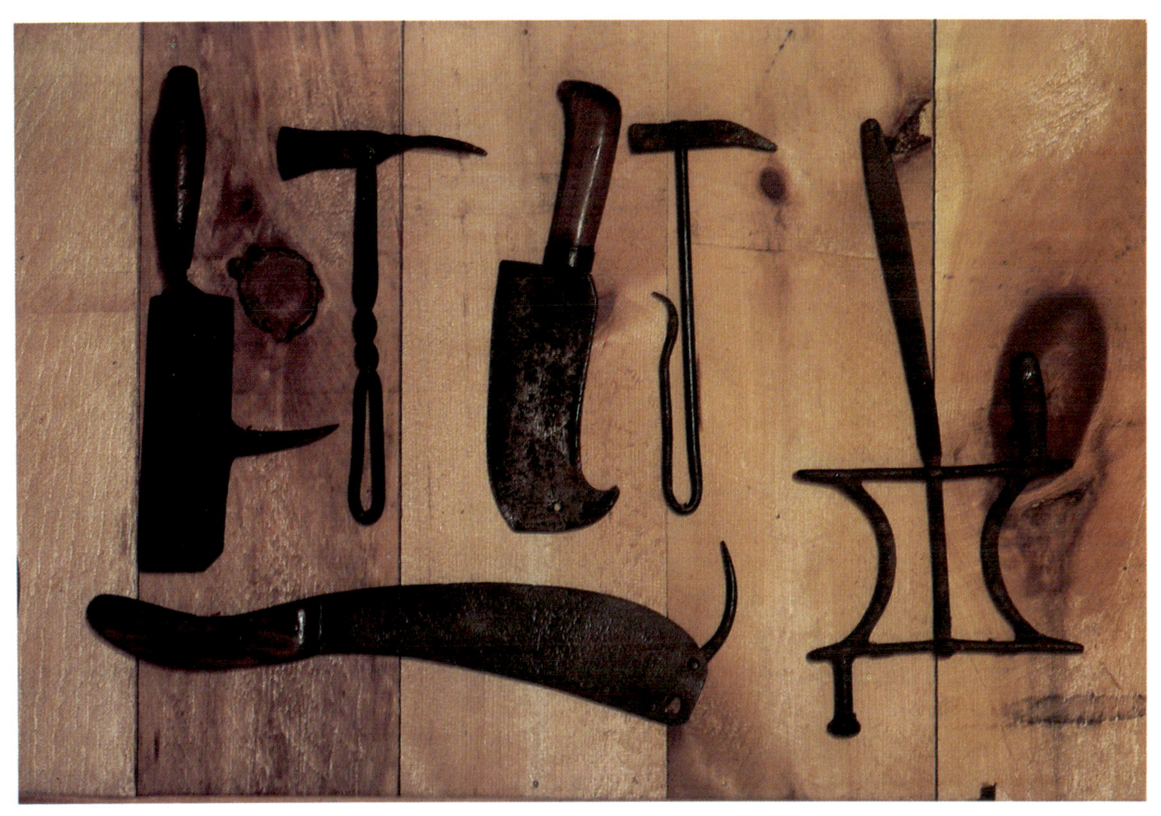

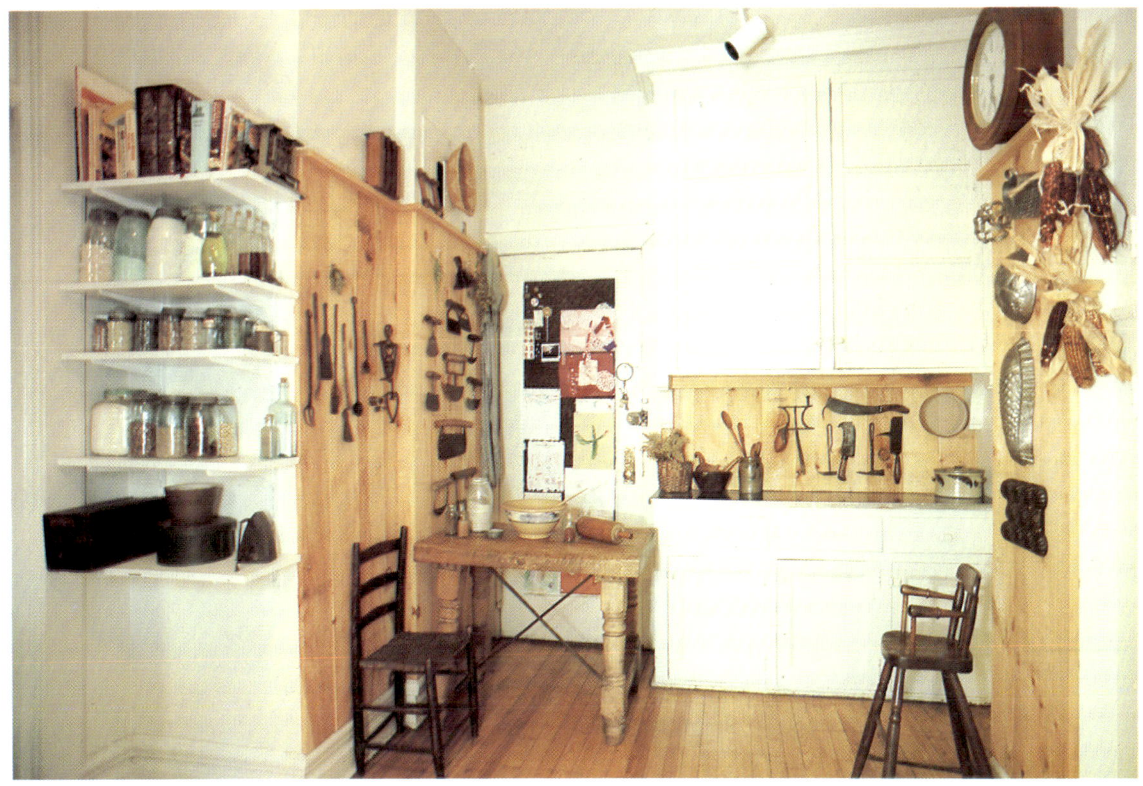

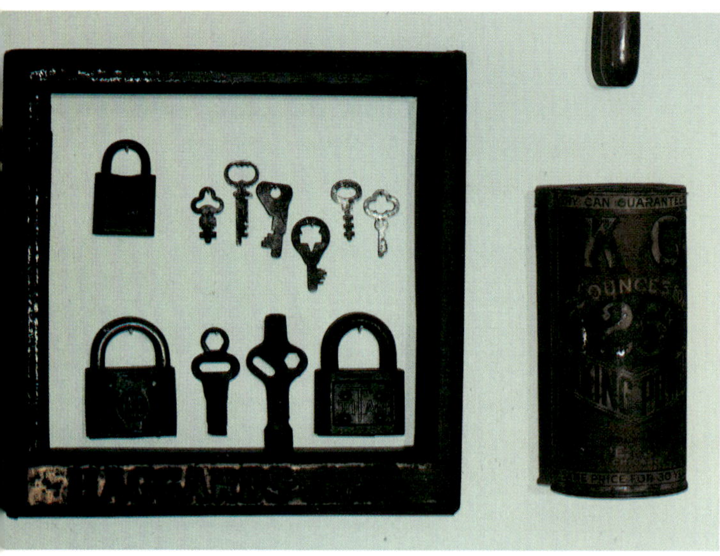
K C
OUNCES

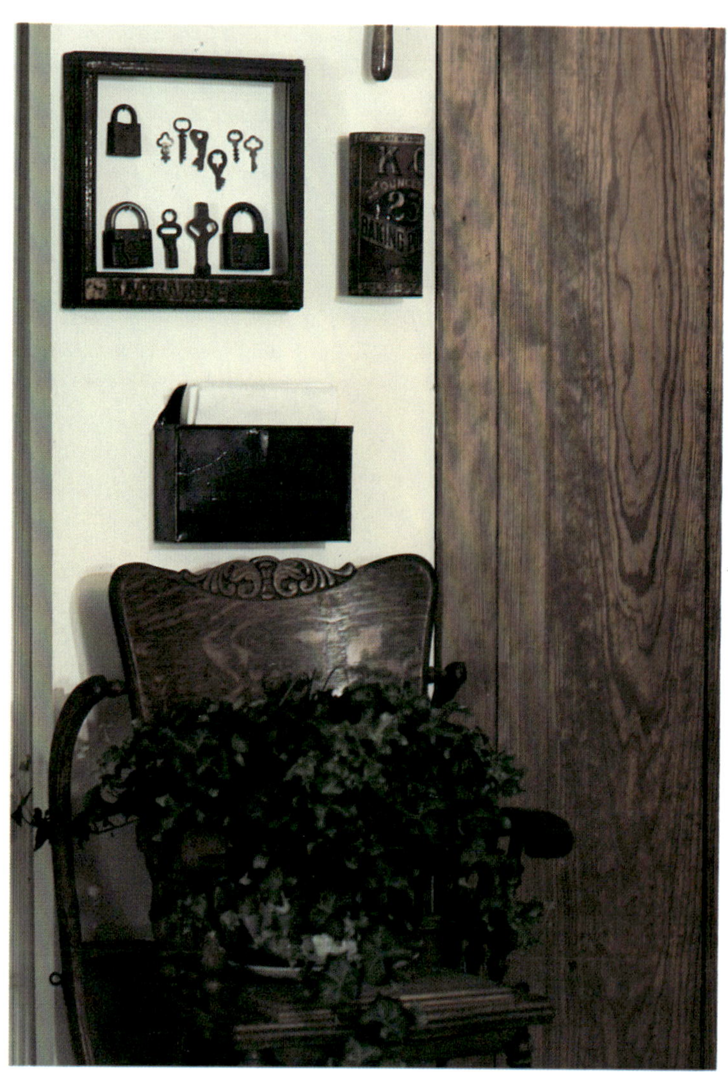

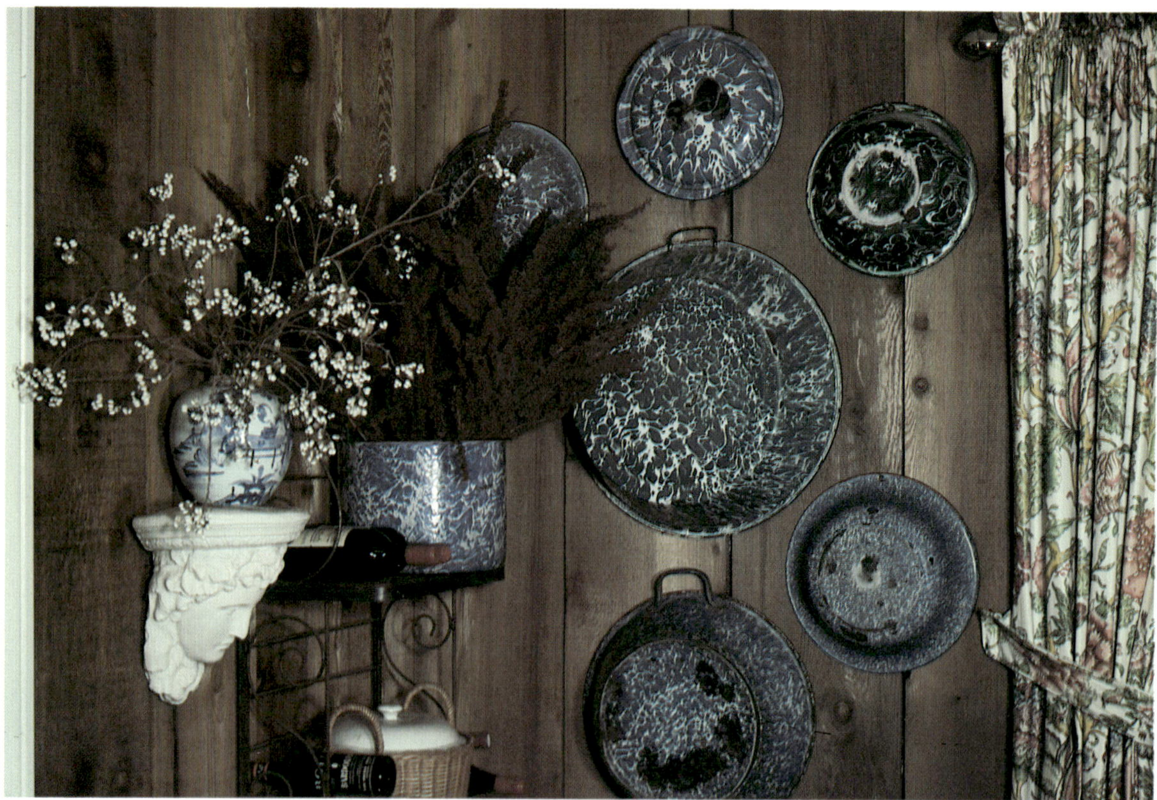

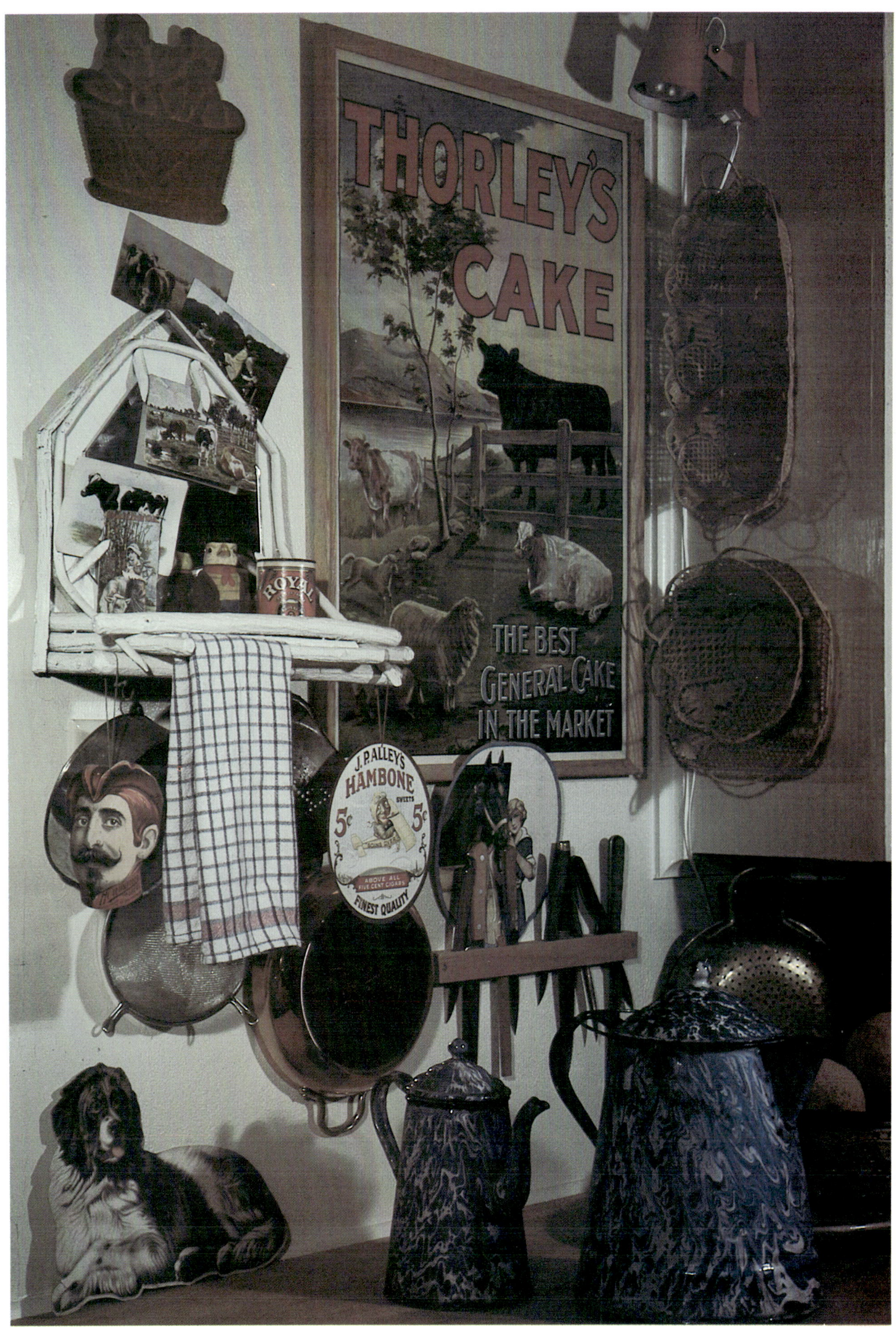
THORLEY'S
CAKE
THE BEST
GENERAL CAKE
IN THE MARKET
ROYAL
J. P. ALLEY'S
HAMBONE
SWEETS
5¢
5¢
ABOVE ALL
FIVE CENT CIGARS
FINEST QUALITY

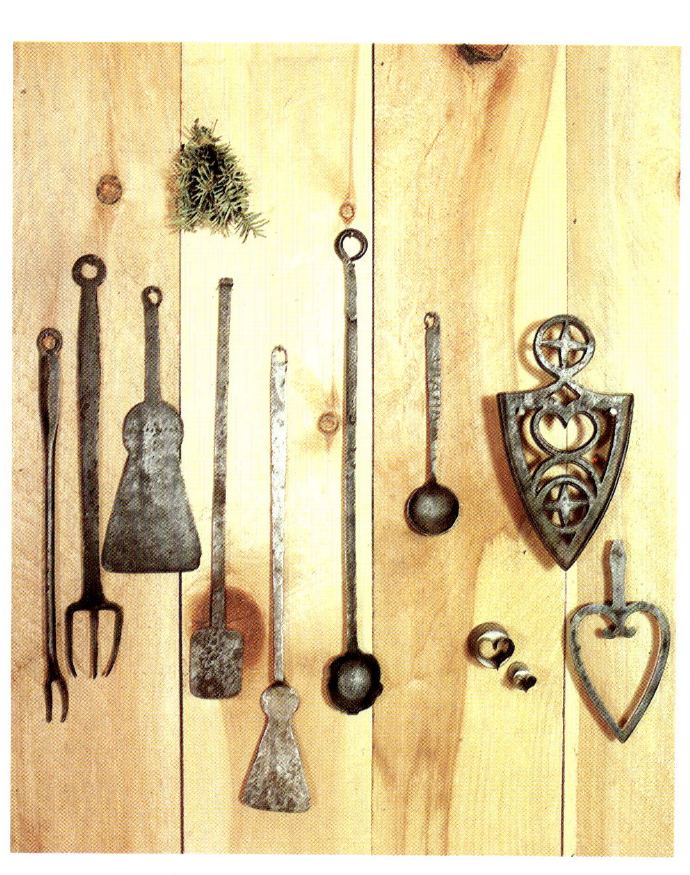

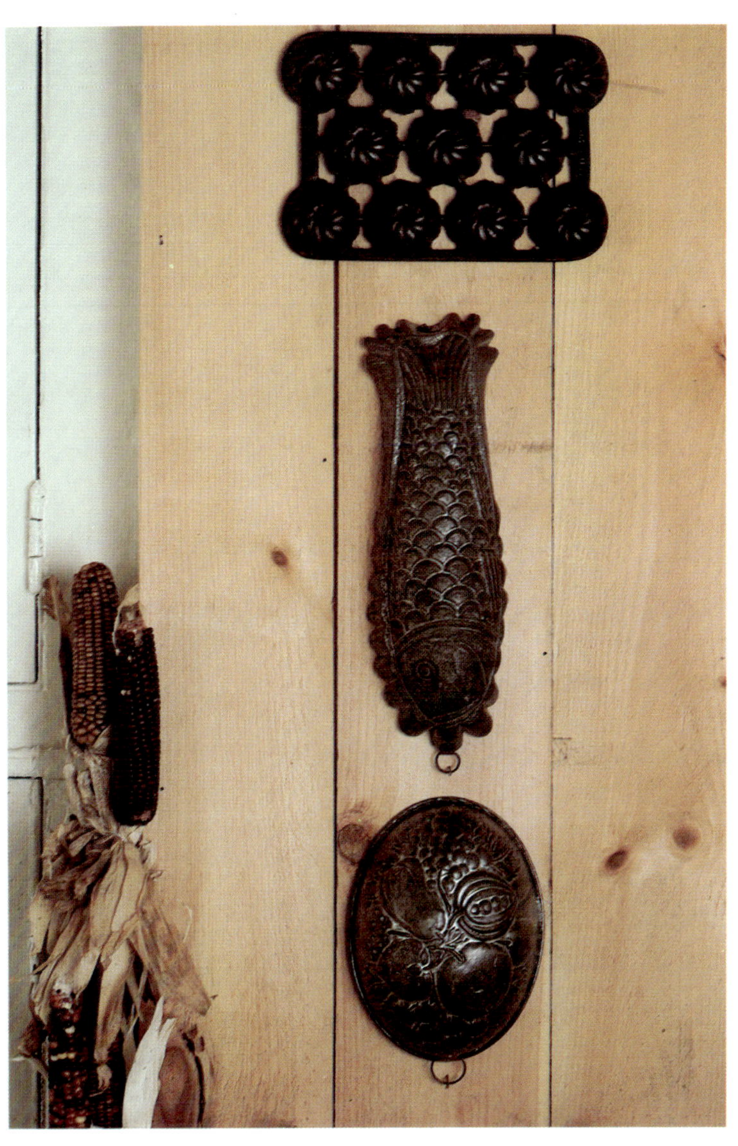

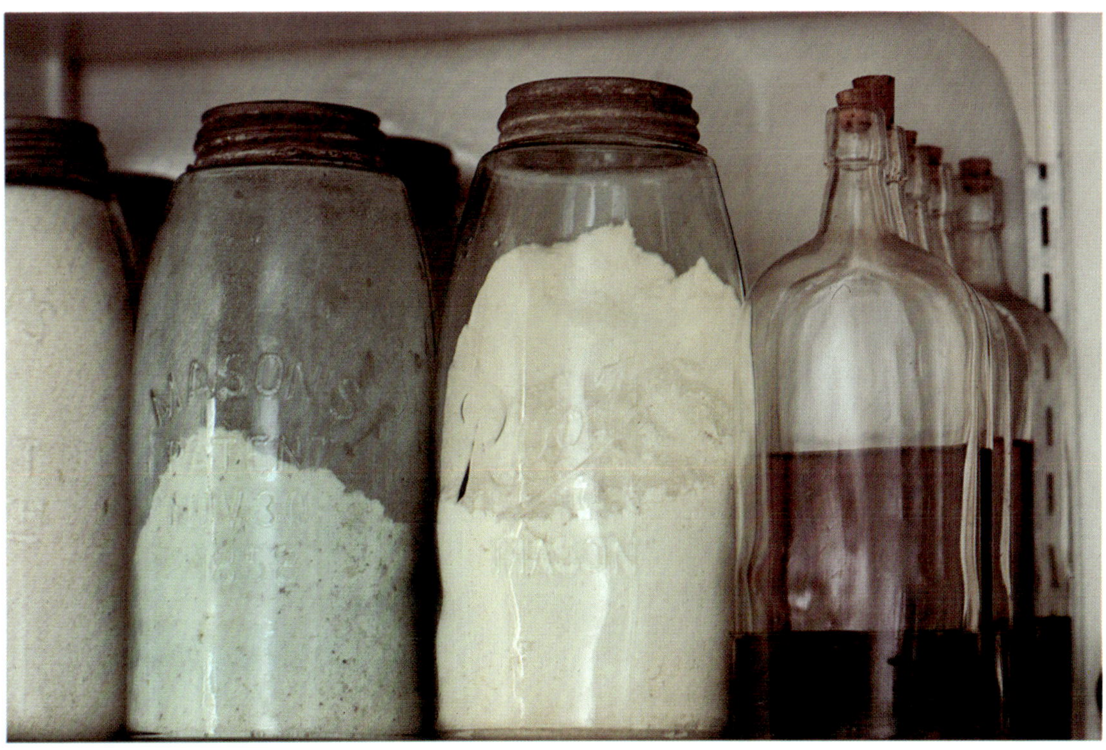
MASON'S
MASON

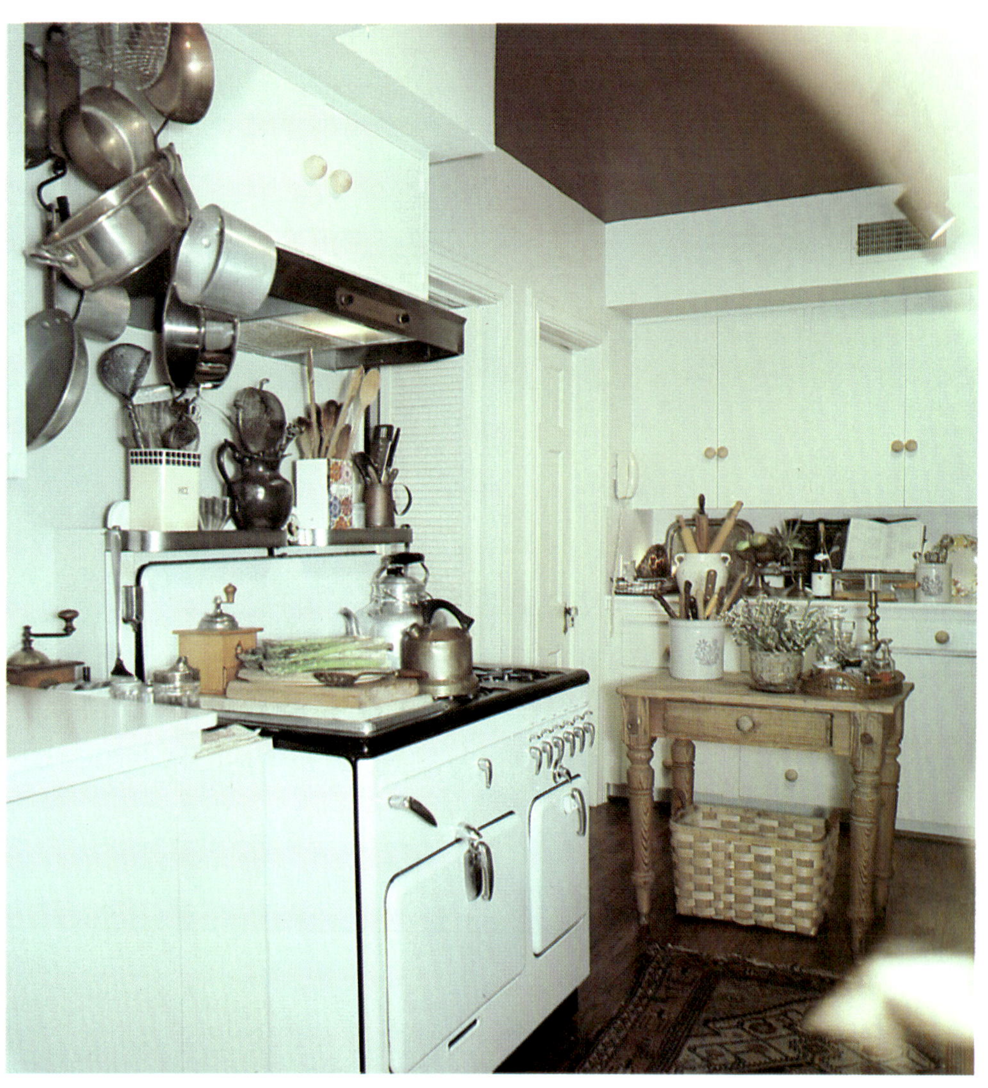

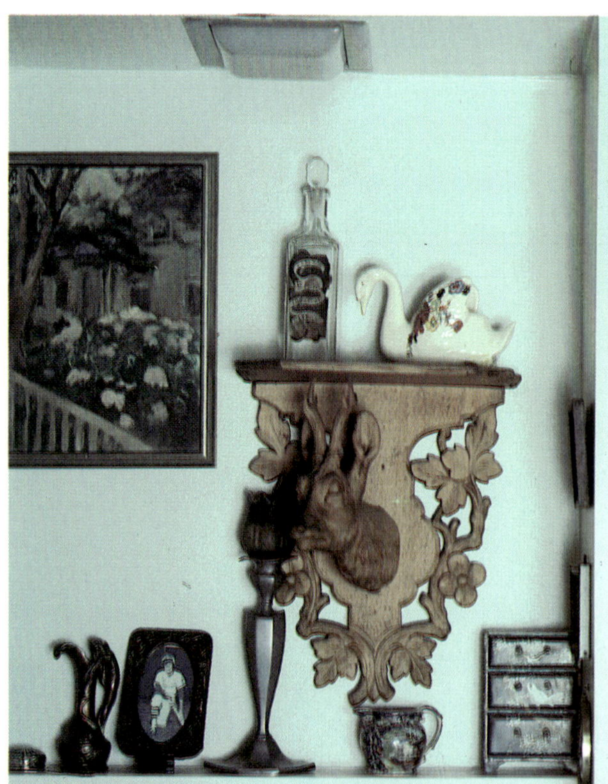

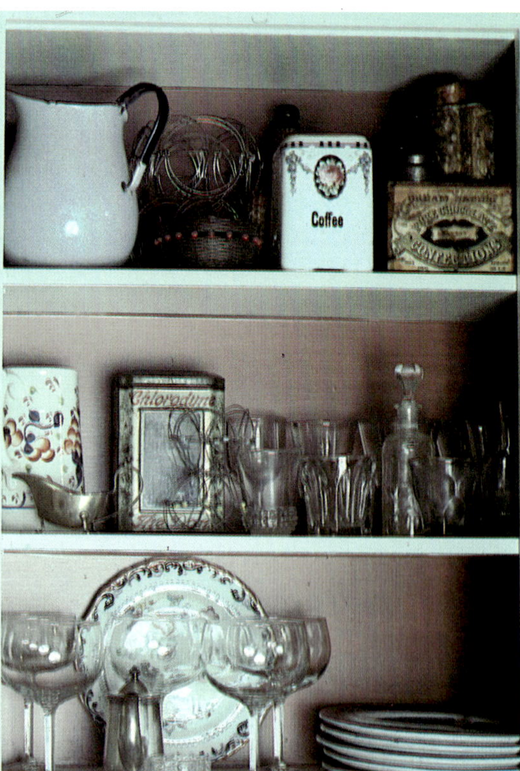
Coffee

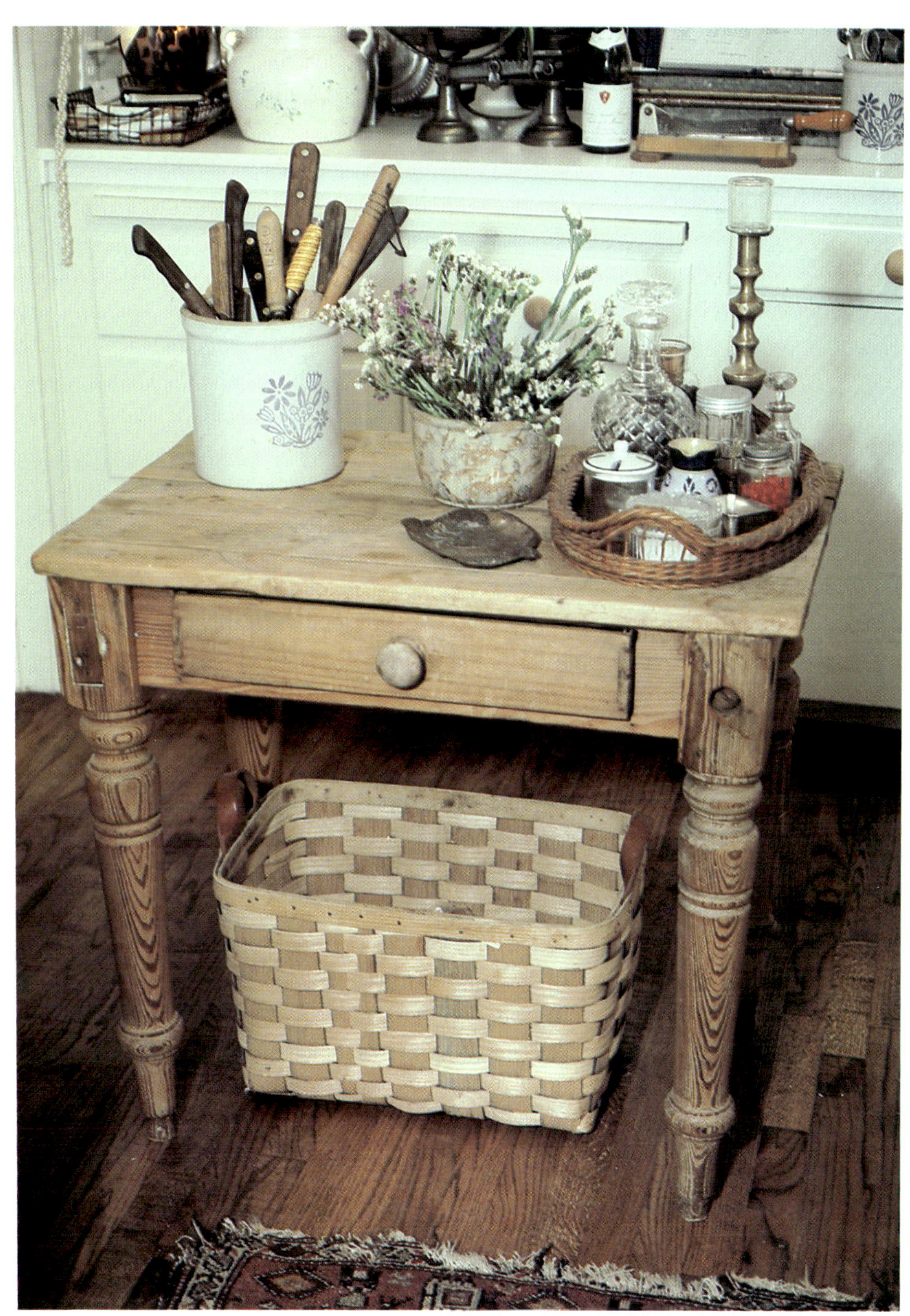

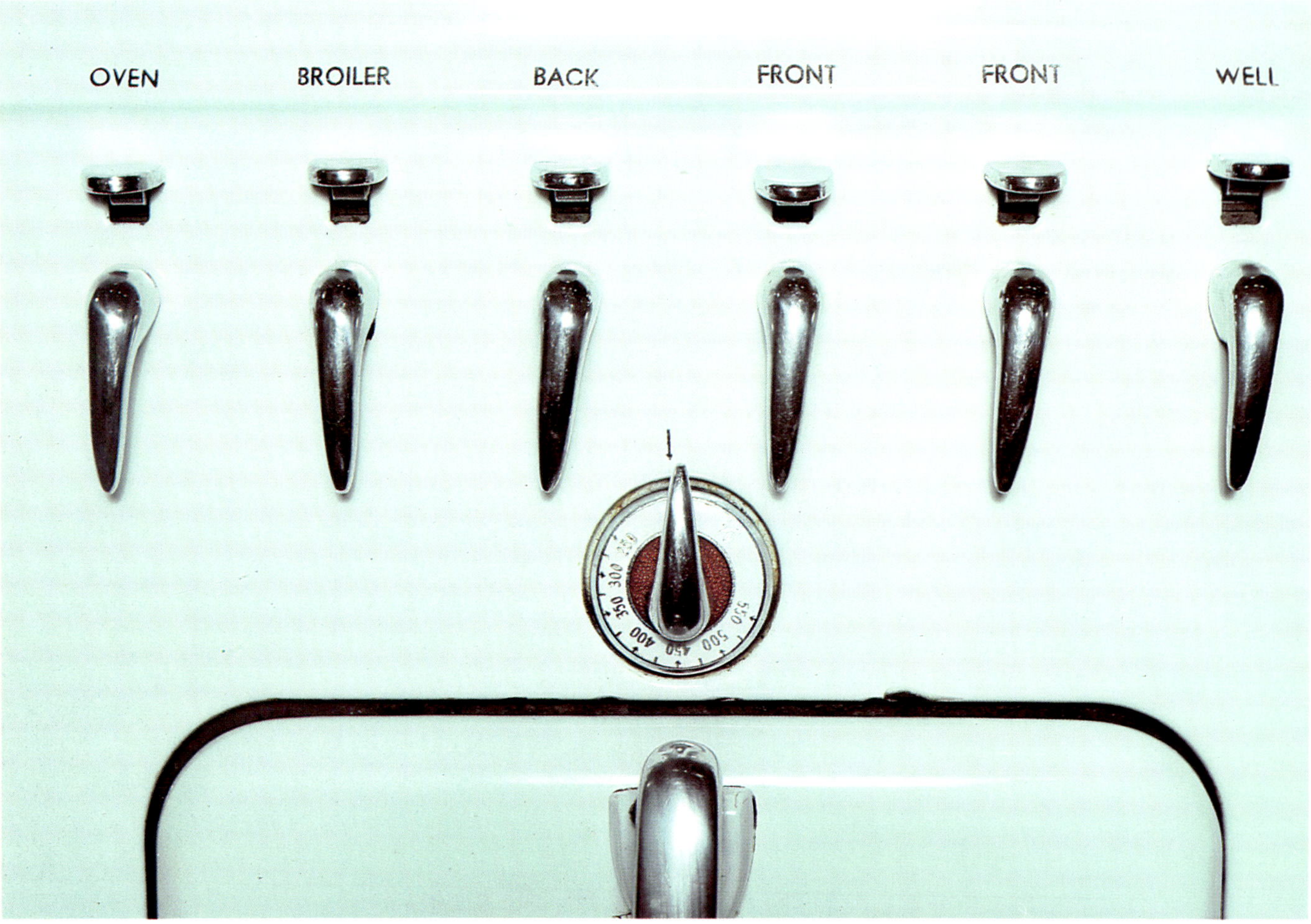

OVEN
BROILER
BACK
FRONT
FRONT
WELL

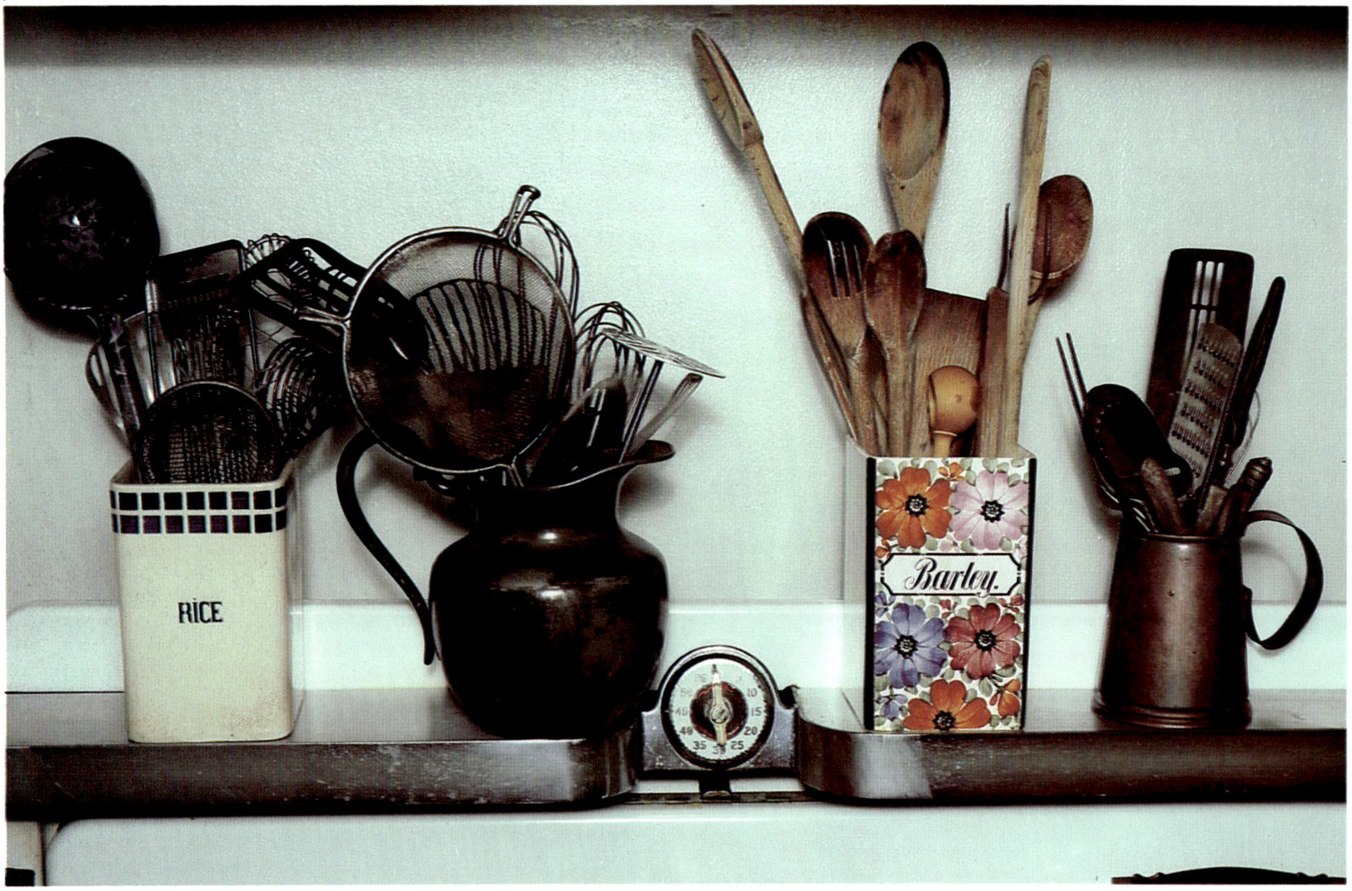

RICE
Barley

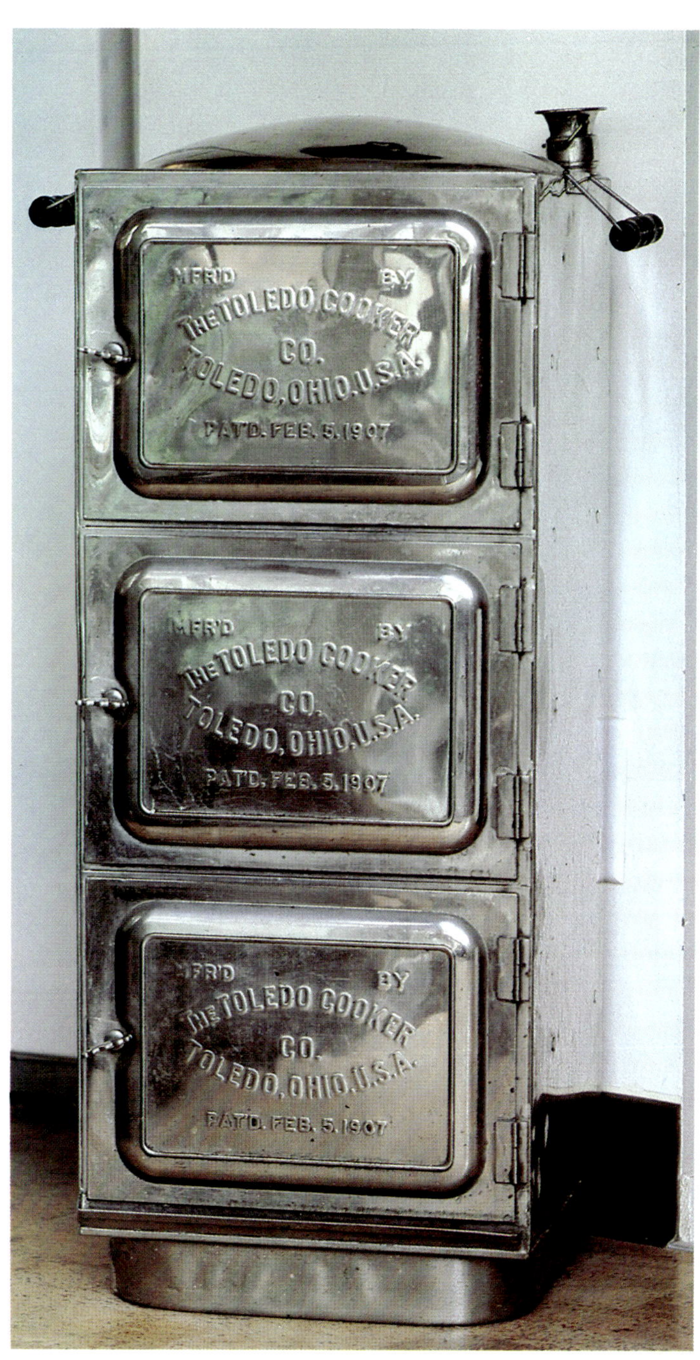
MFR'D BY
THE TOLEDO COOKER
CO.
TOLEDO, OHIO, U.S.A.
PAT'D. FEB. 5, 1907
MFR'D BY
THE TOLEDO COOKER
CO.
TOLEDO, OHIO, U.S.A.
PAT'D. FEB. 5, 1907
MFR'D BY
THE TOLEDO COOKER
CO.
TOLEDO, OHIO, U.S.A.
PAT'D. FEB. 5, 1907

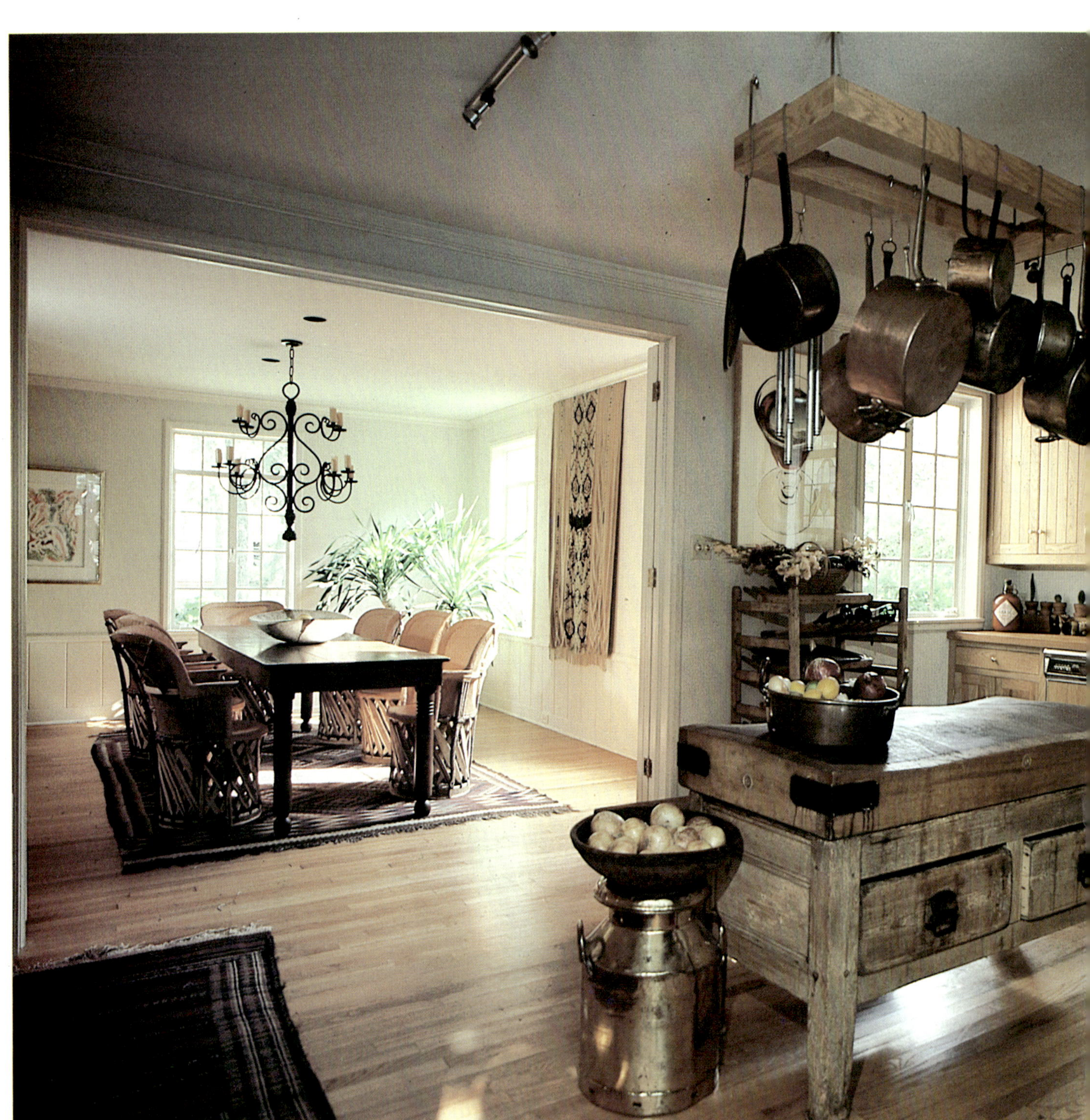

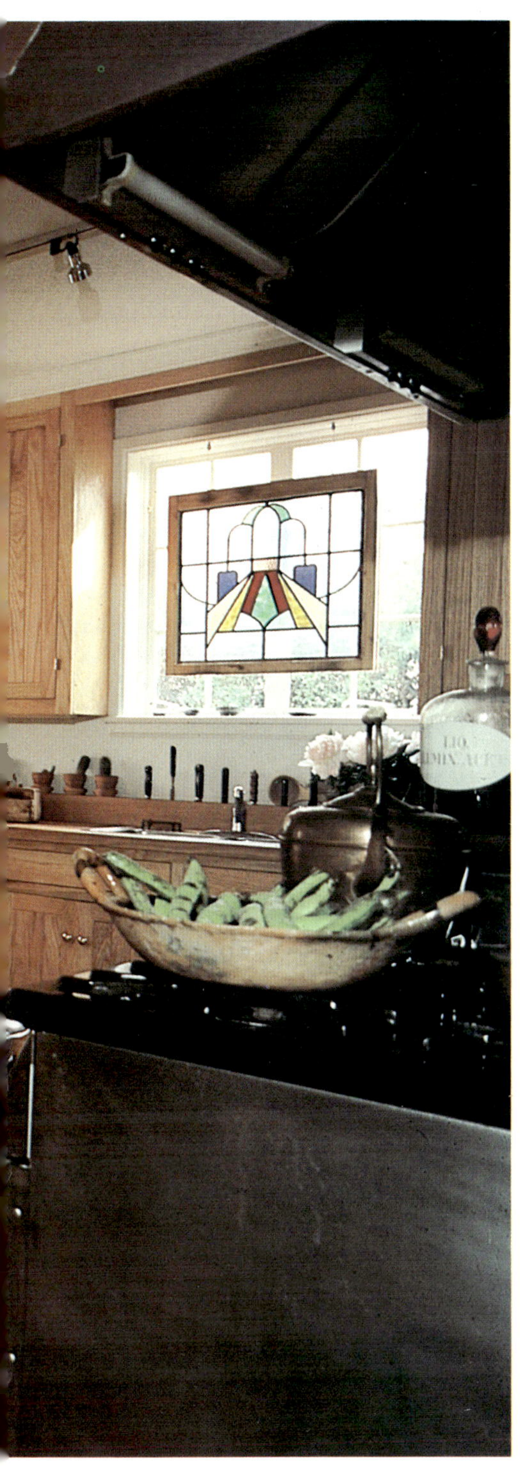

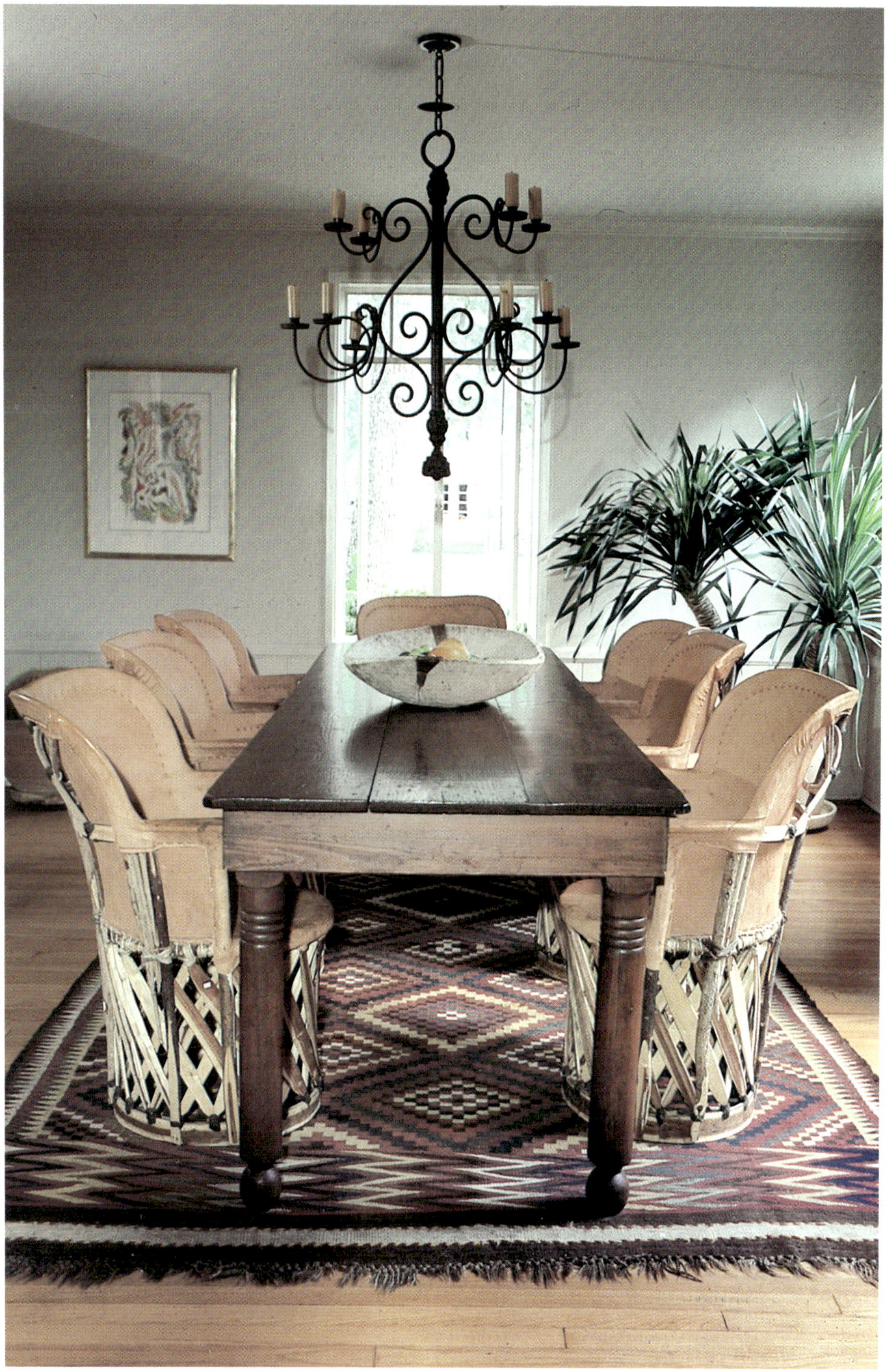

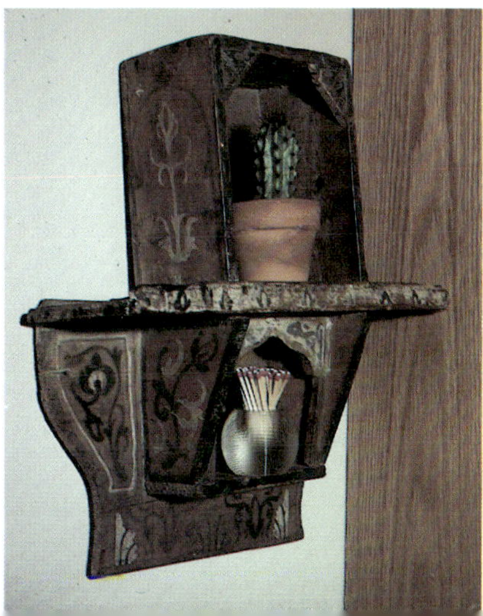

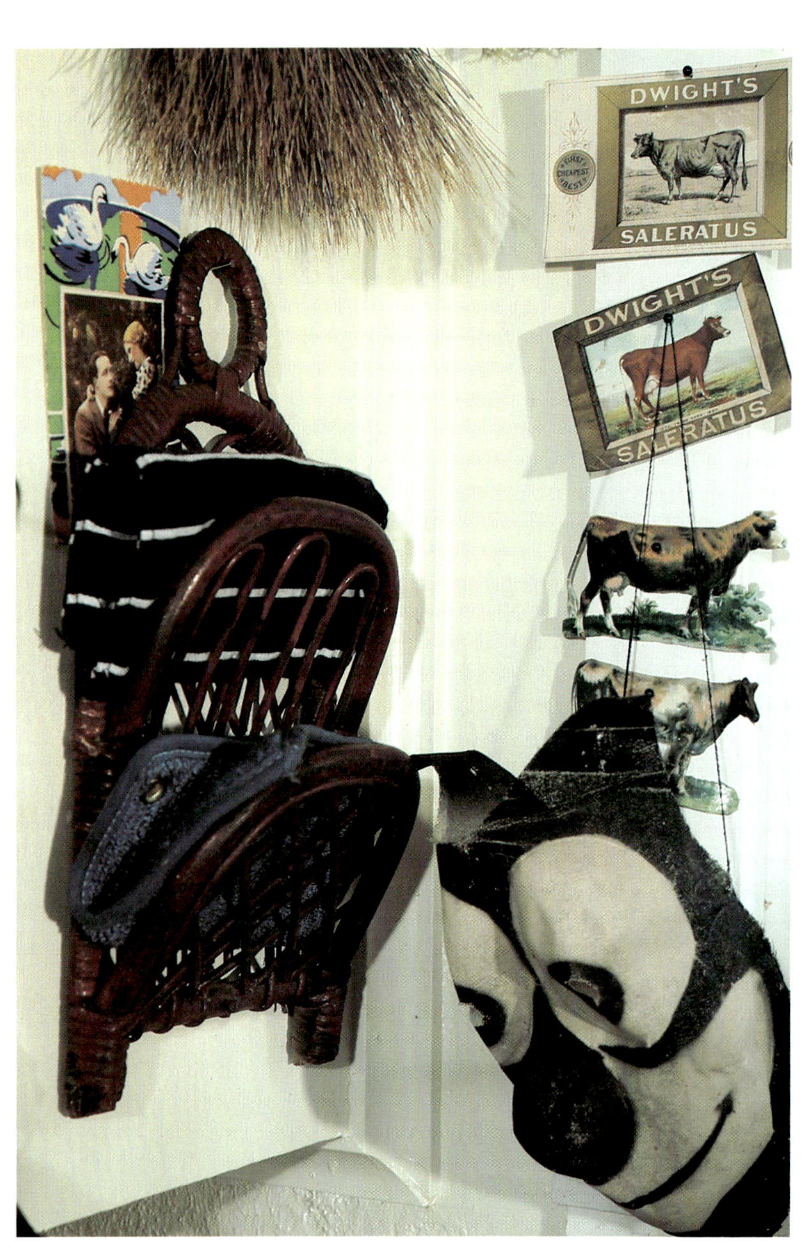
DWIGHT'S
SALERATUS
DWIGHT'S
SALERATUS

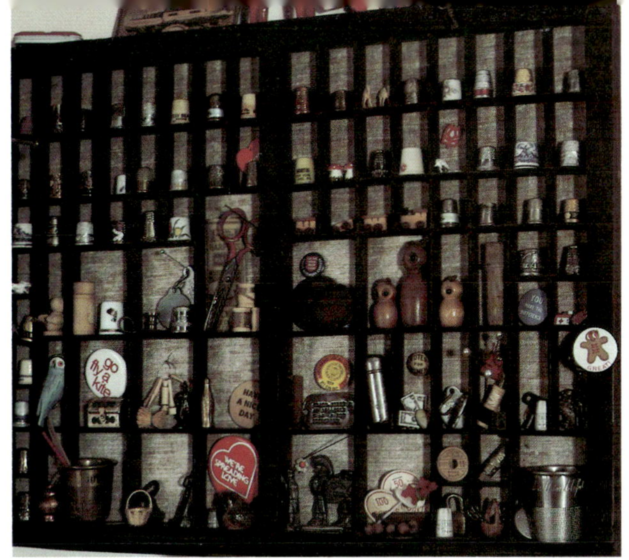
go fly a kite
WE'RE SPREADING LOVE

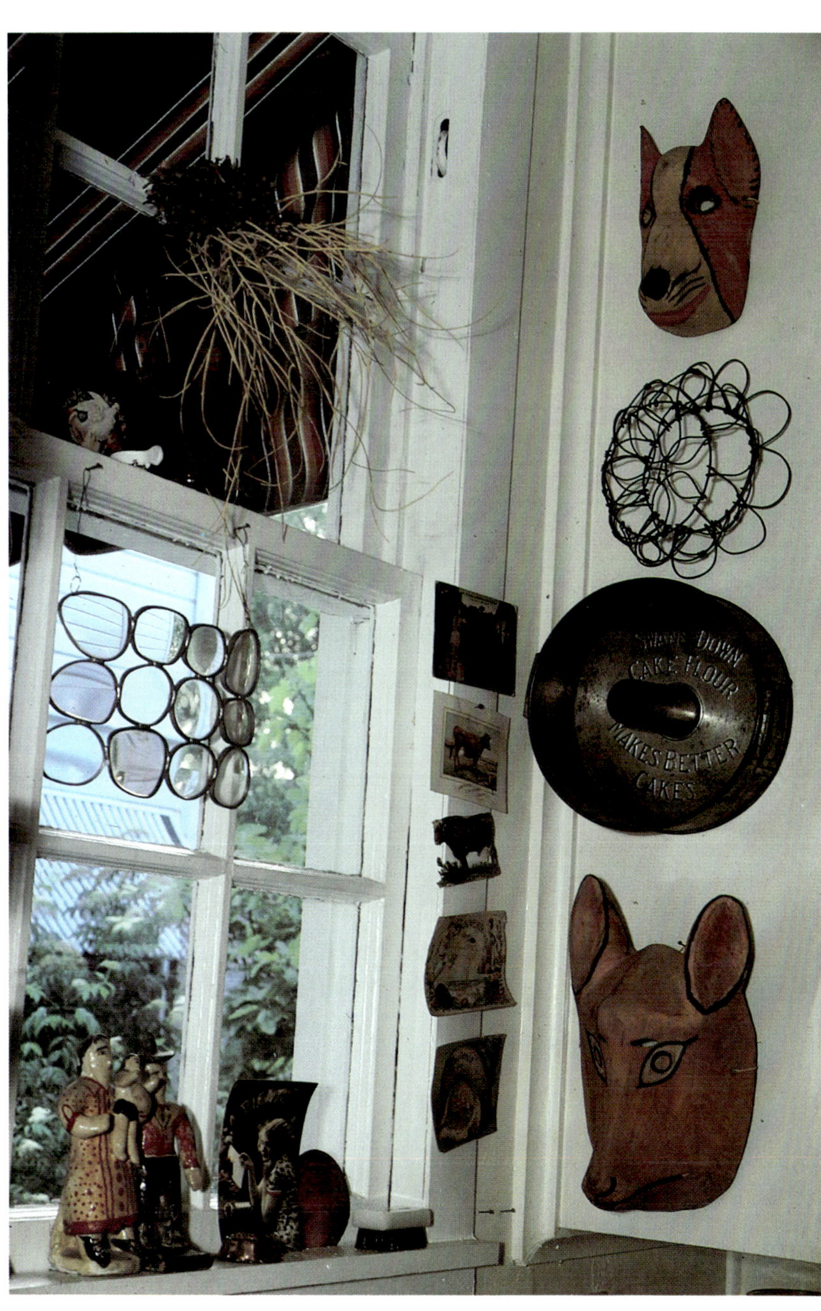
SWANS DOWN
CAKE FLOUR
MAKES BETTER
CAKES

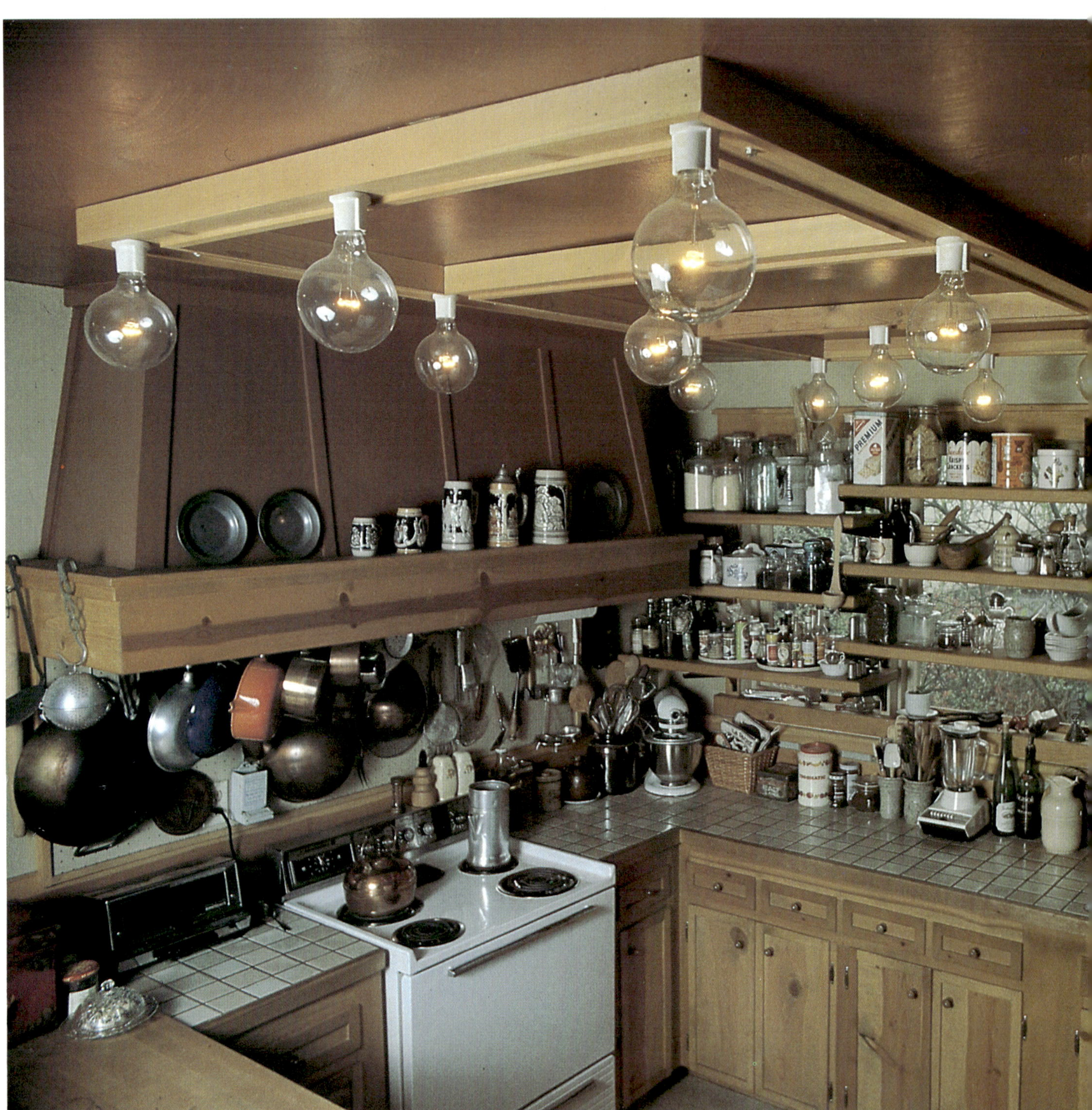
PREMIUM

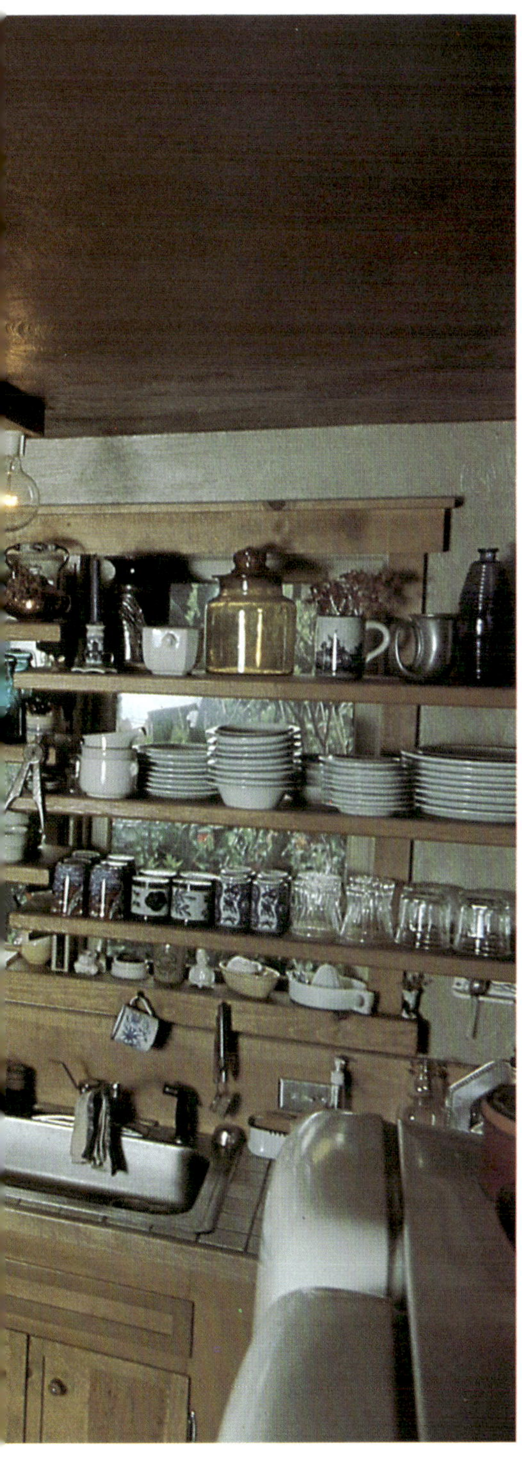

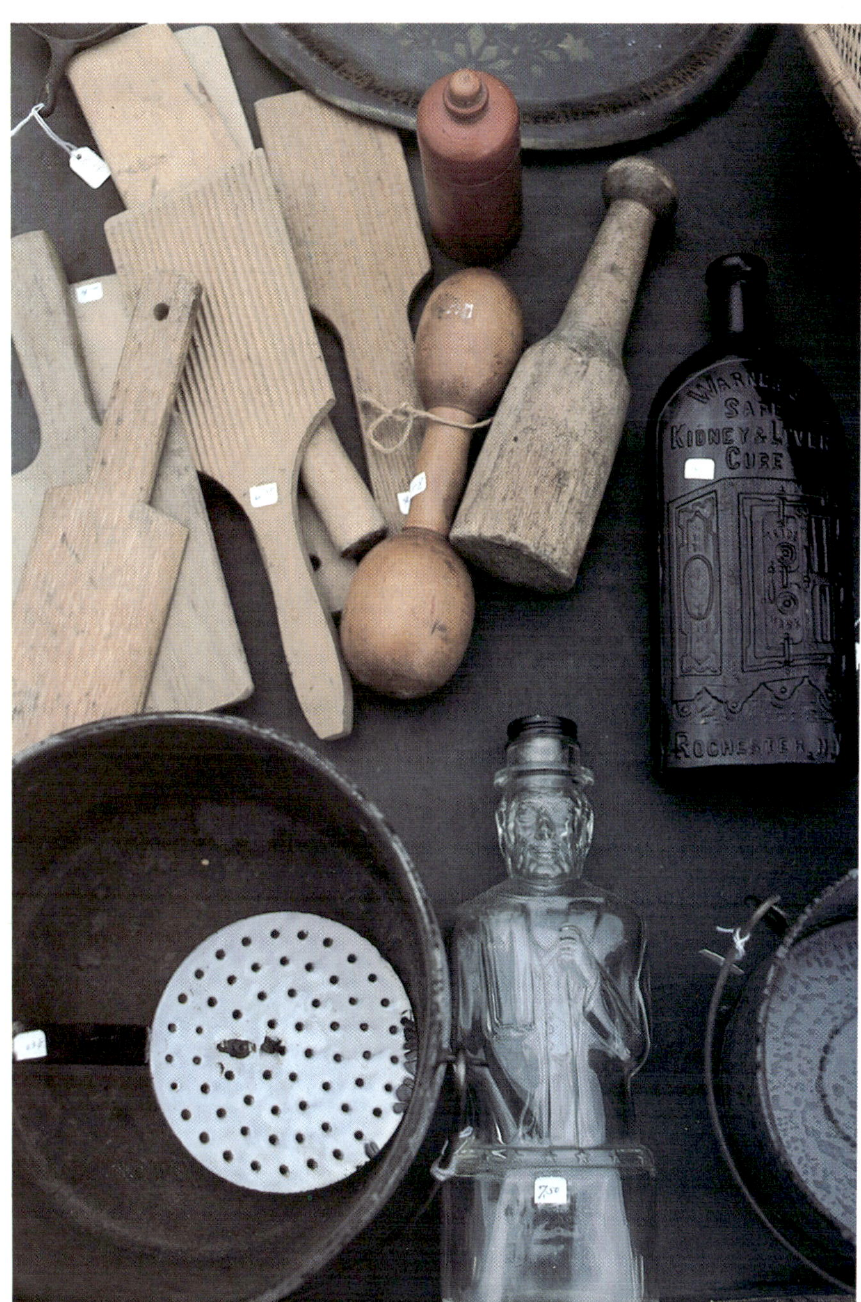
SAFE
KIDNEY & LIVER
CURE

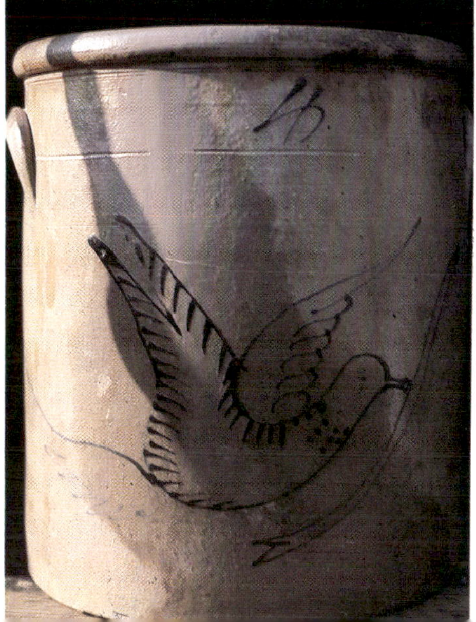

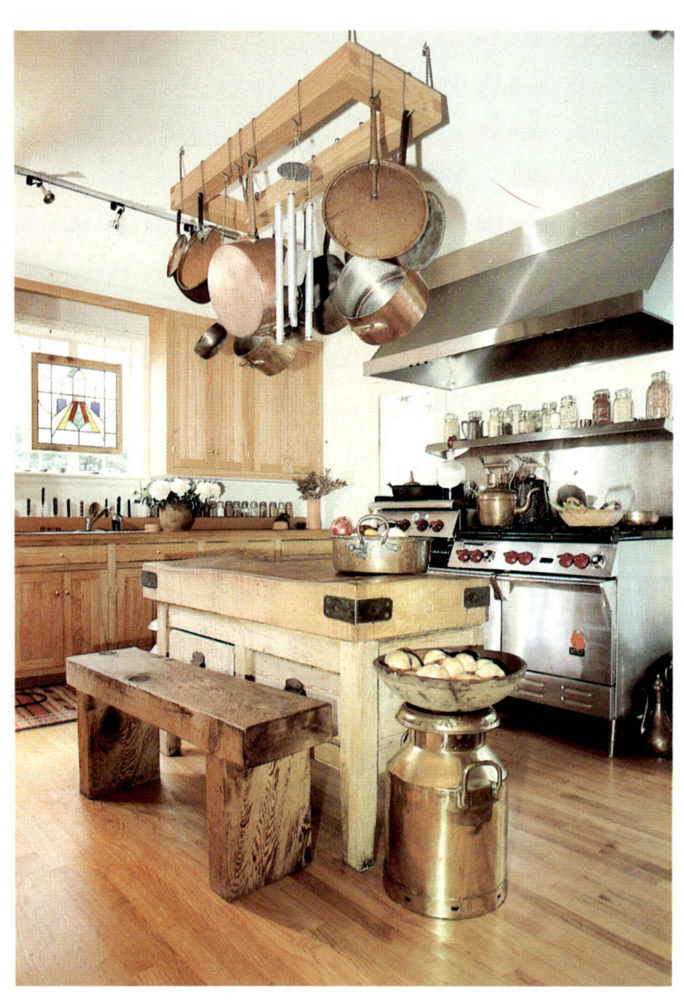

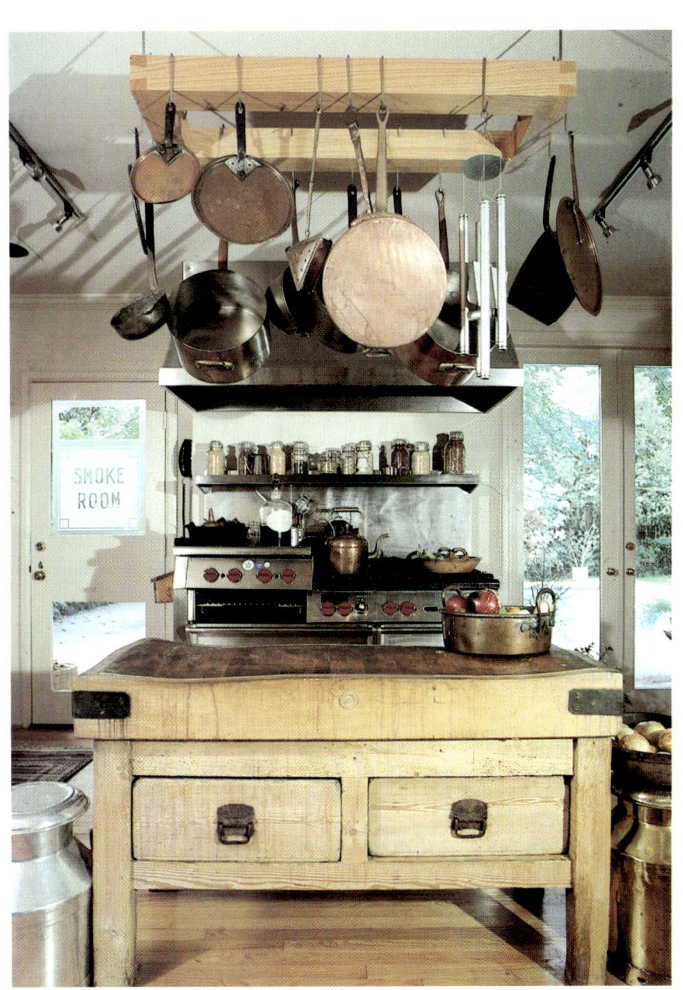
SMOKE
ROOM

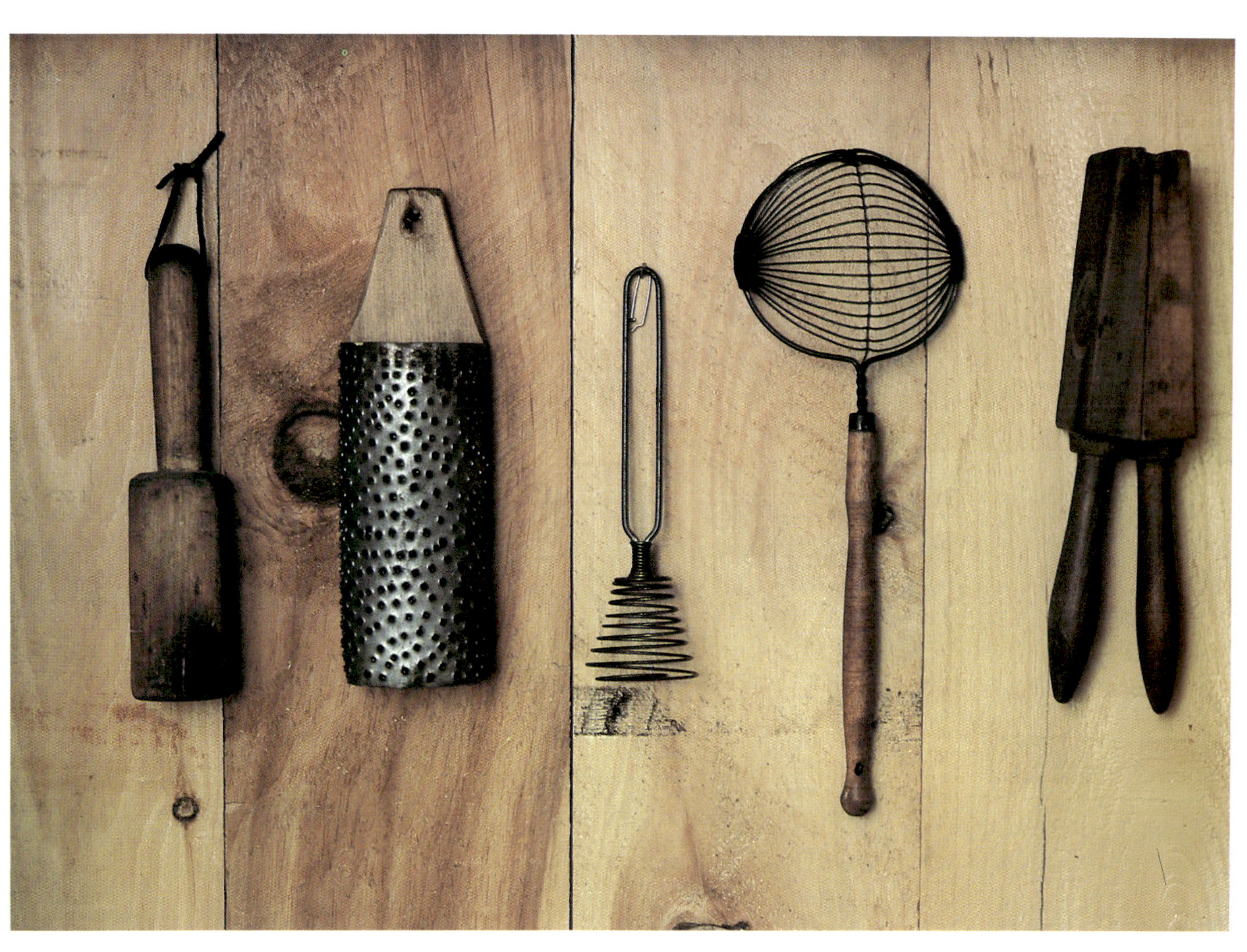

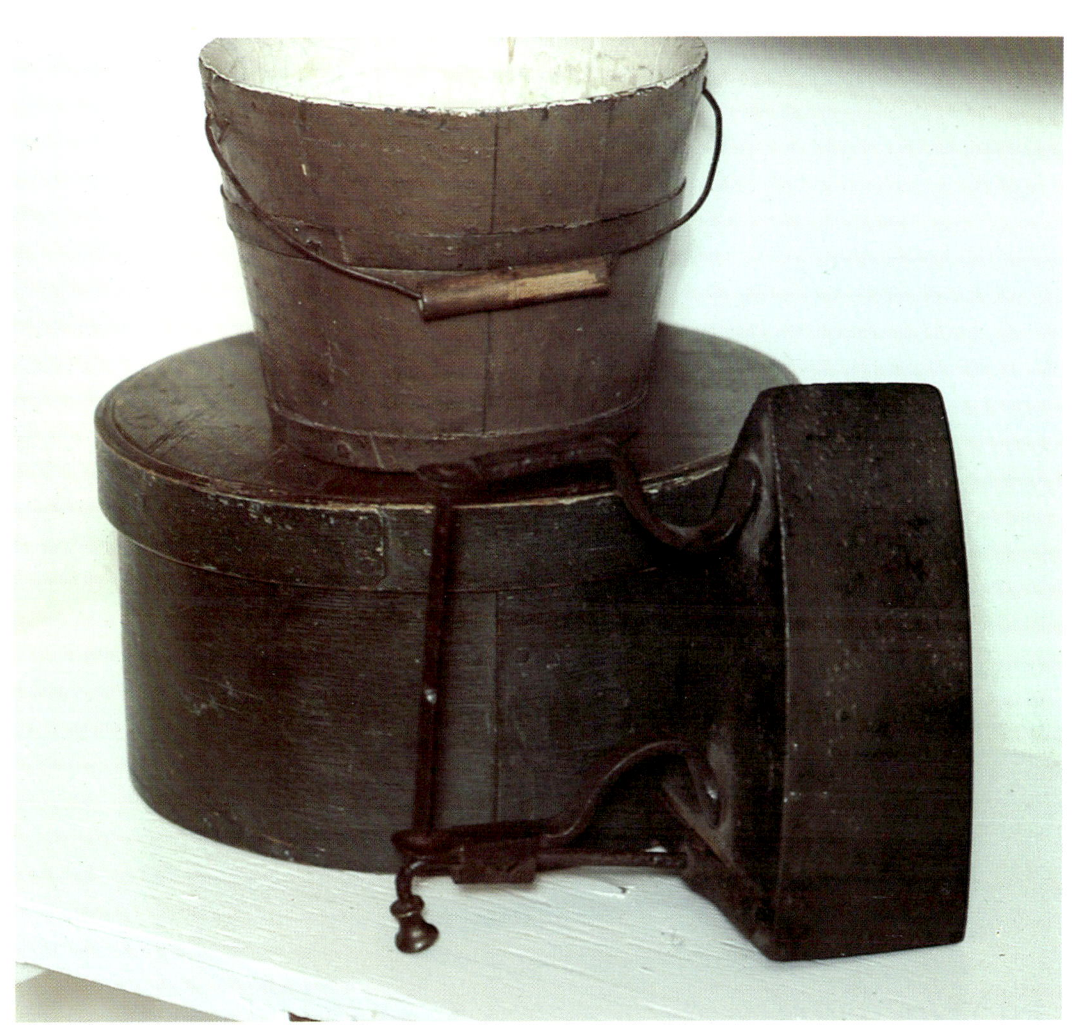

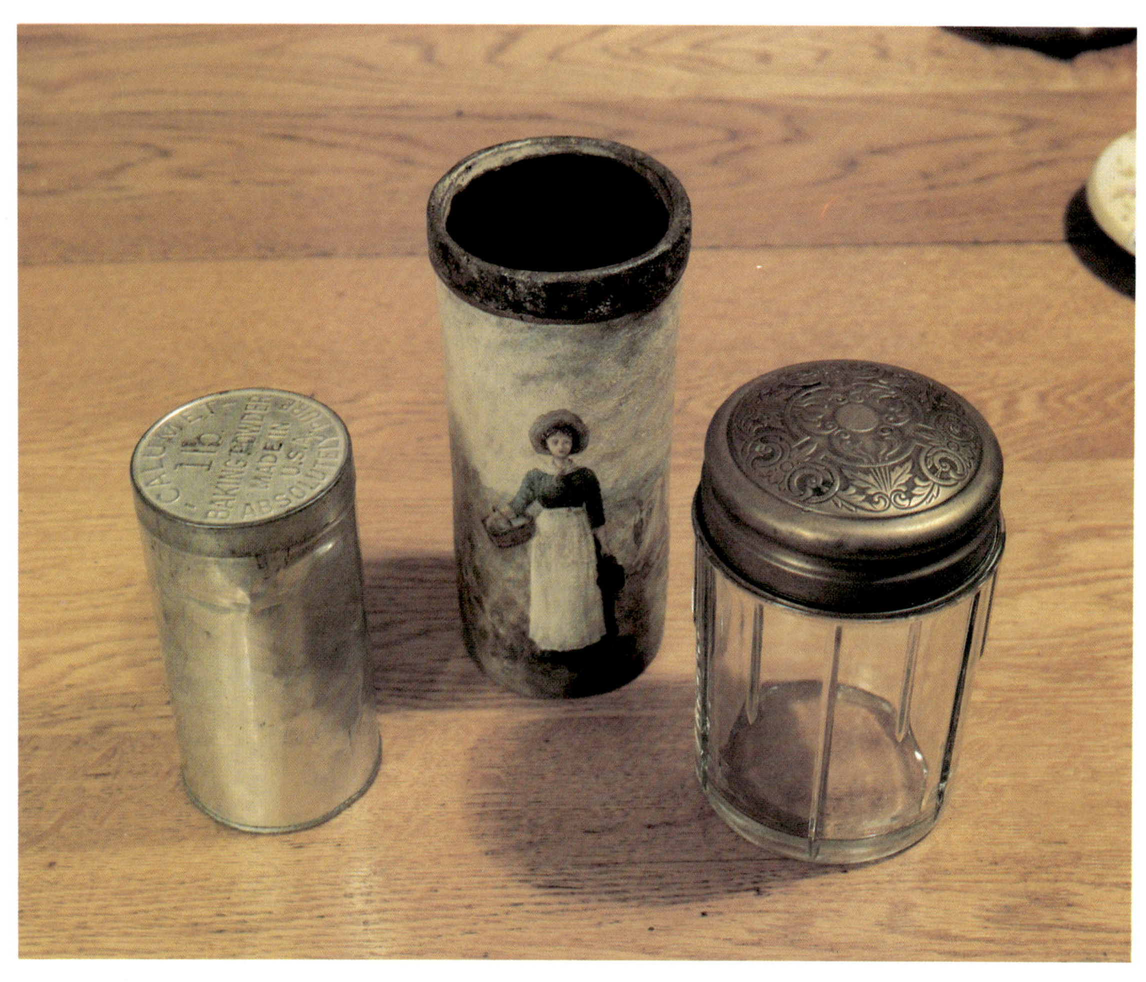
CALUMET
1 lb
BAKING POWDER
MADE IN
U.S.A.
ABSOLUTELY

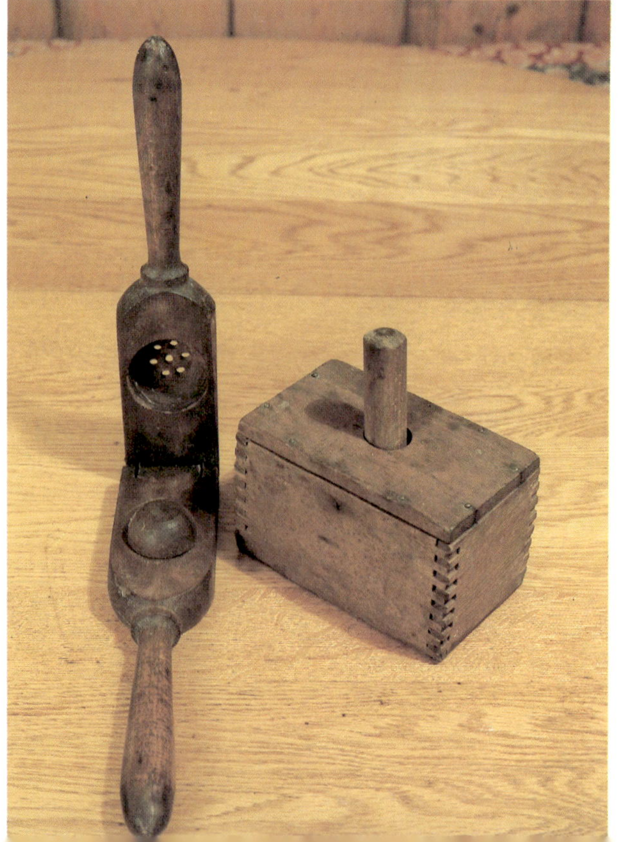

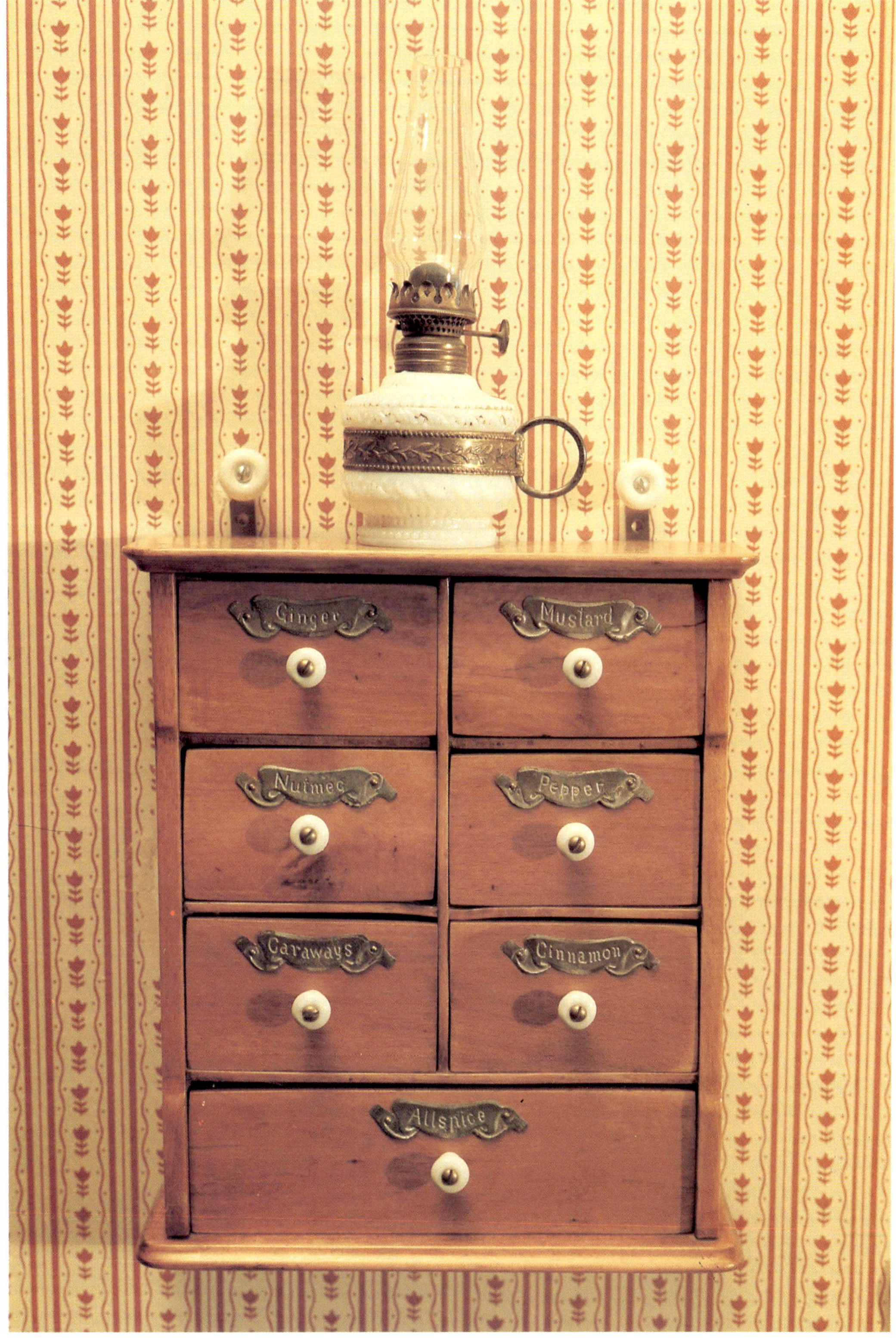
Ginger
Mustard
Nutmeg
Pepper
Caraways
Cinnamon
Allspice

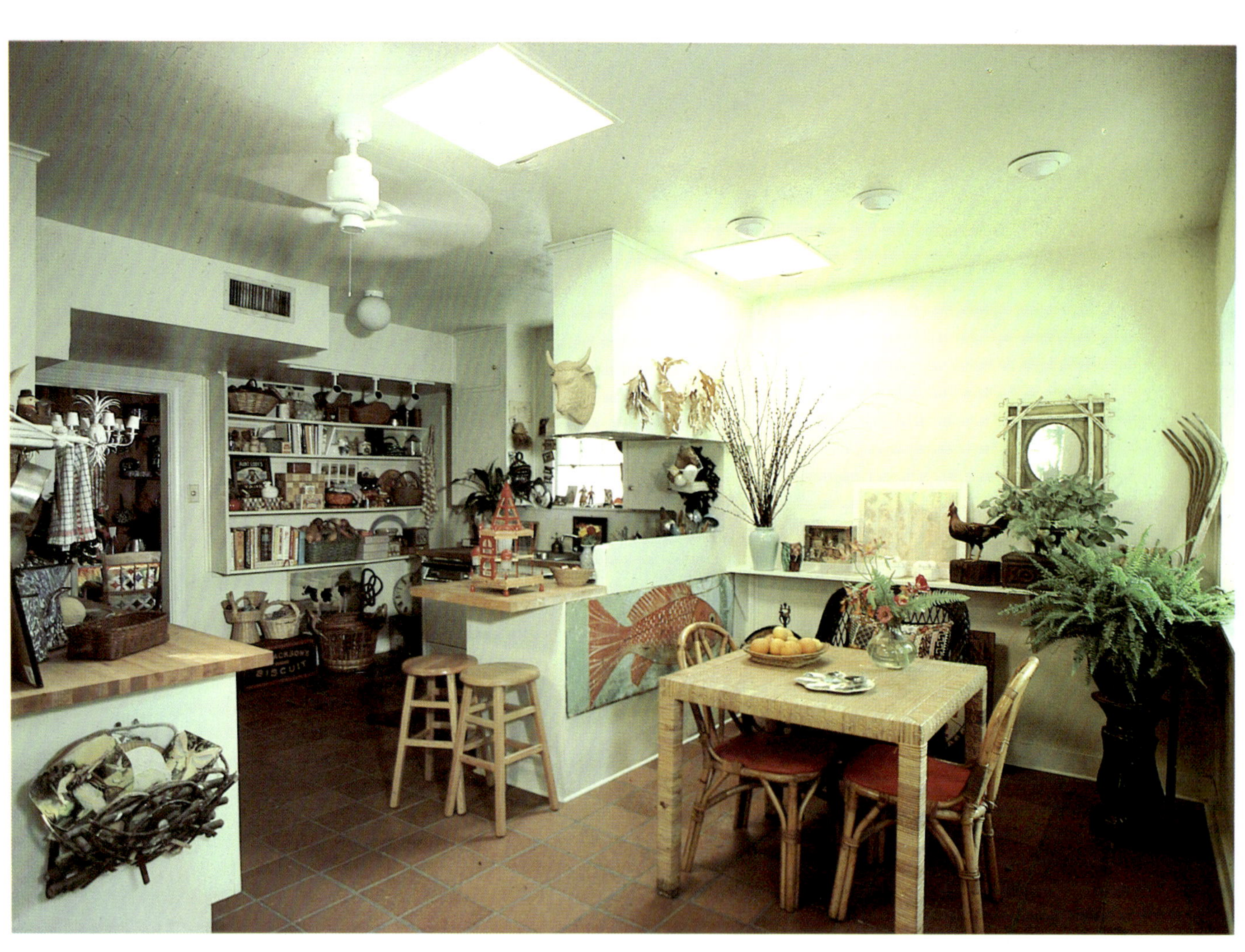
BISCUIT

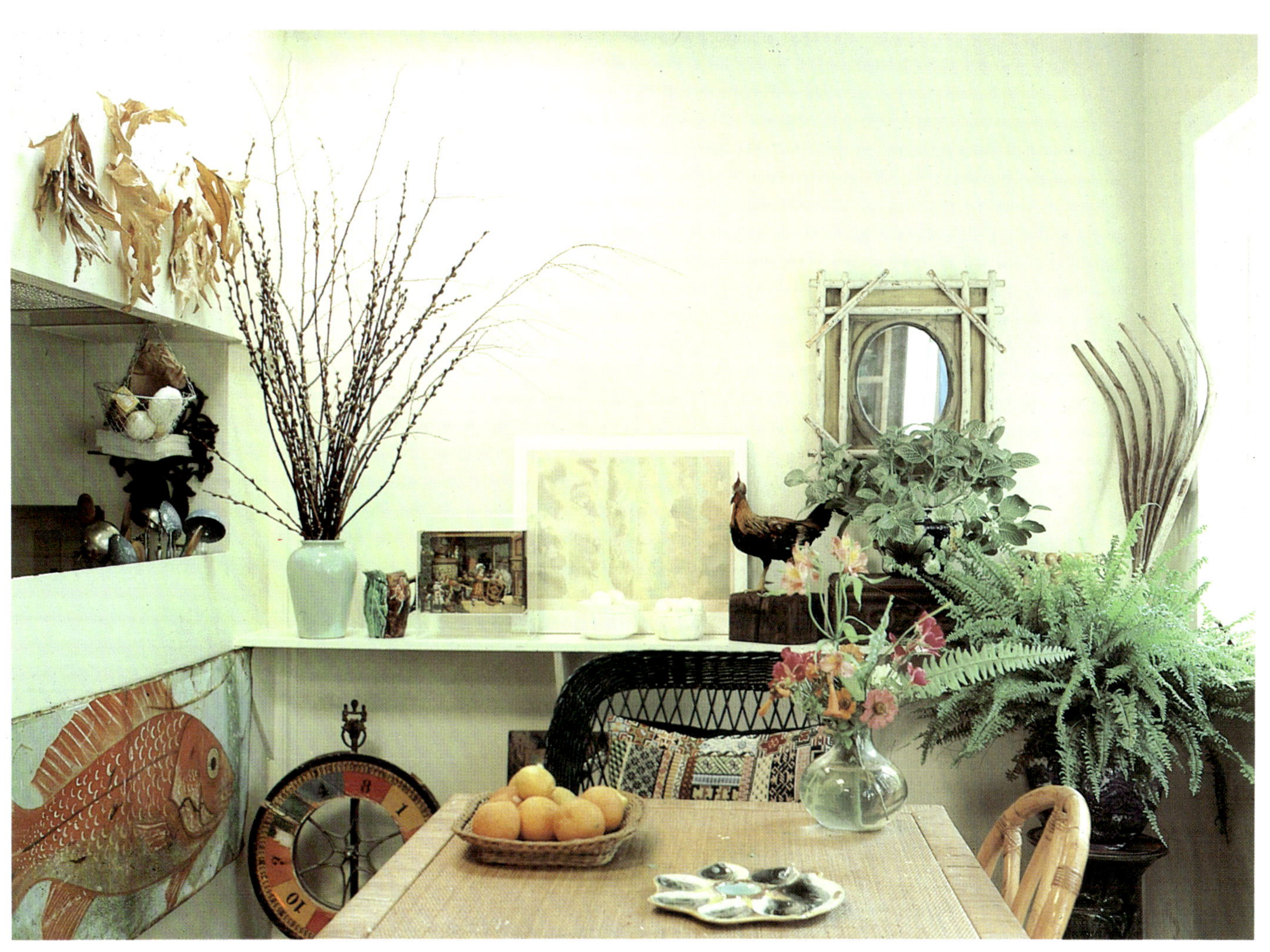

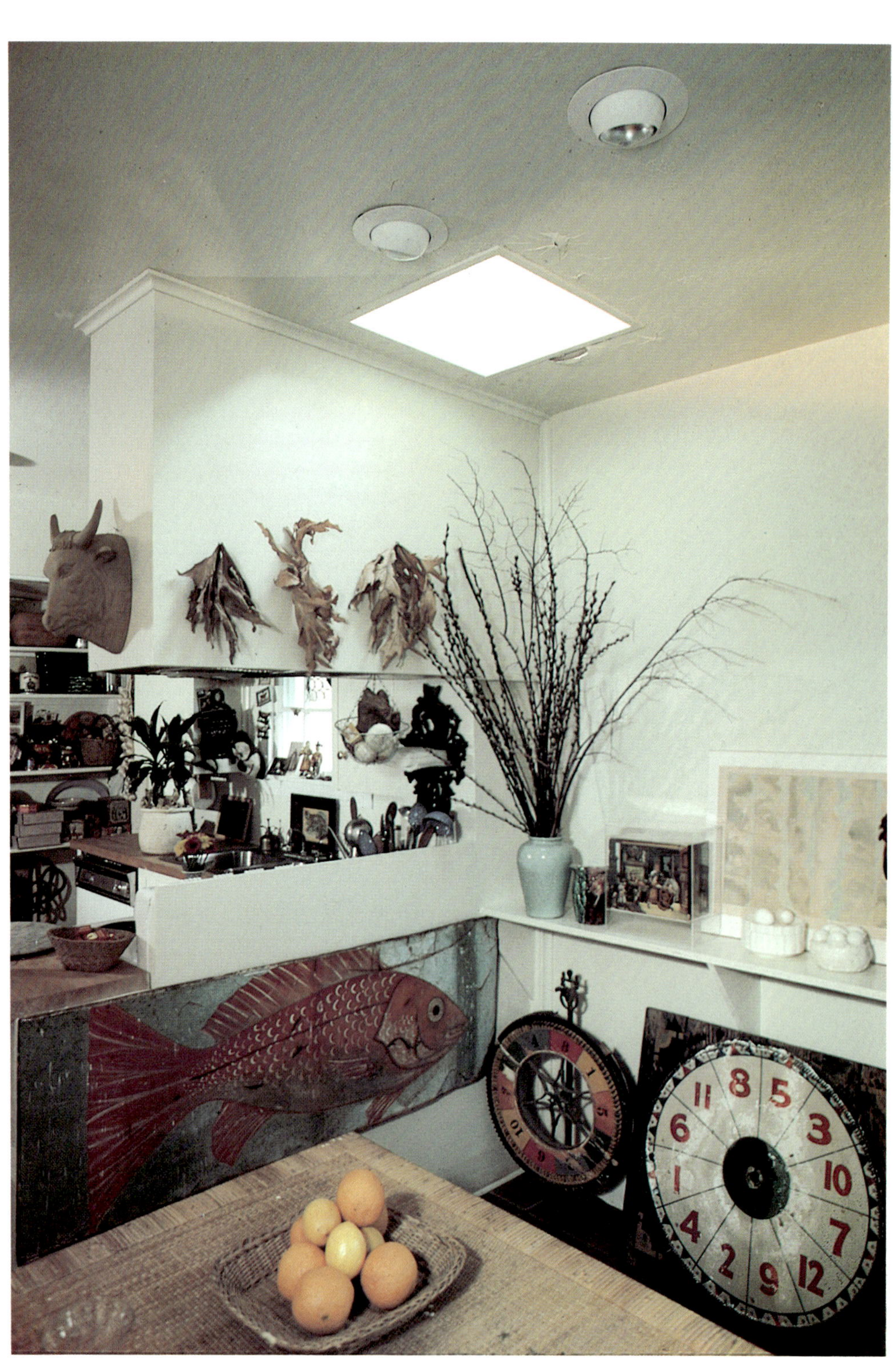

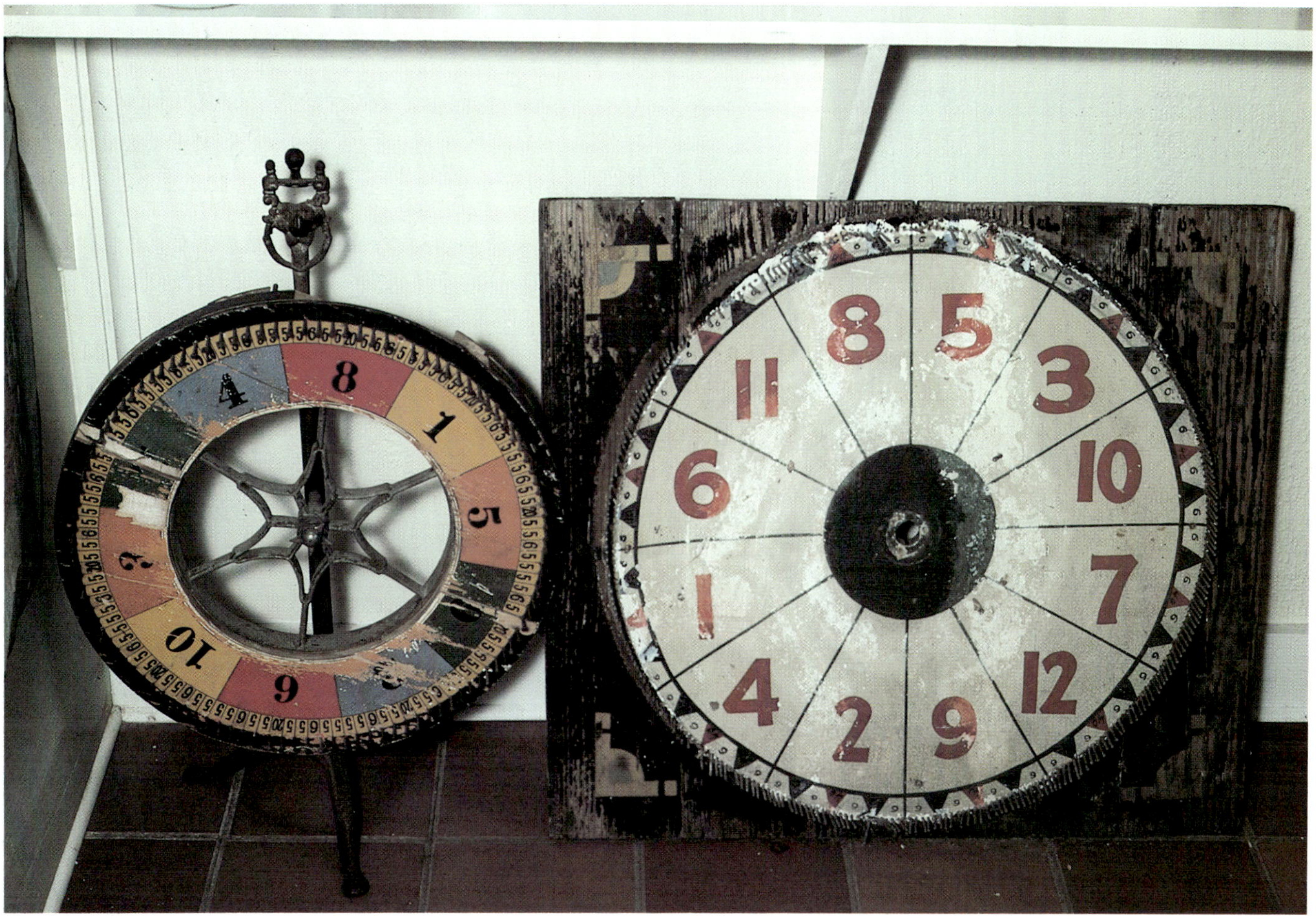

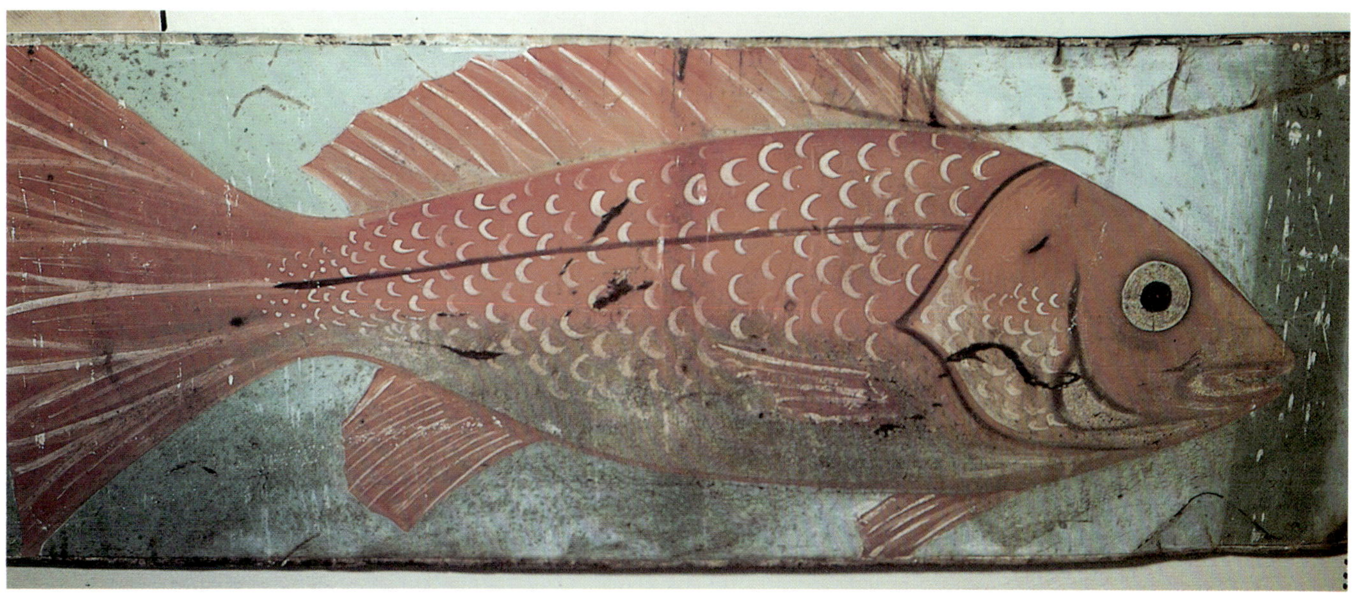

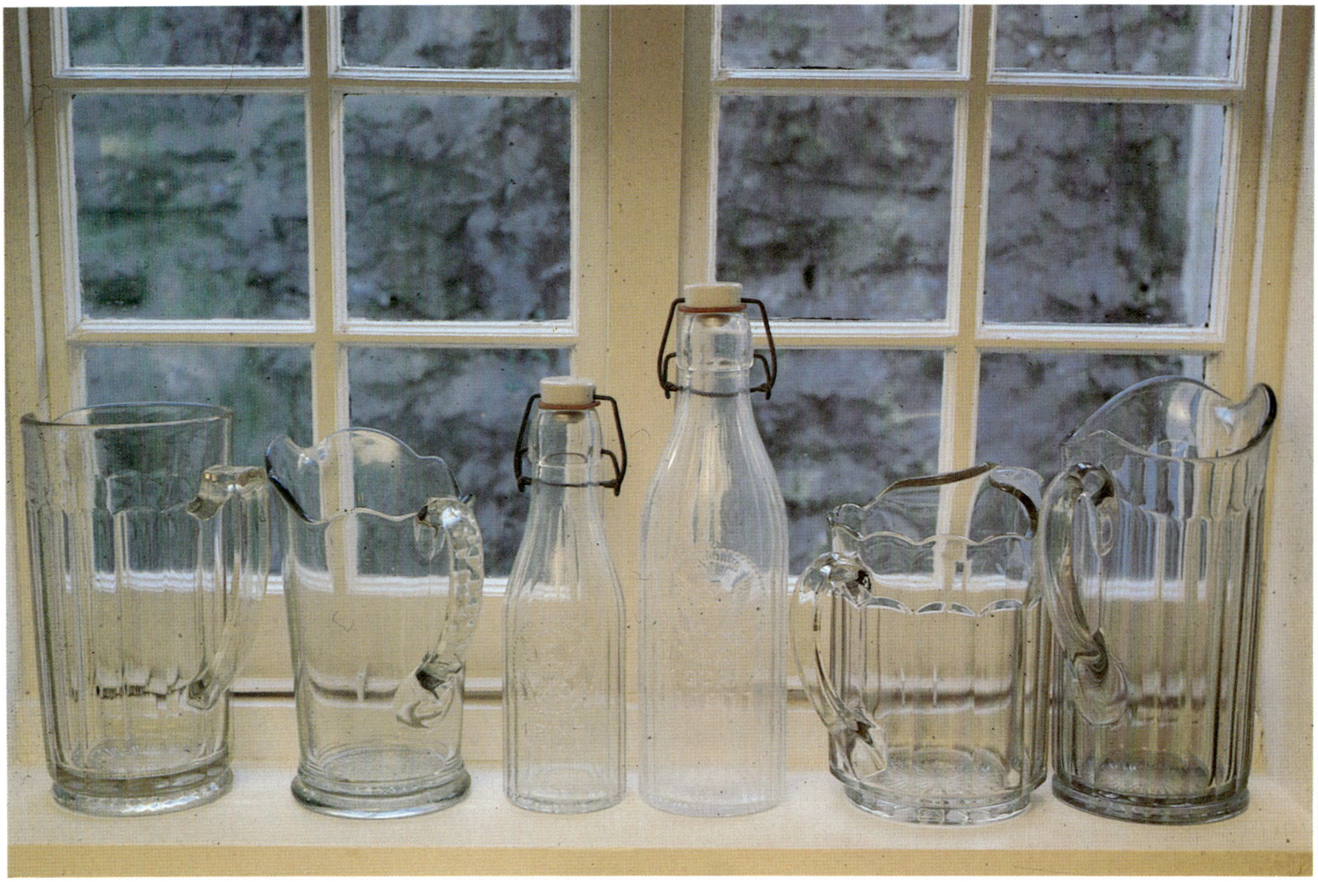

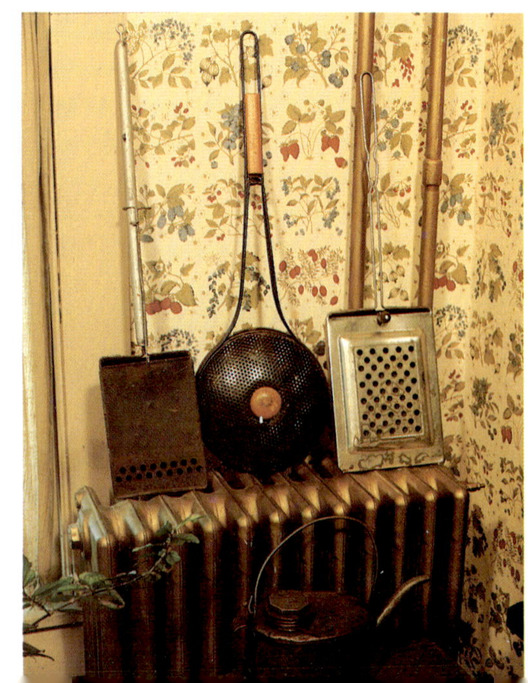

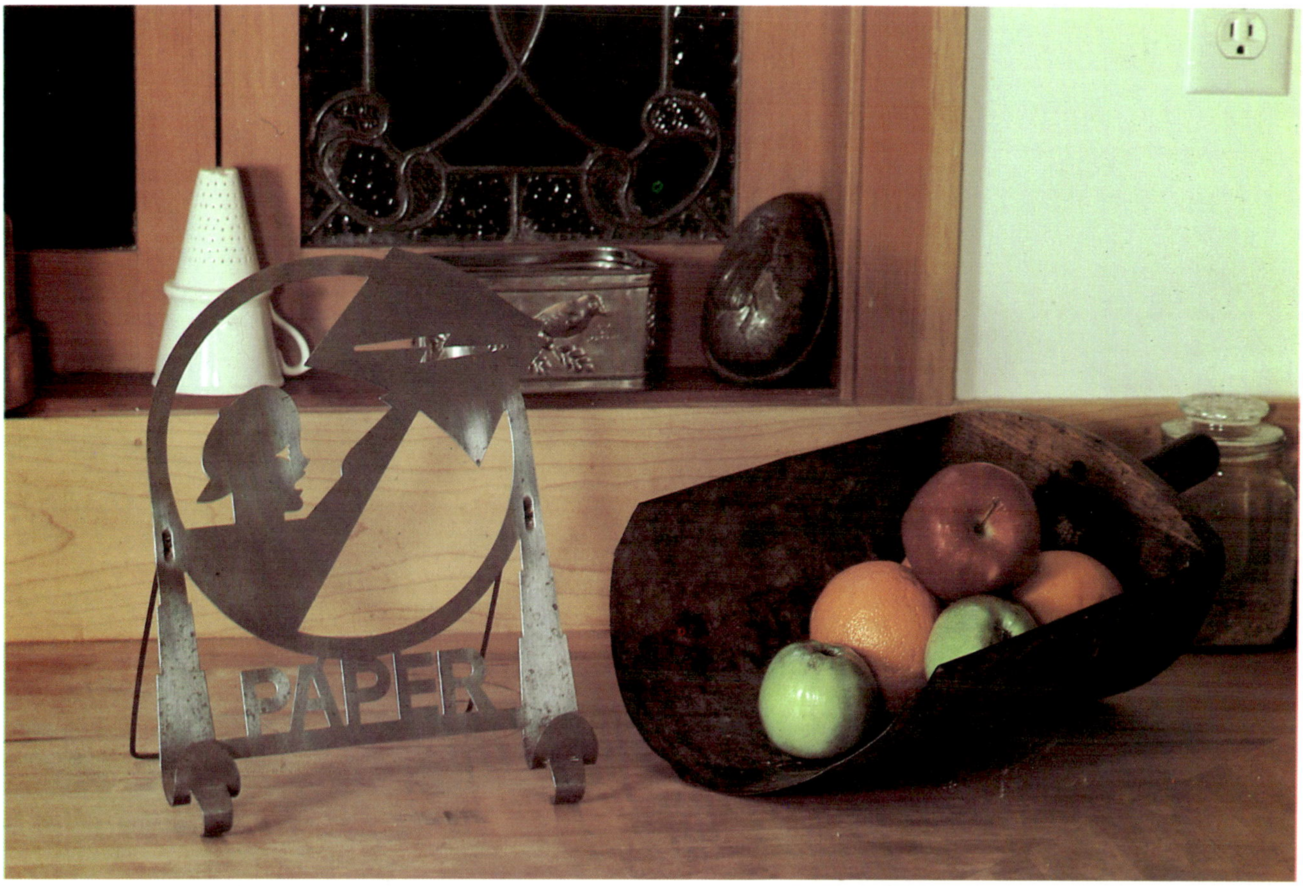

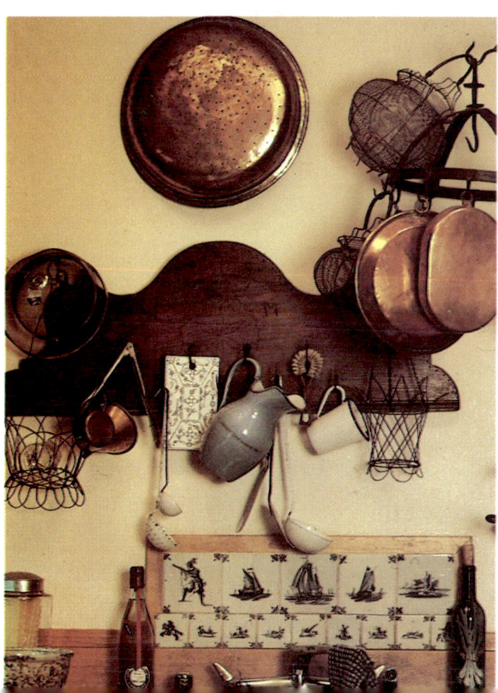

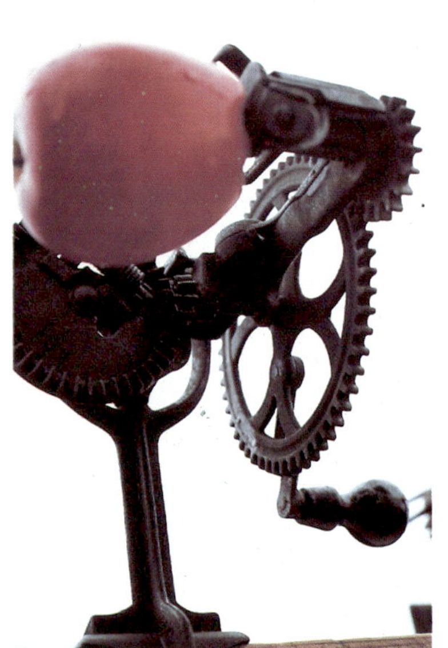

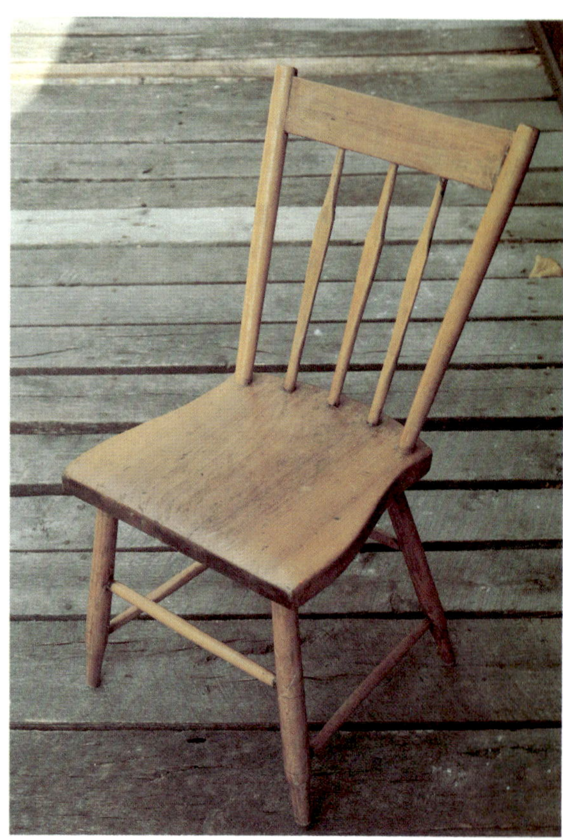

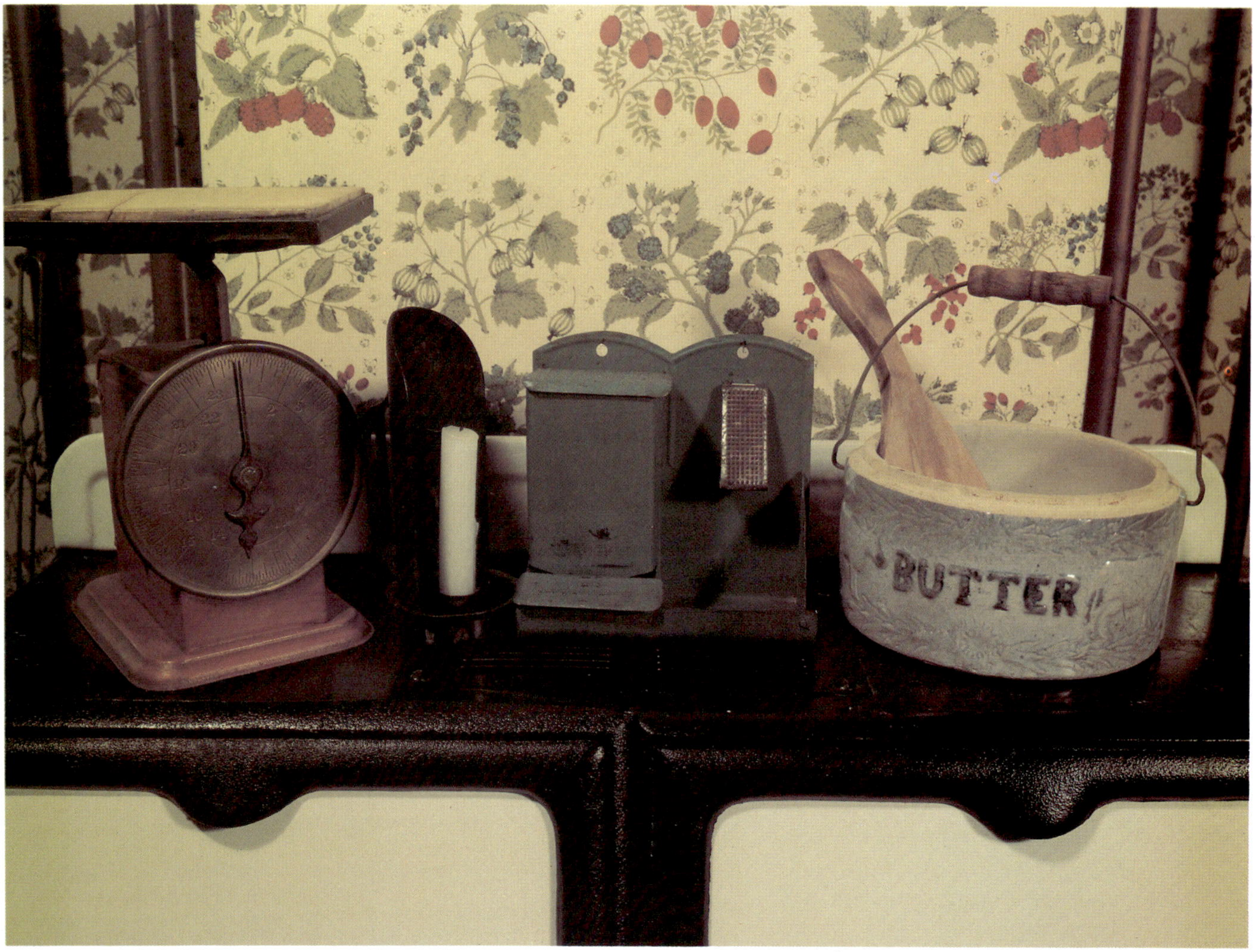

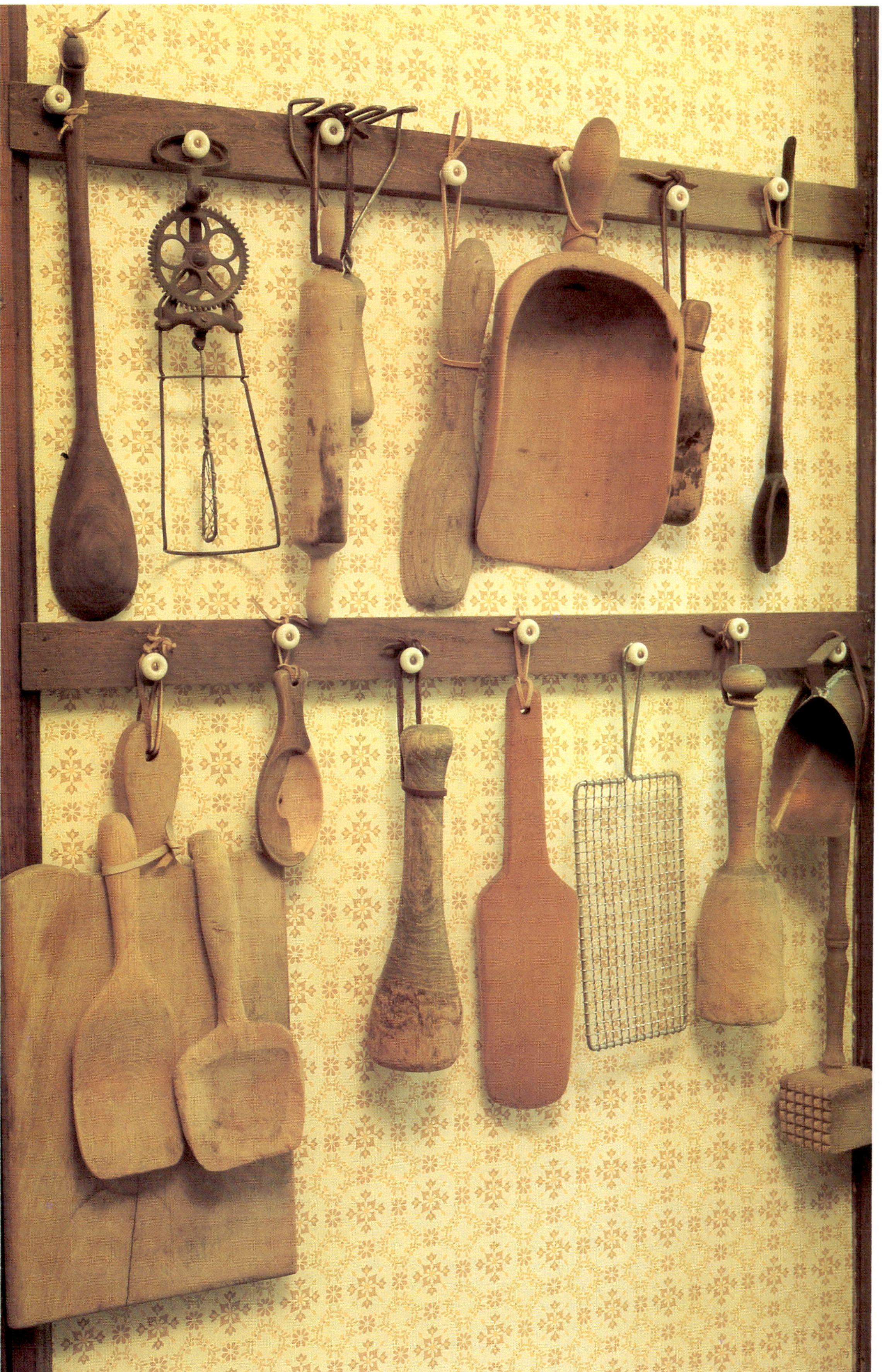

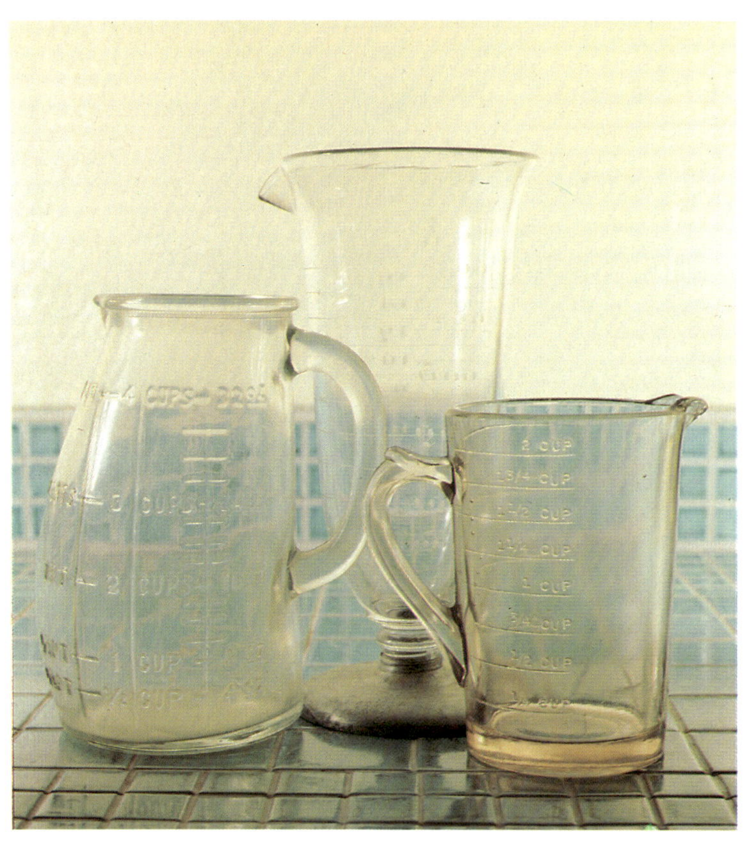
2 CUP
1 3/4 CUP
1 1/2 CUP
1 1/4 CUP
1 CUP
3/4 CUP
1/2 CUP

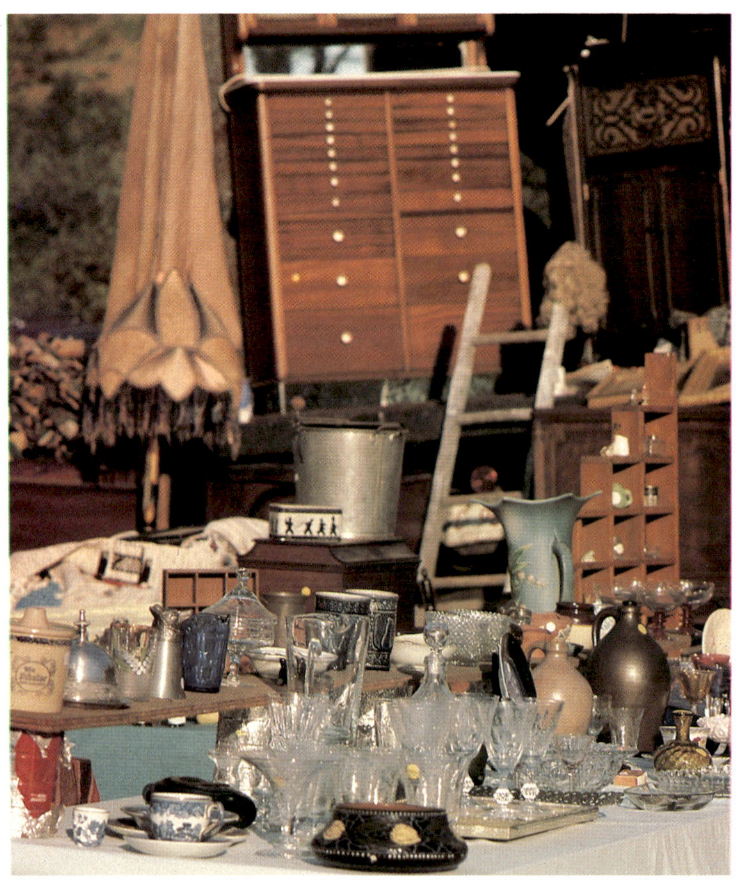

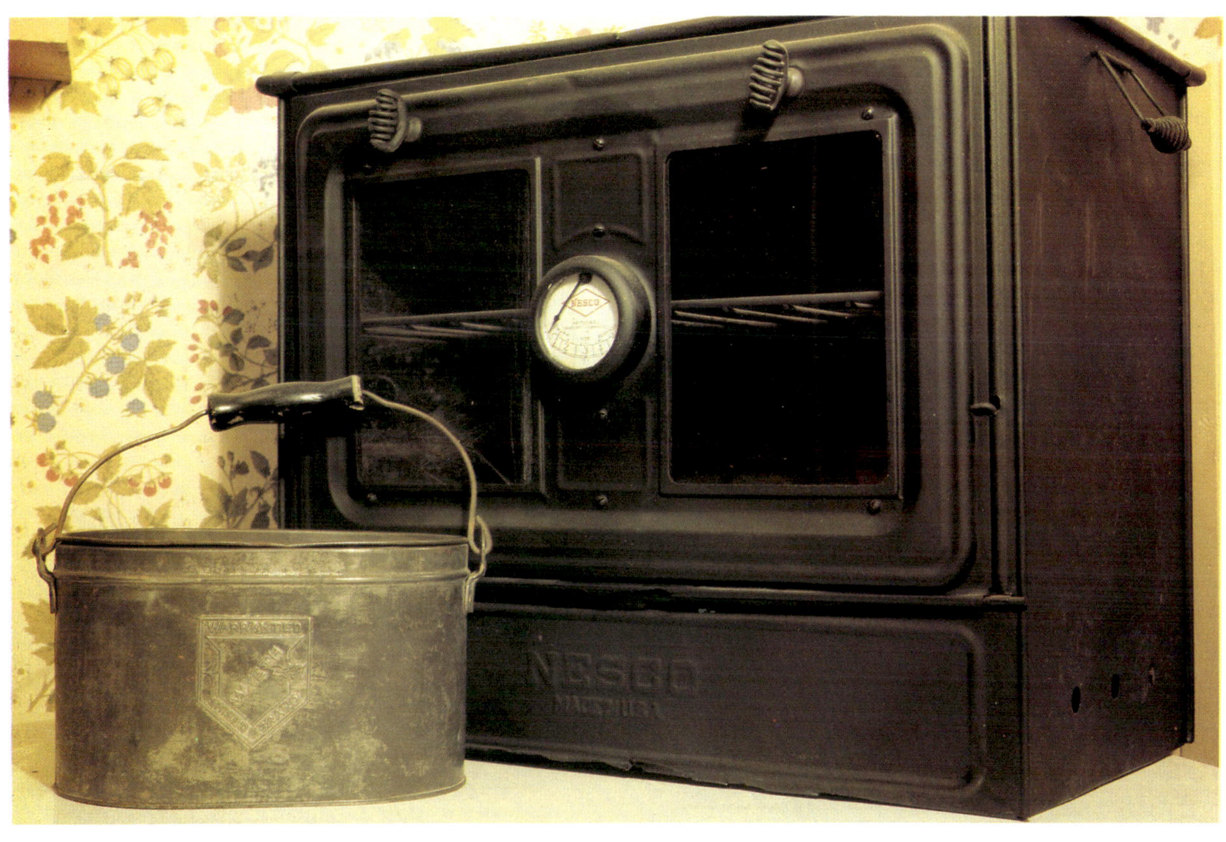
NESCO
WARRANTED

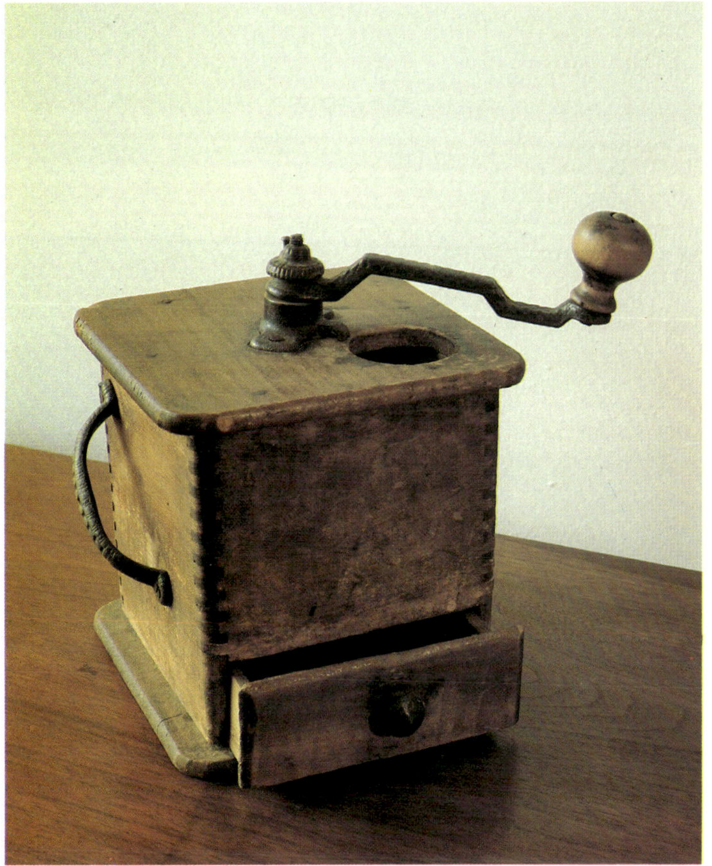

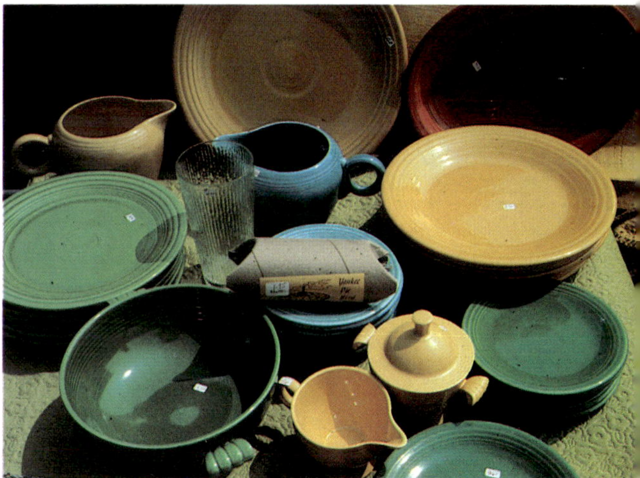

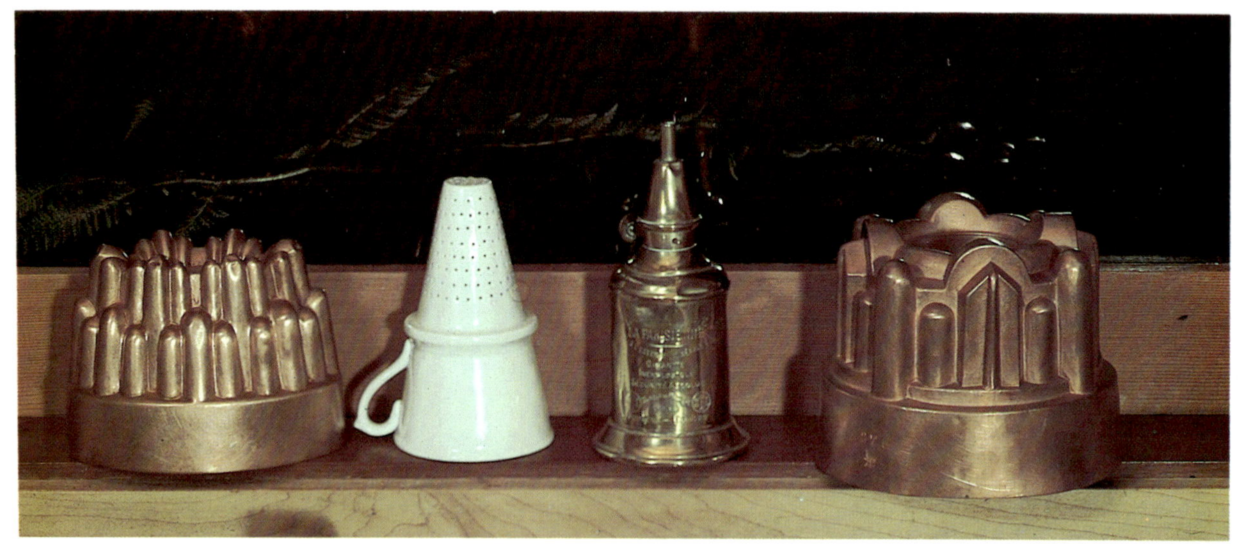

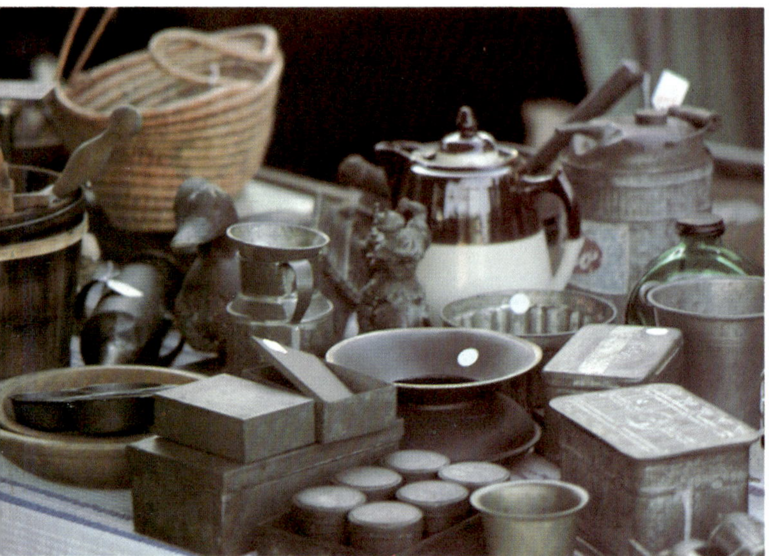

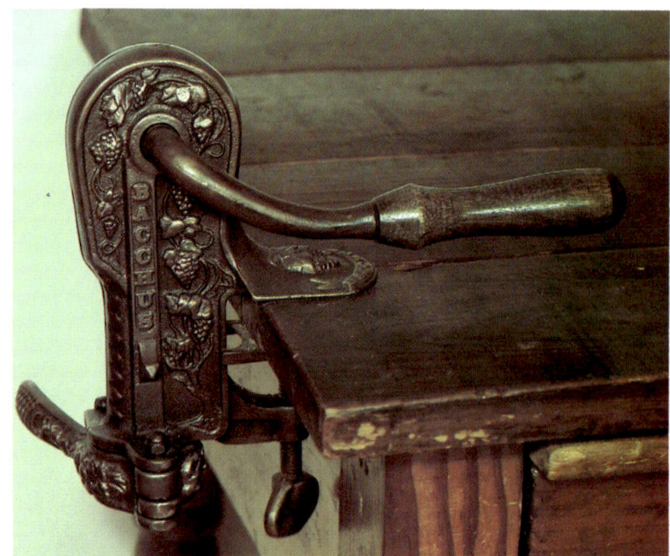
BACCHUS

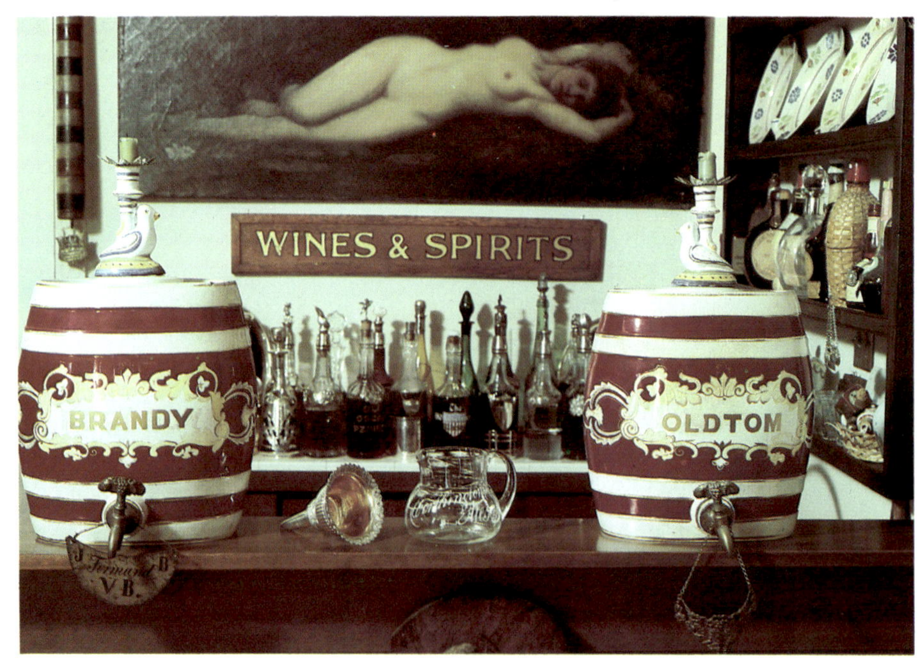
WINES & SPIRITS
BRANDY
OLDTOM

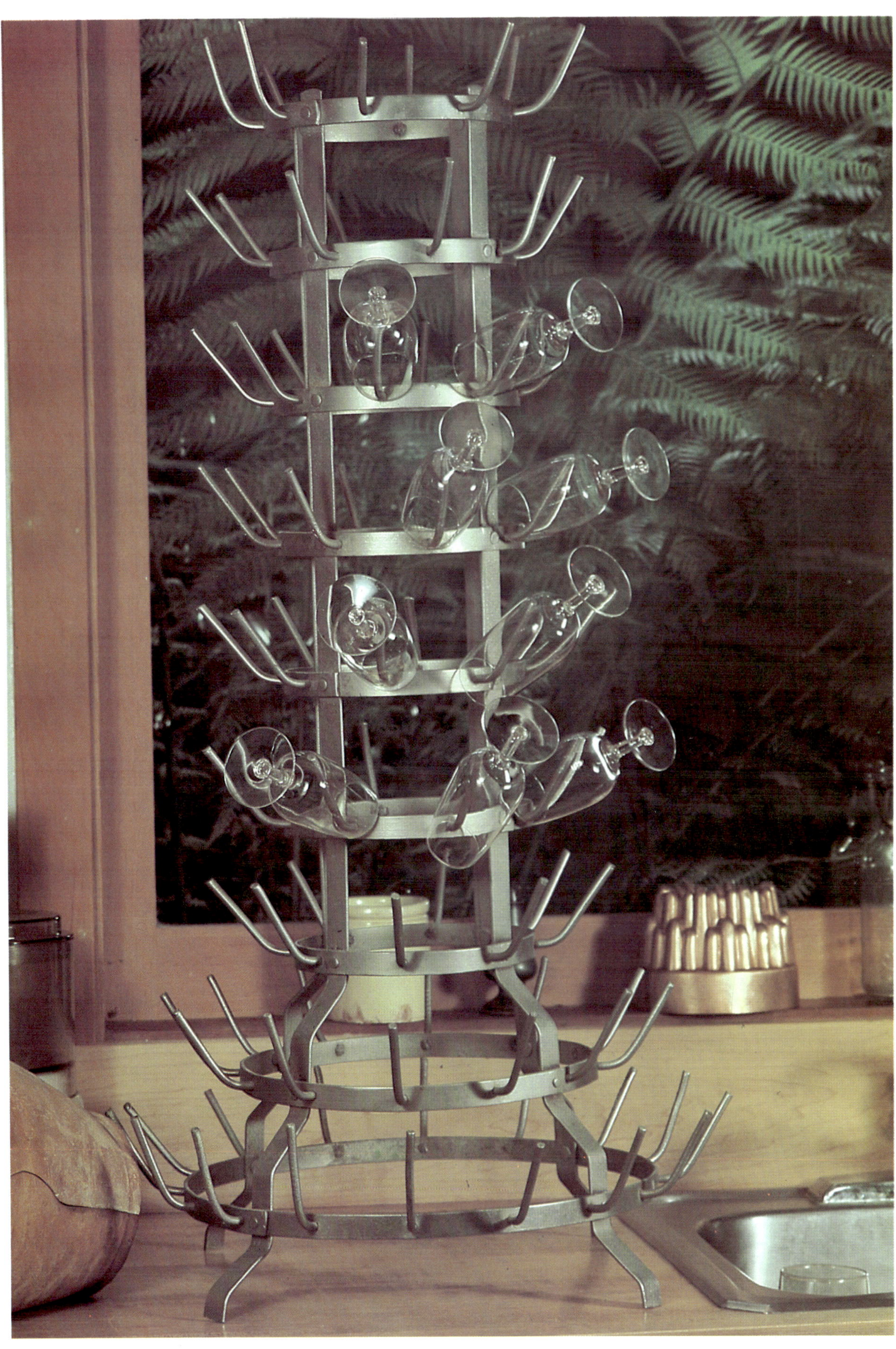

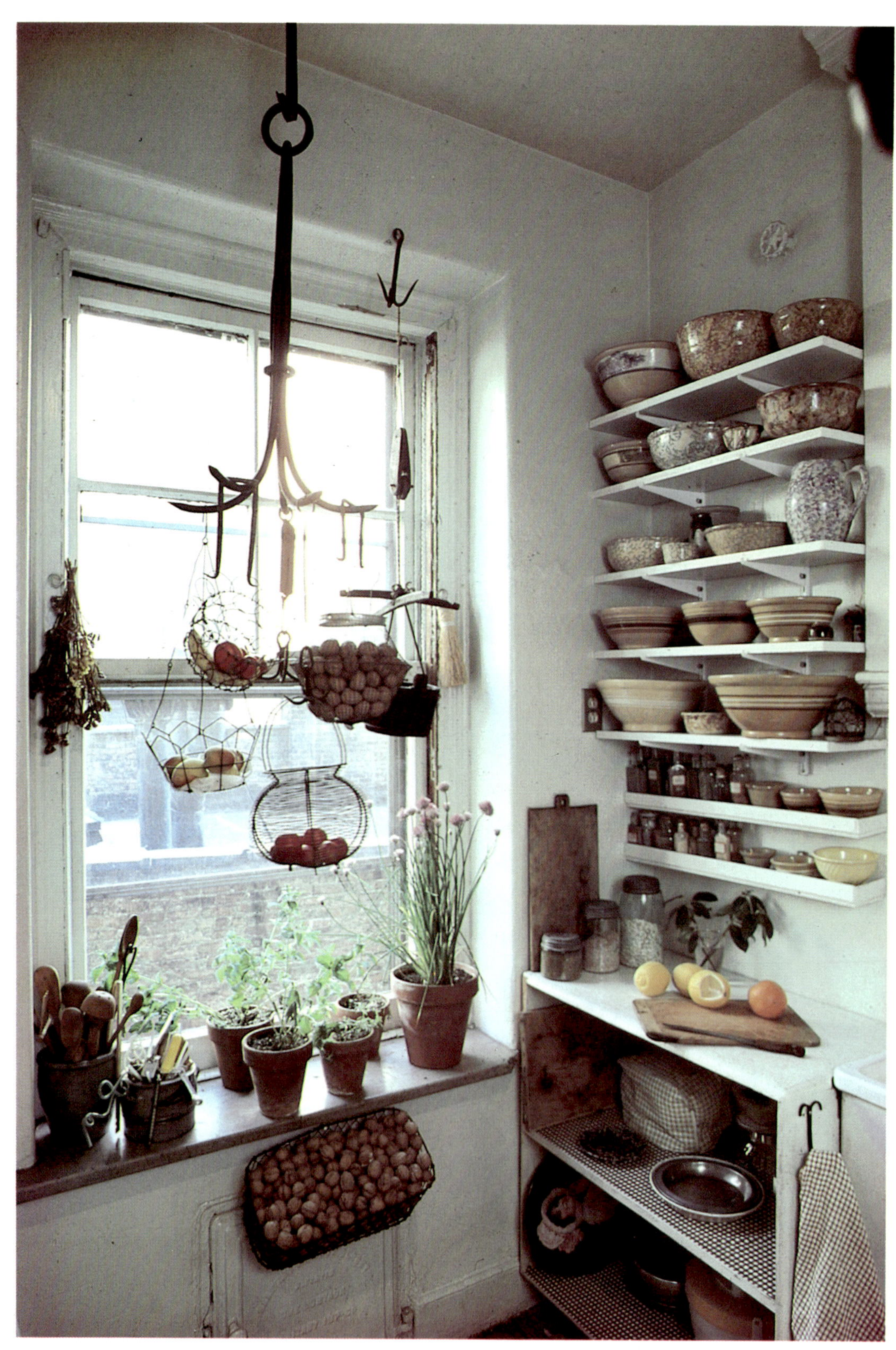

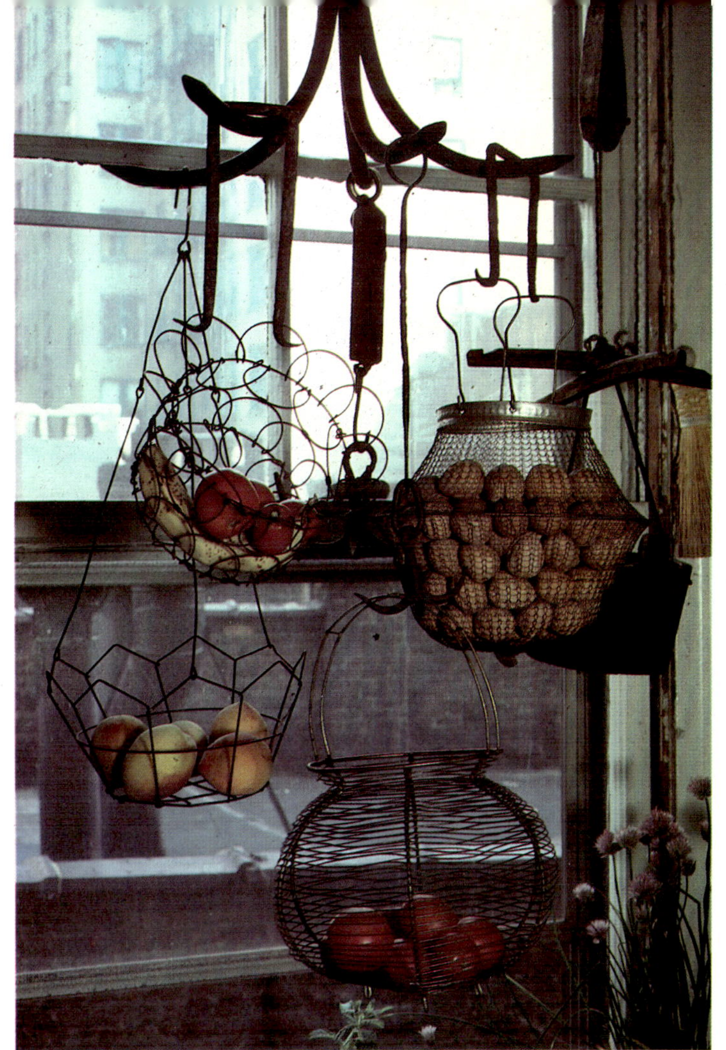

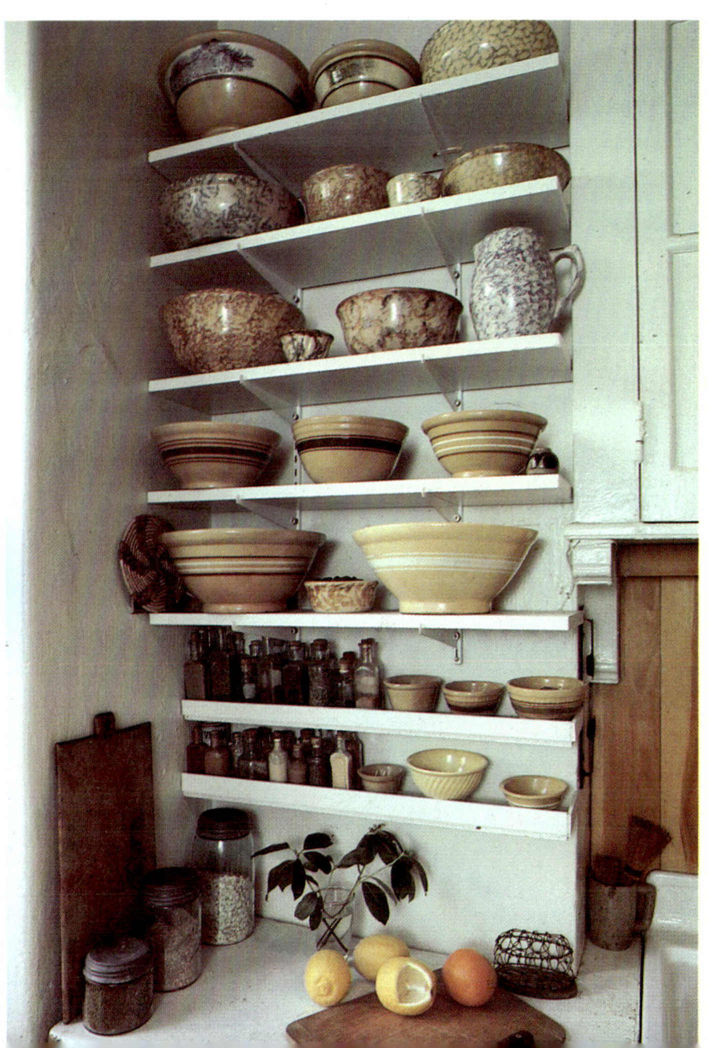

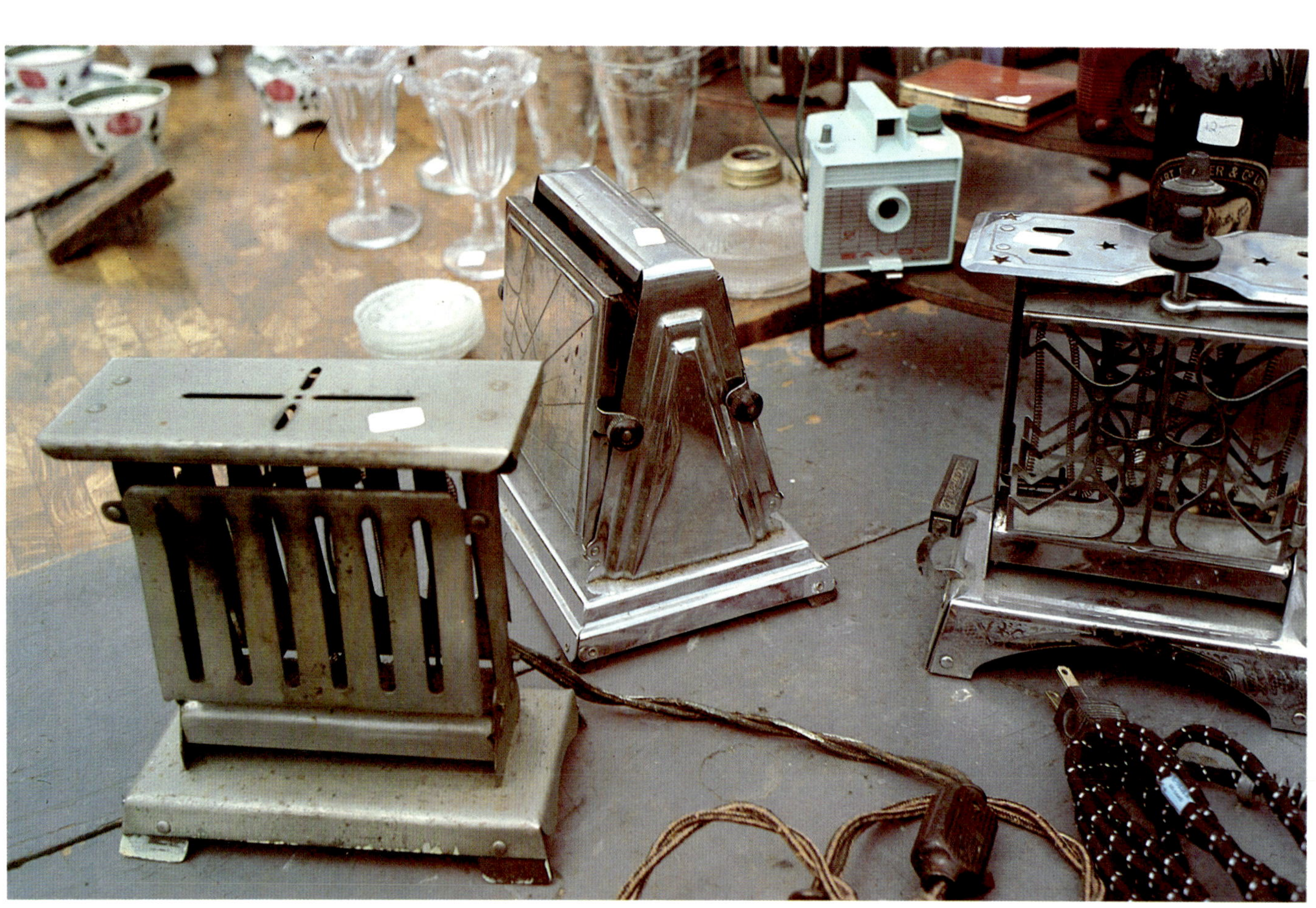

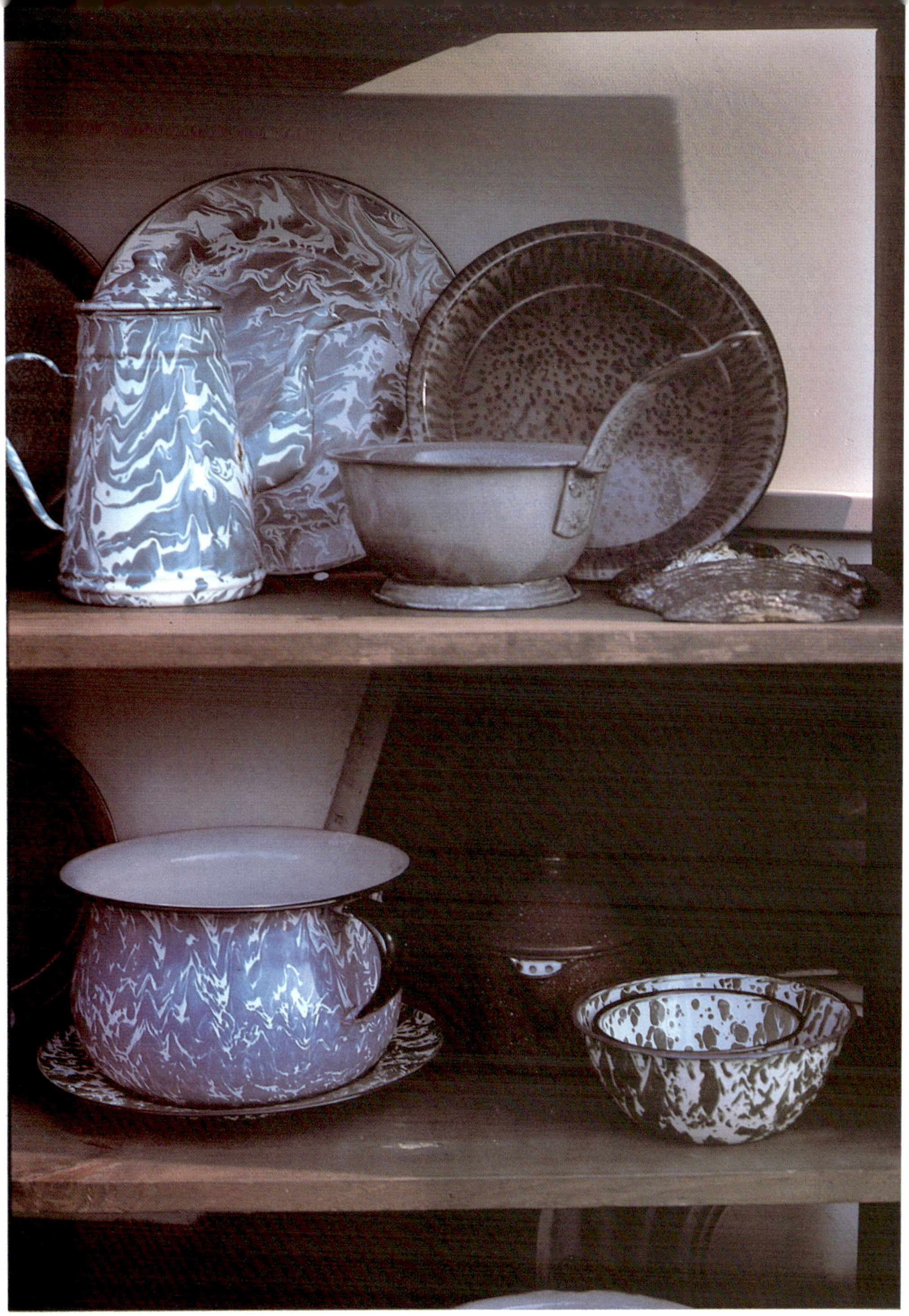

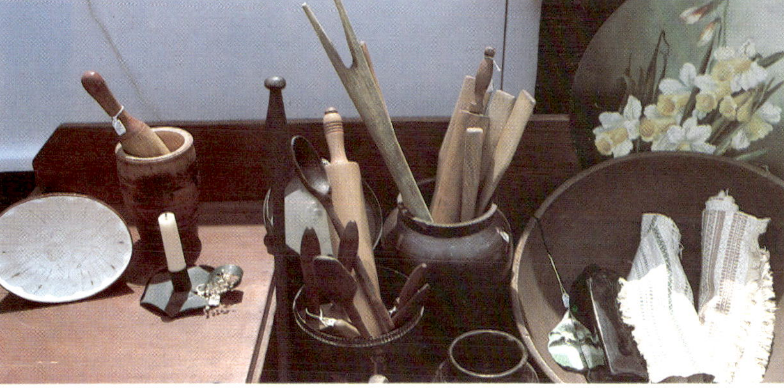

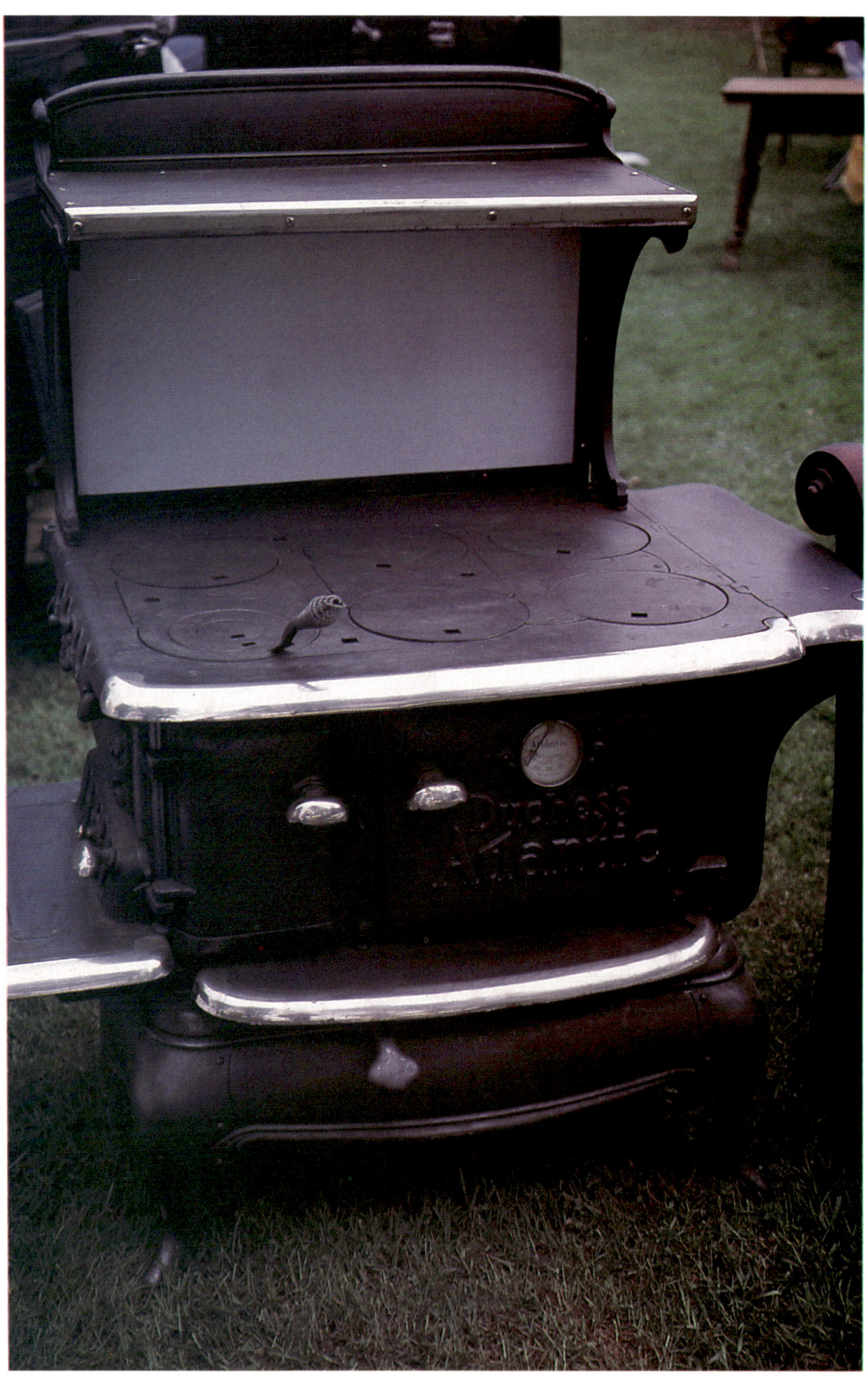

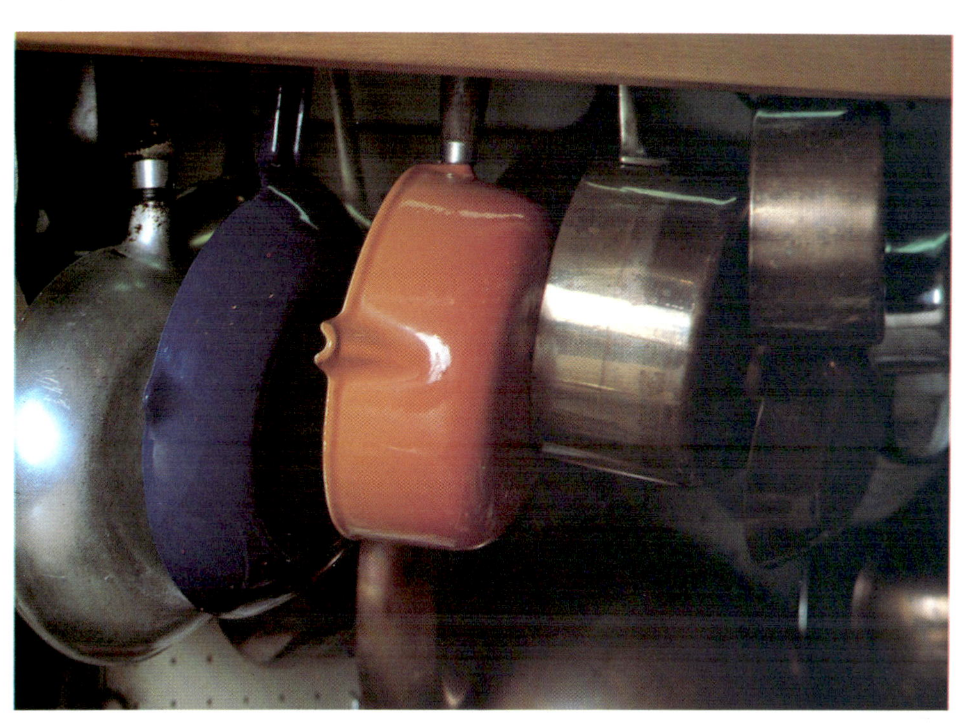

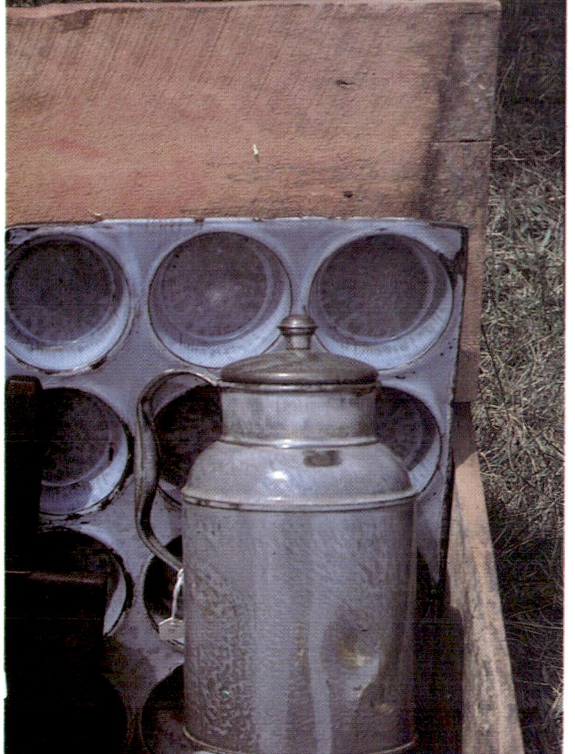

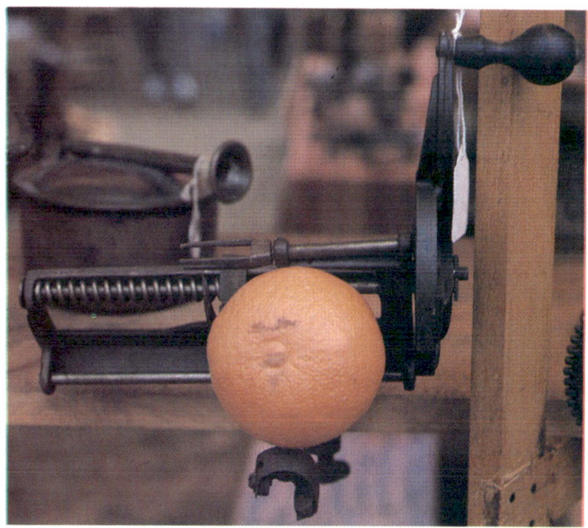

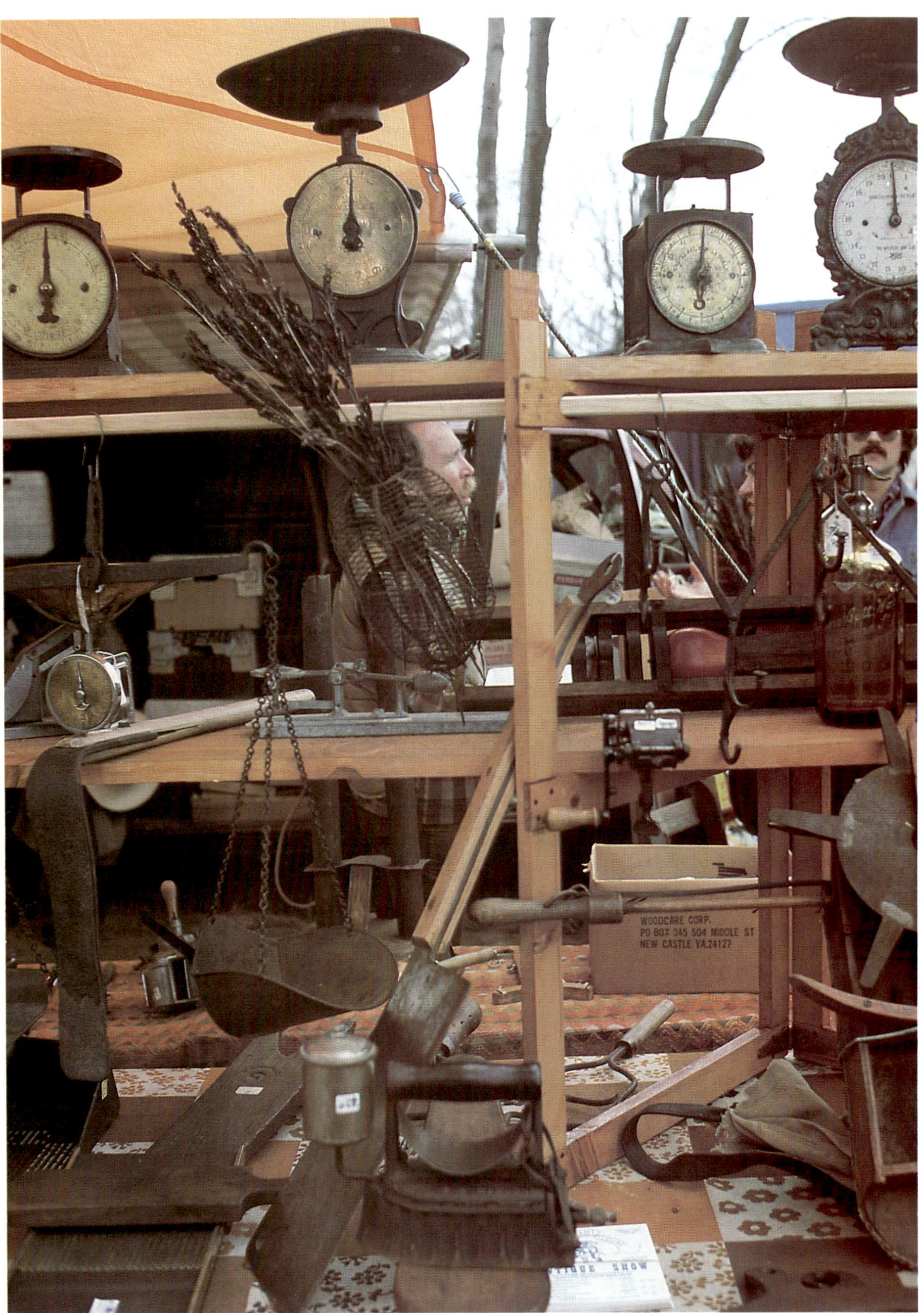
WOODCARE CORP.
PO BOX 345 504 MIDDLE ST
NEW CASTLE VA.24127

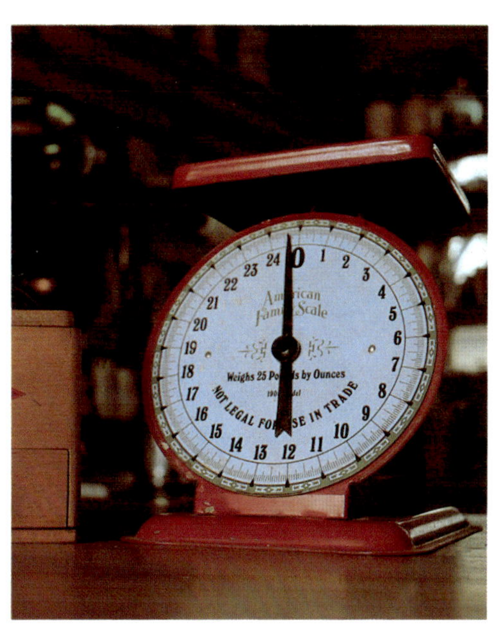

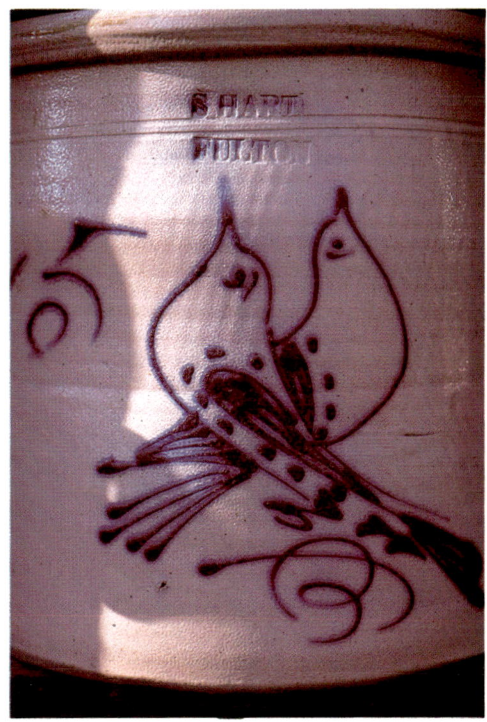

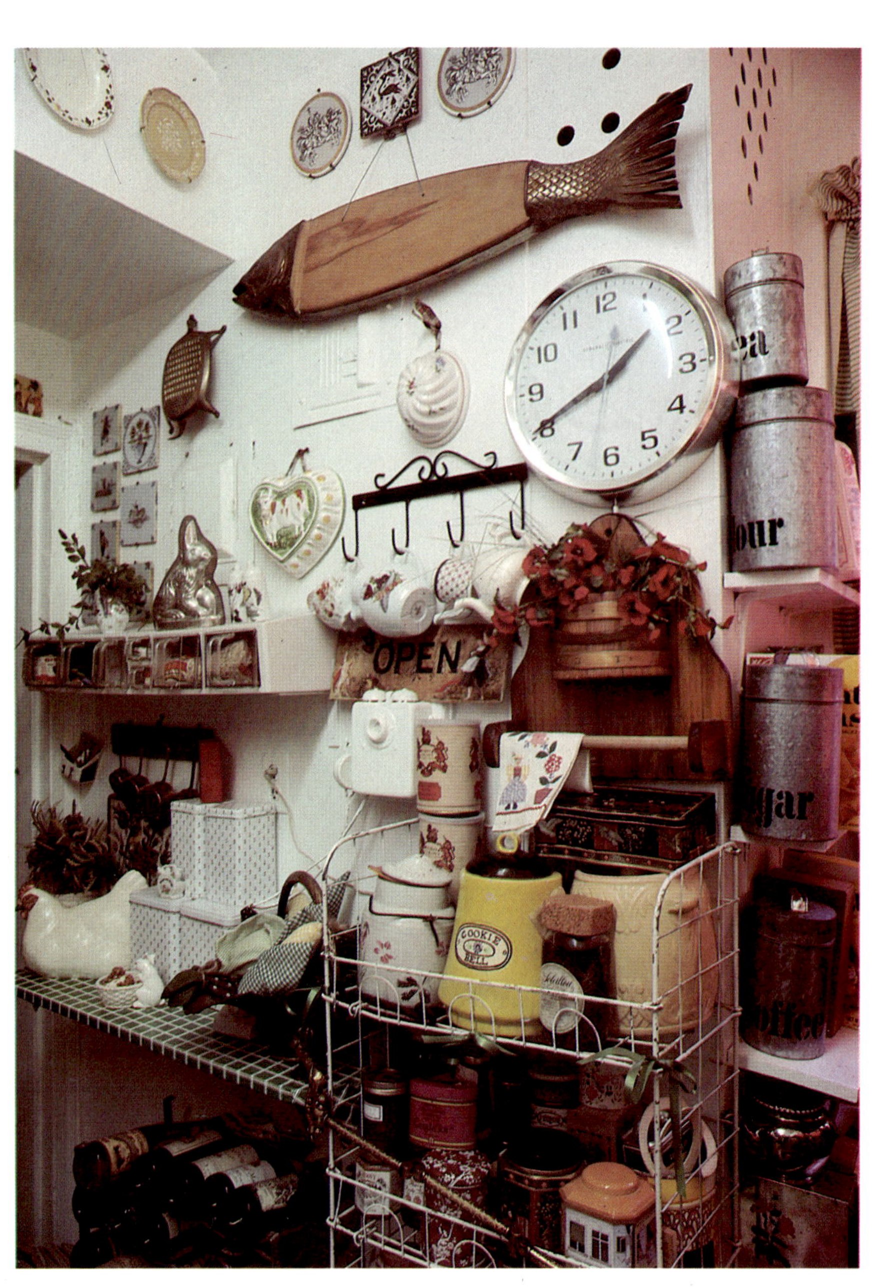
OPEN

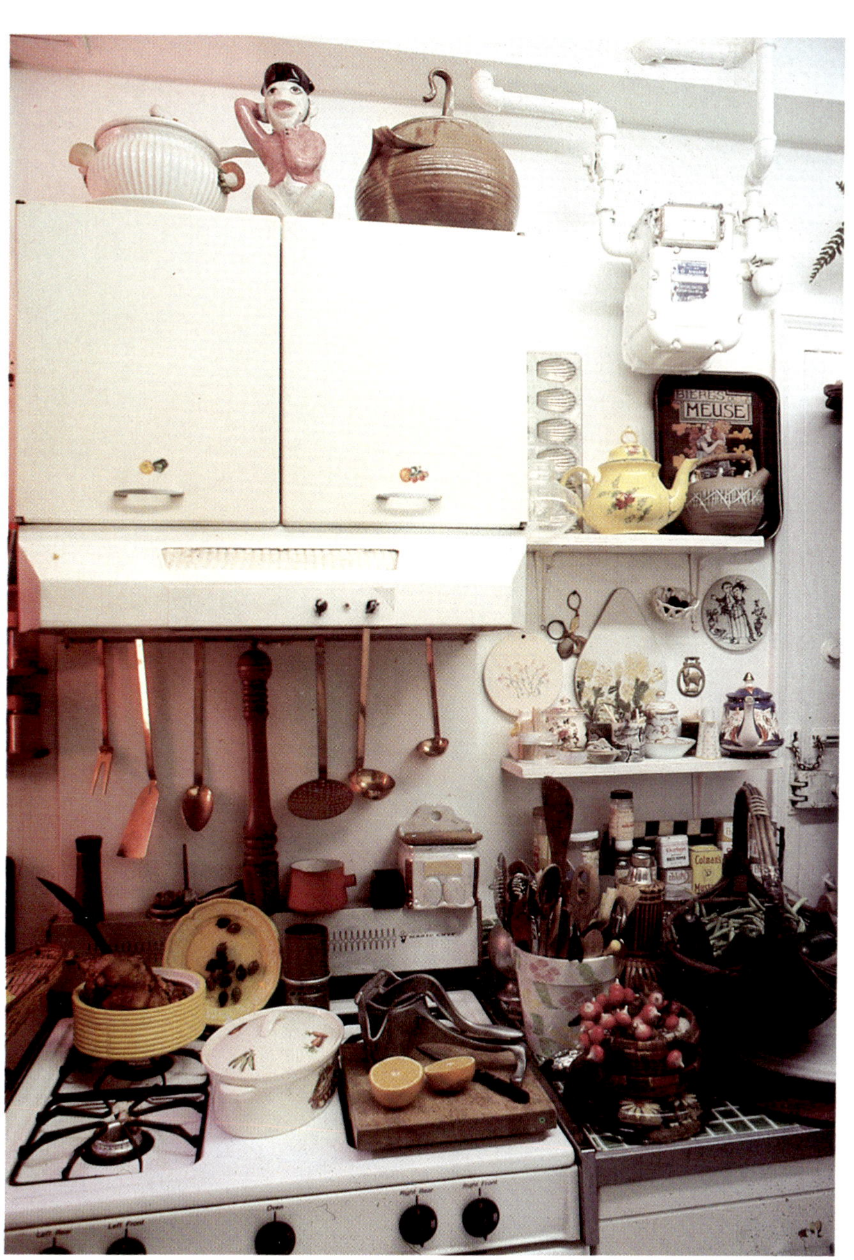
BIERES
MEUSE

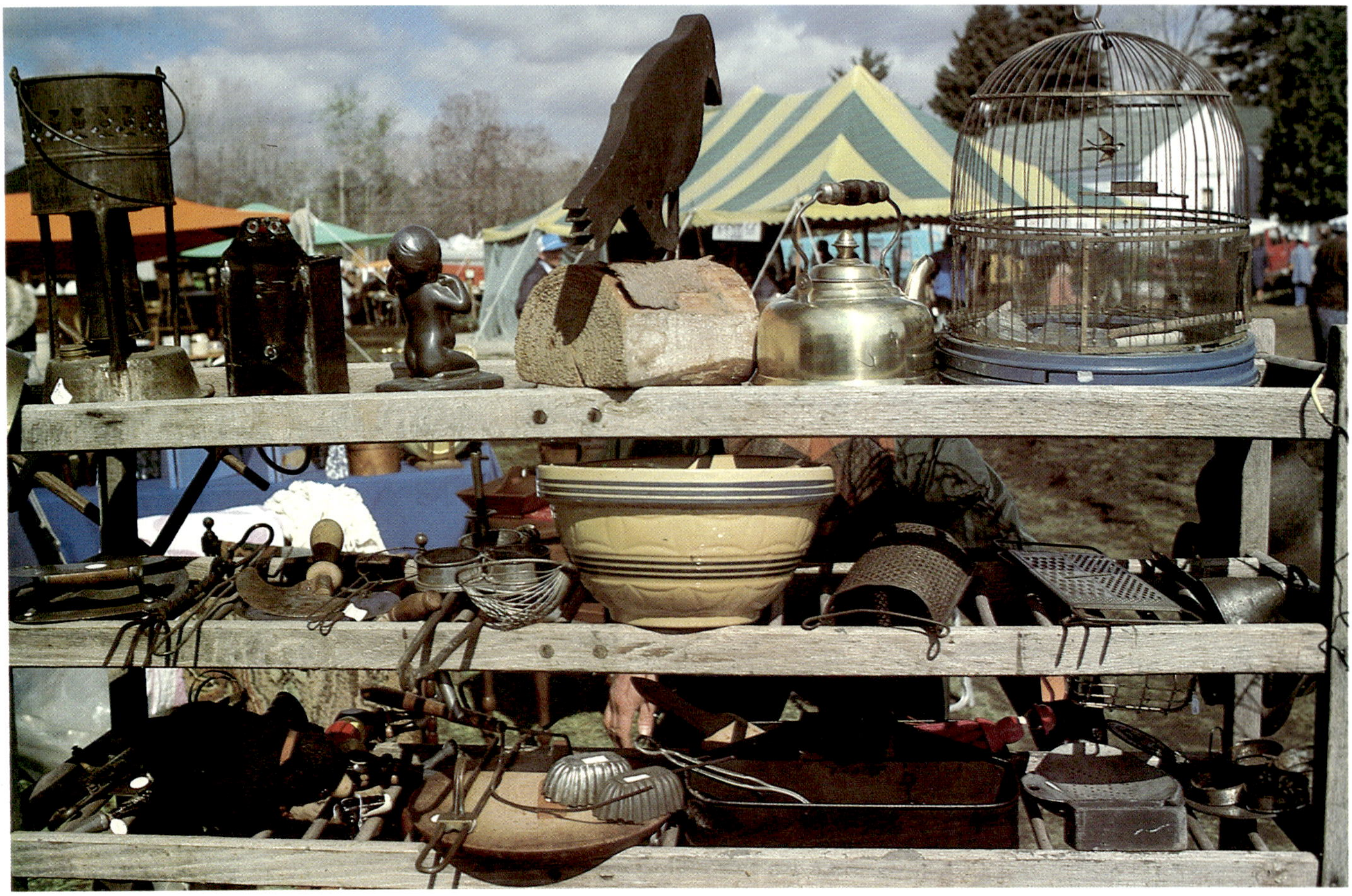

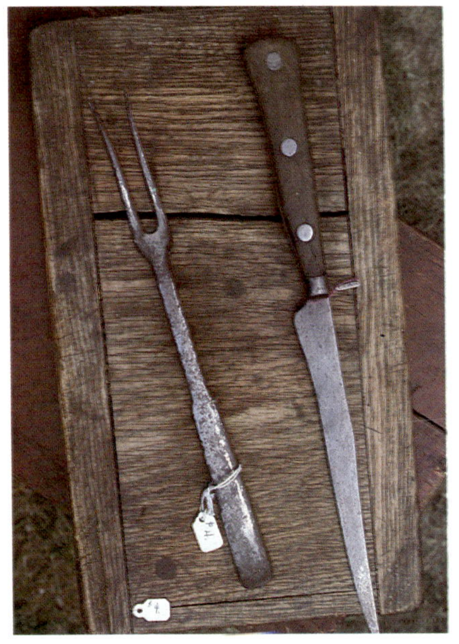

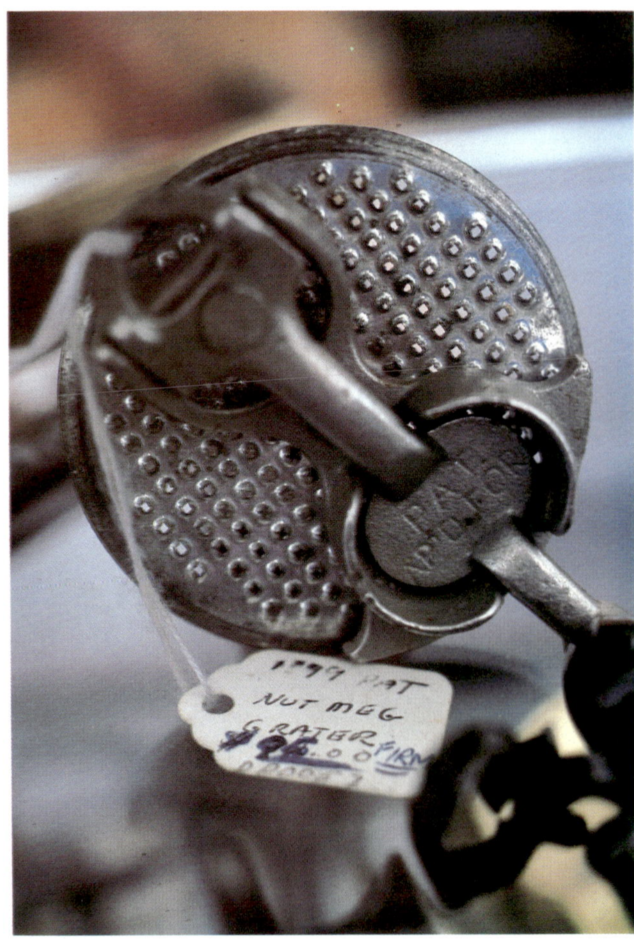
1899 PAT
NUT MEG
GRATER
FIRM

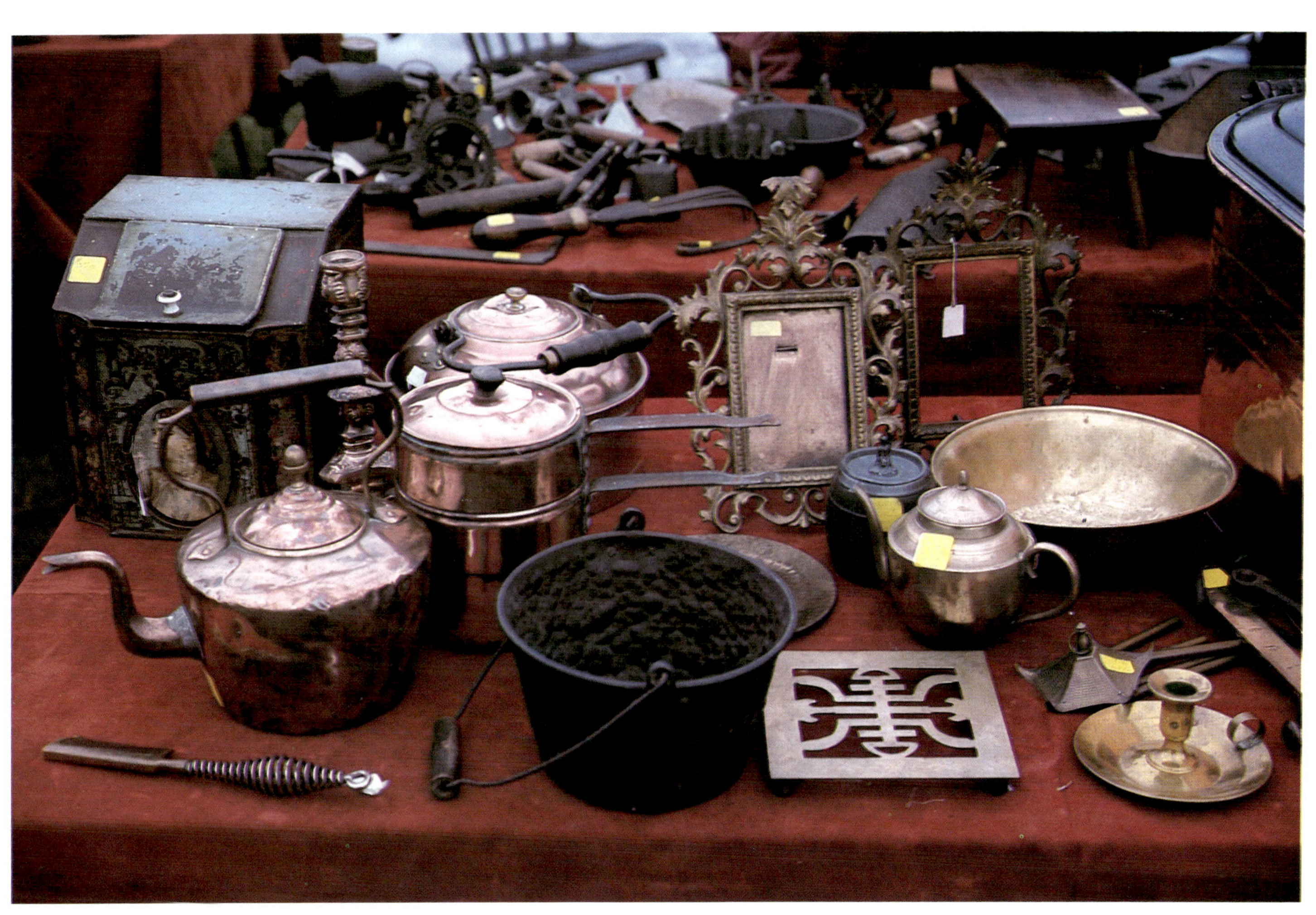

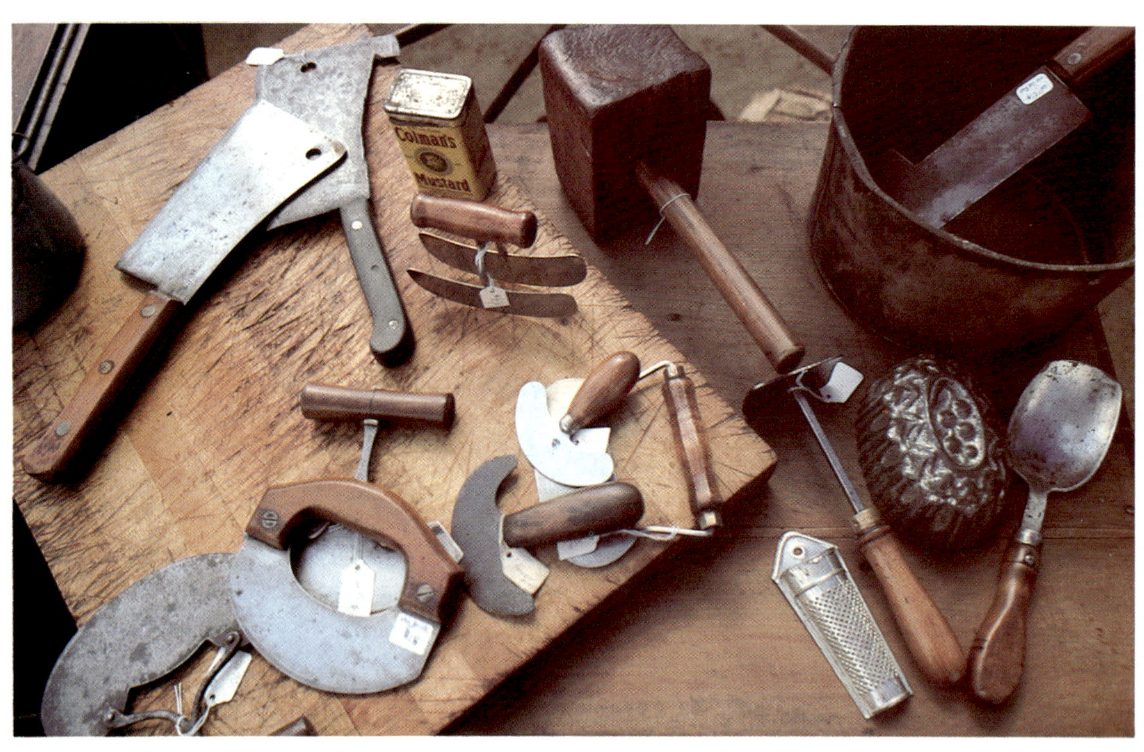
Colman's
Mustard

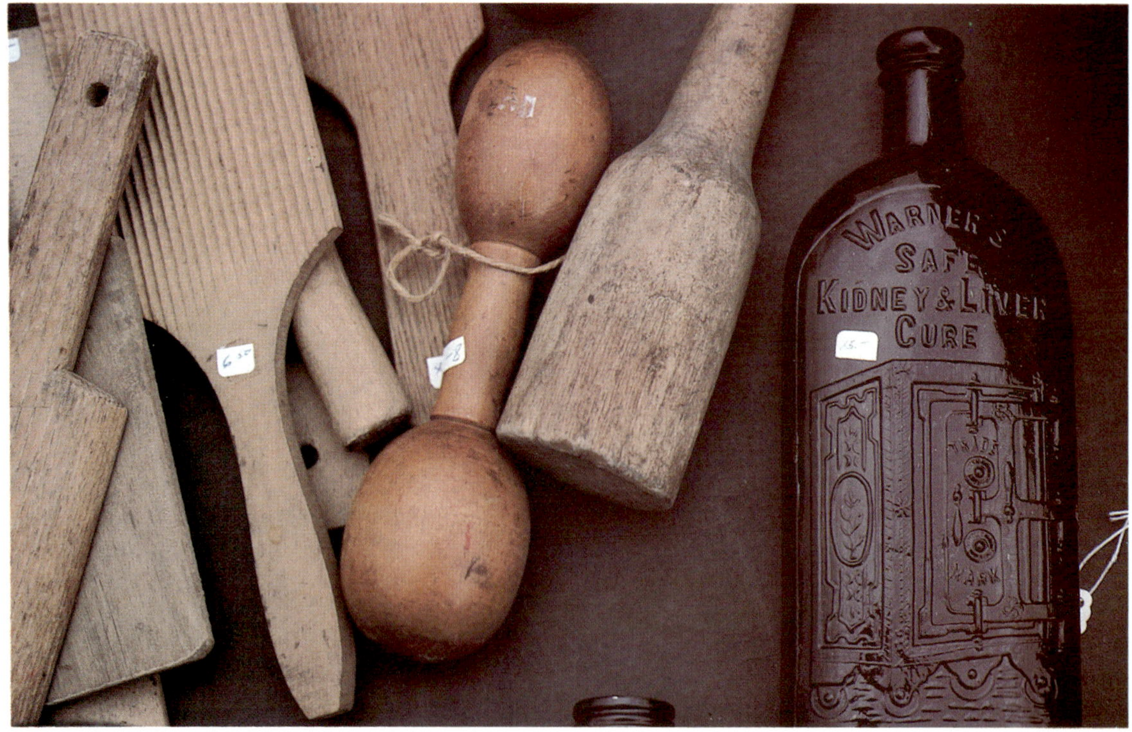
WARNER'S
SAFE
KIDNEY & LIVER
CURE

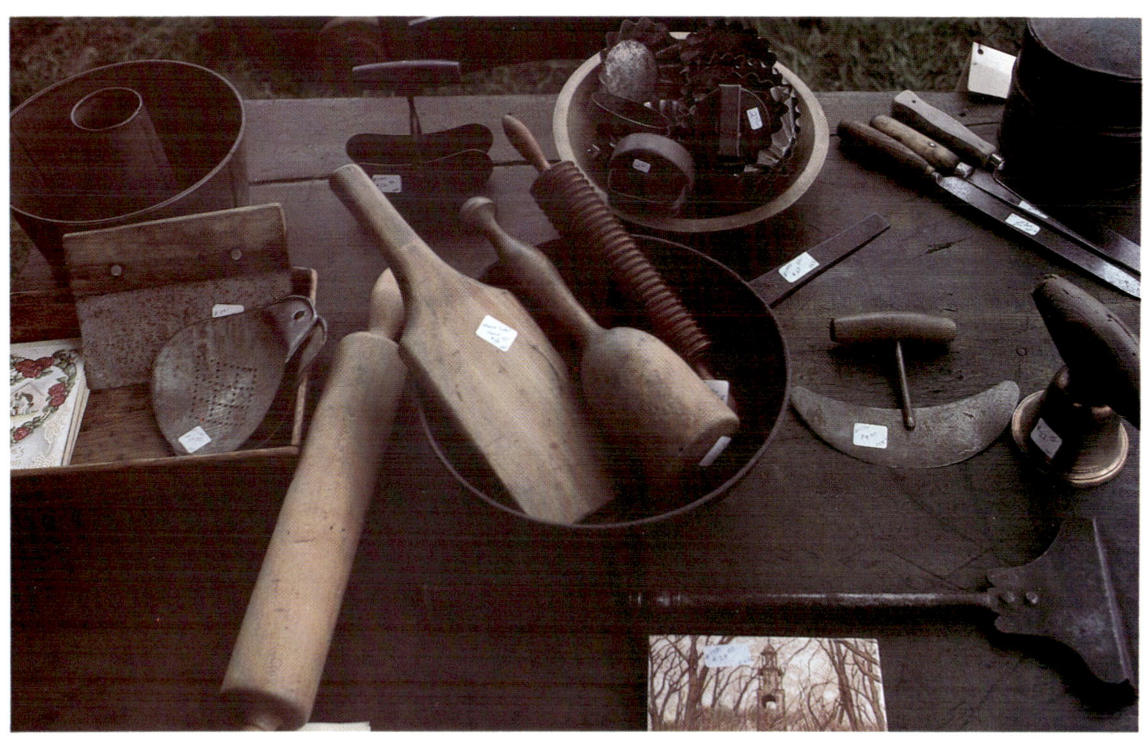

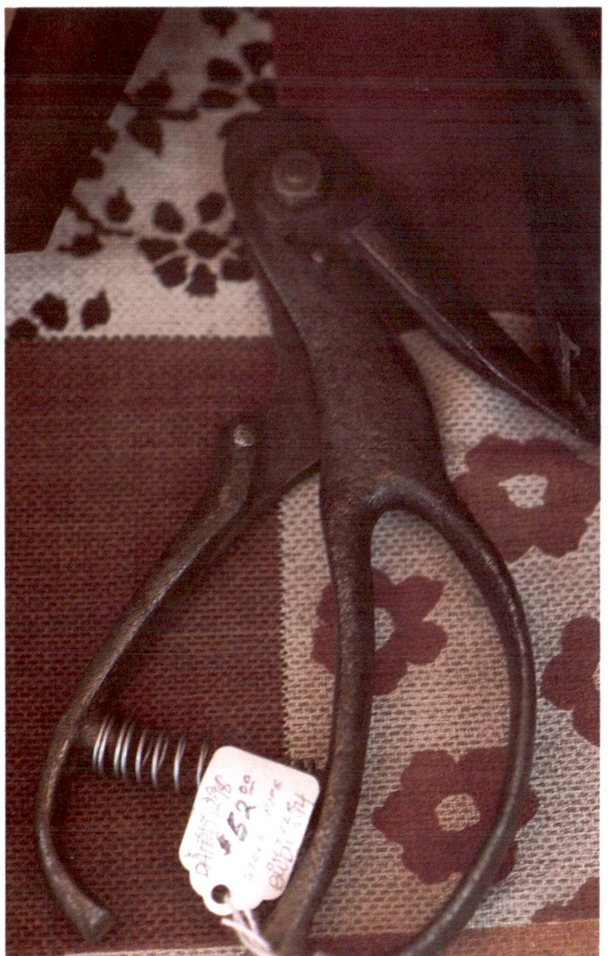

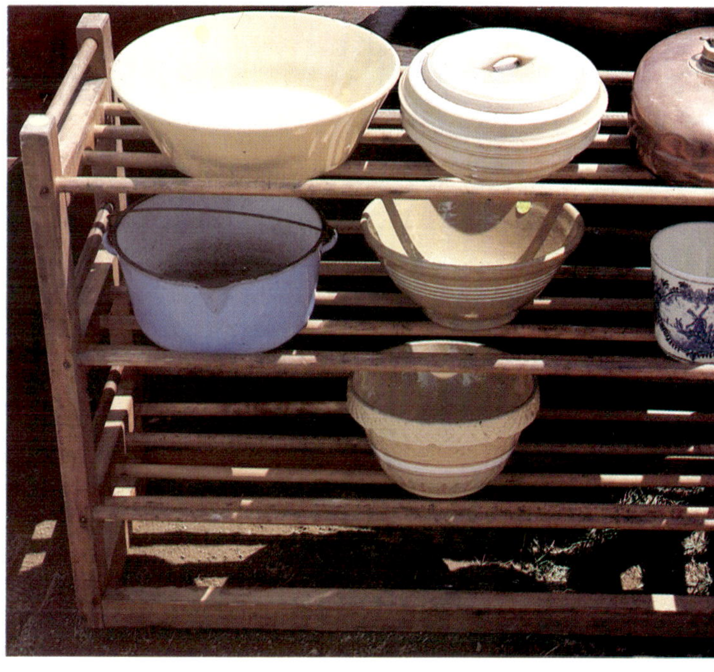

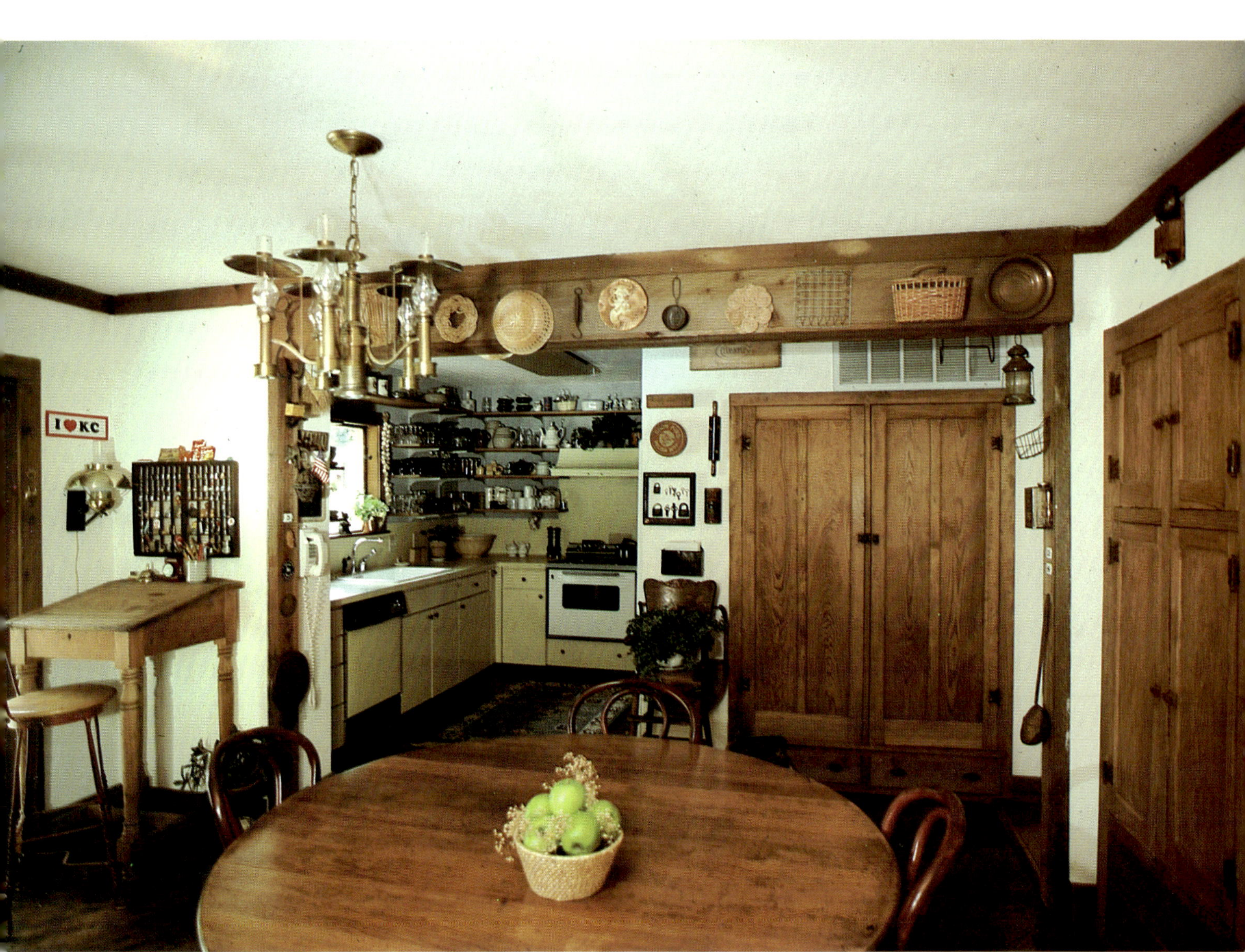
I ♥ KC

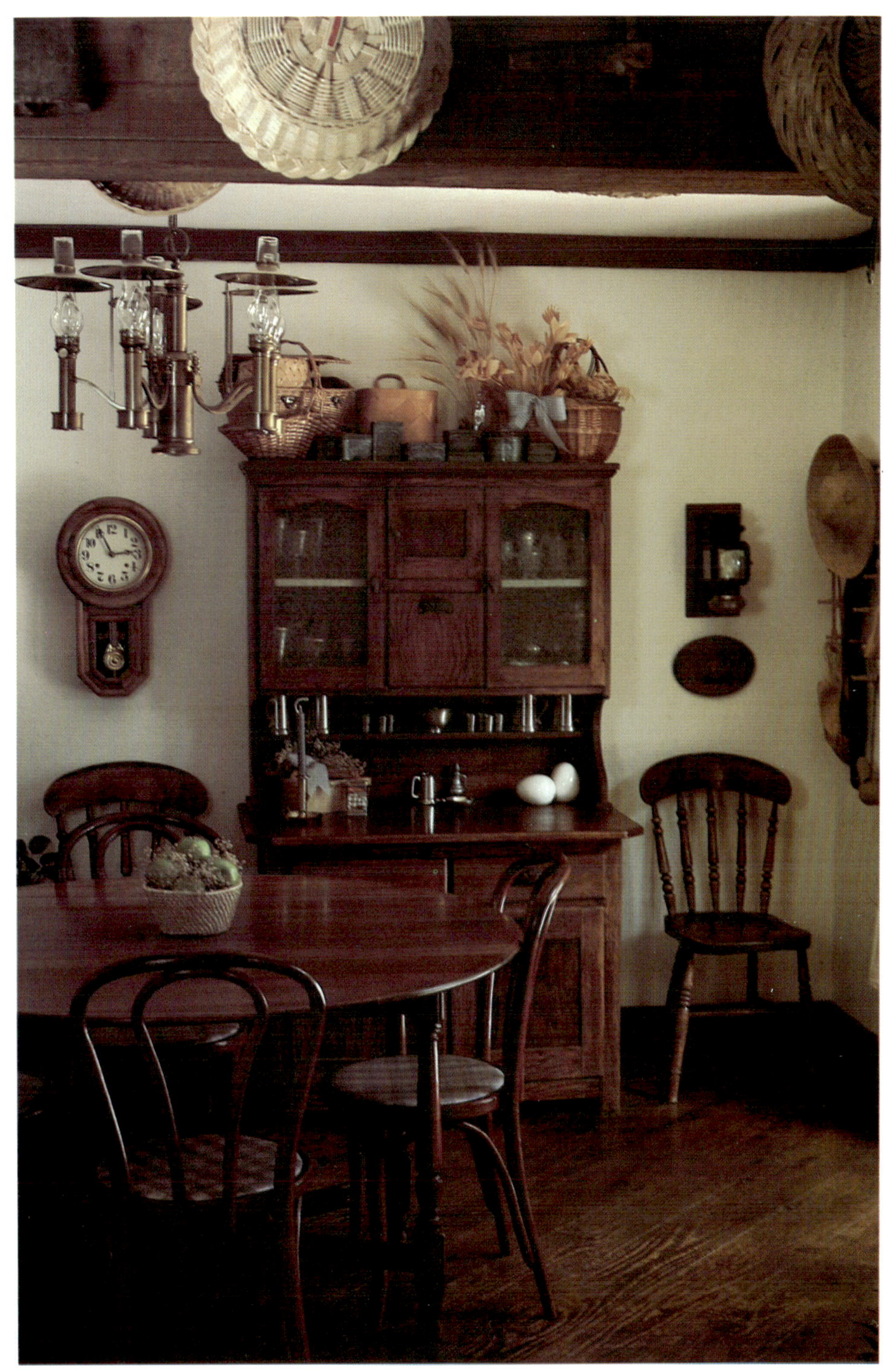

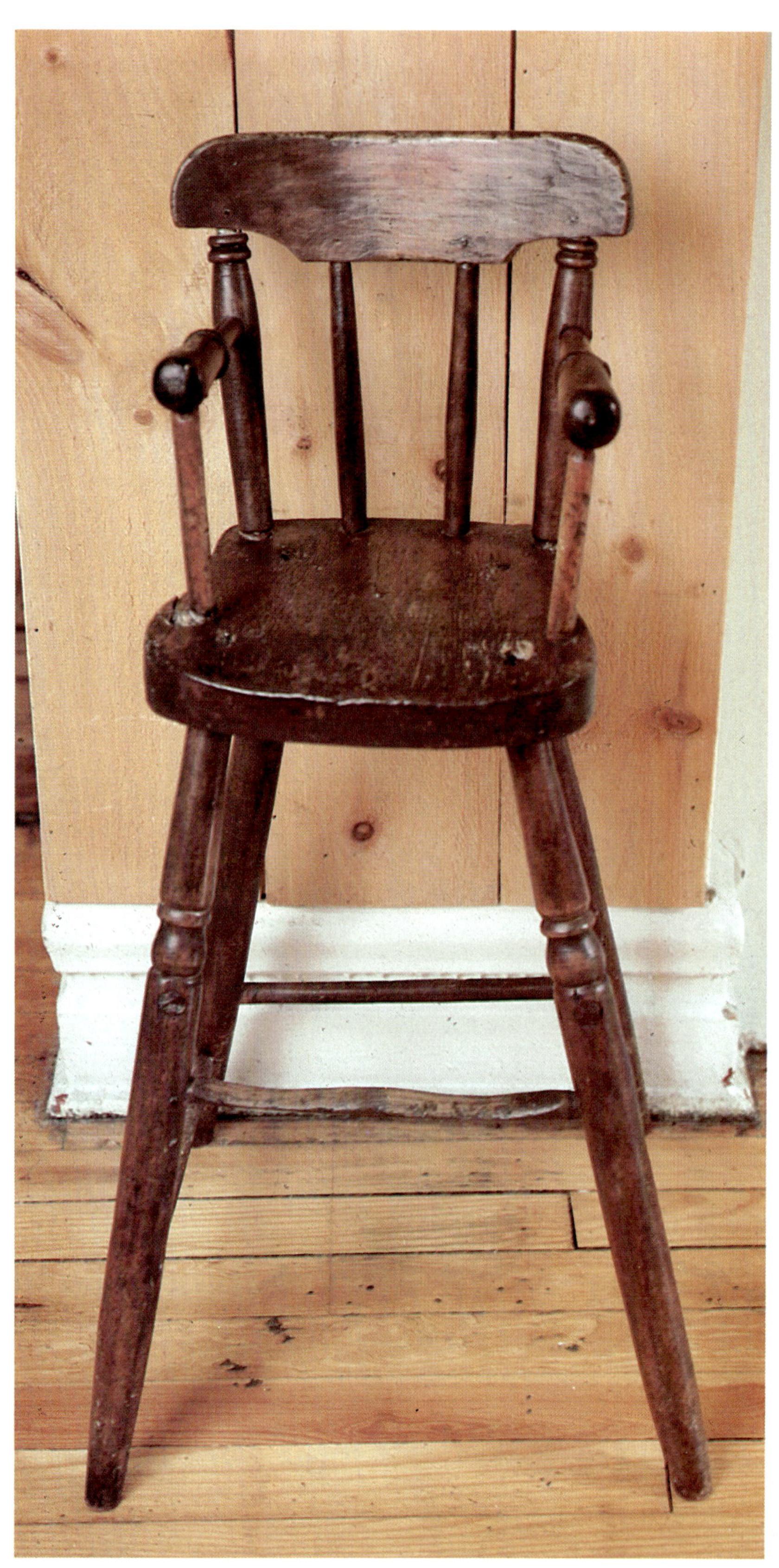

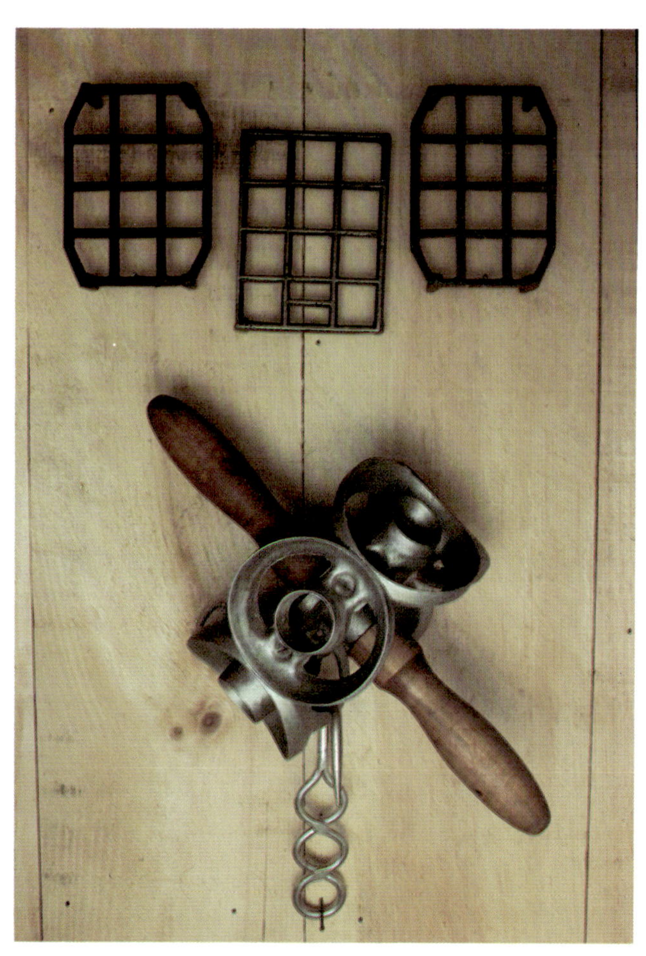

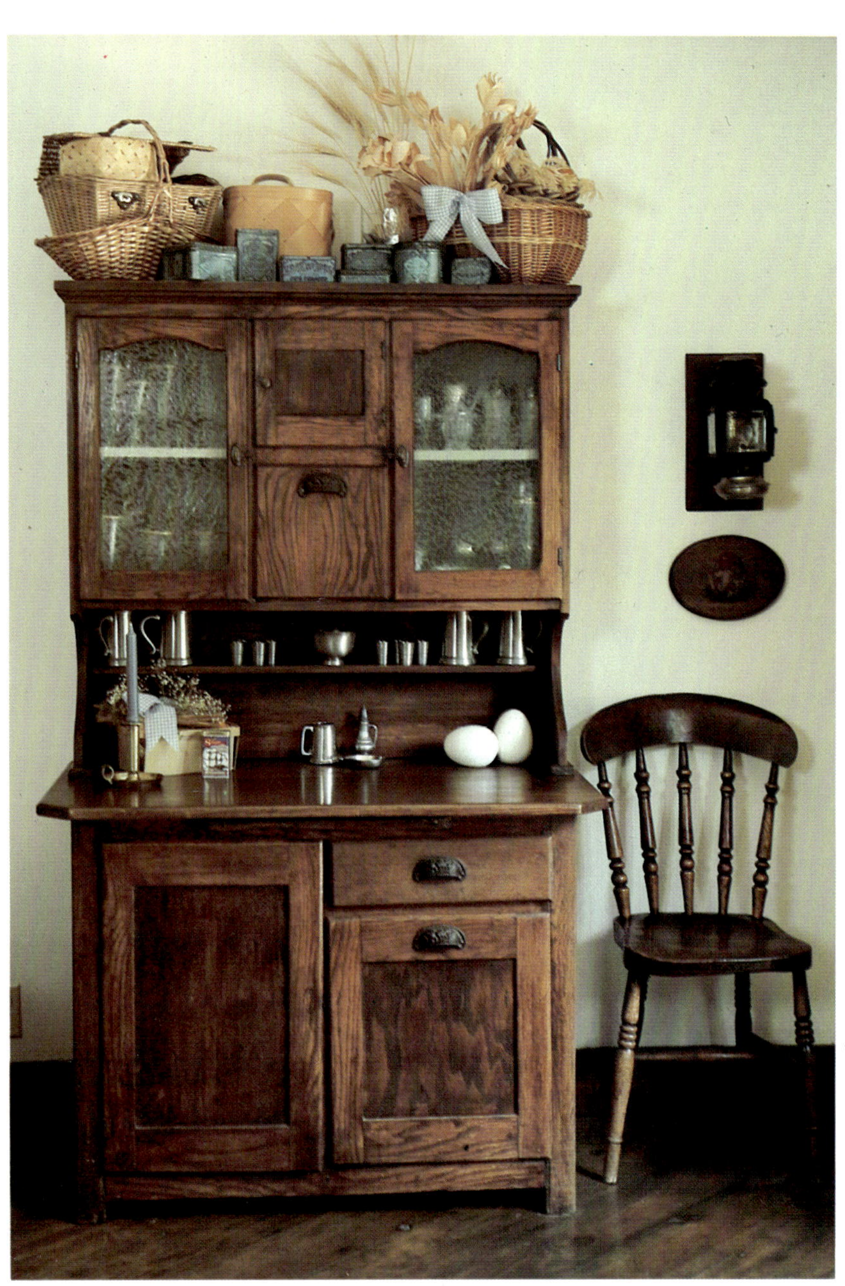

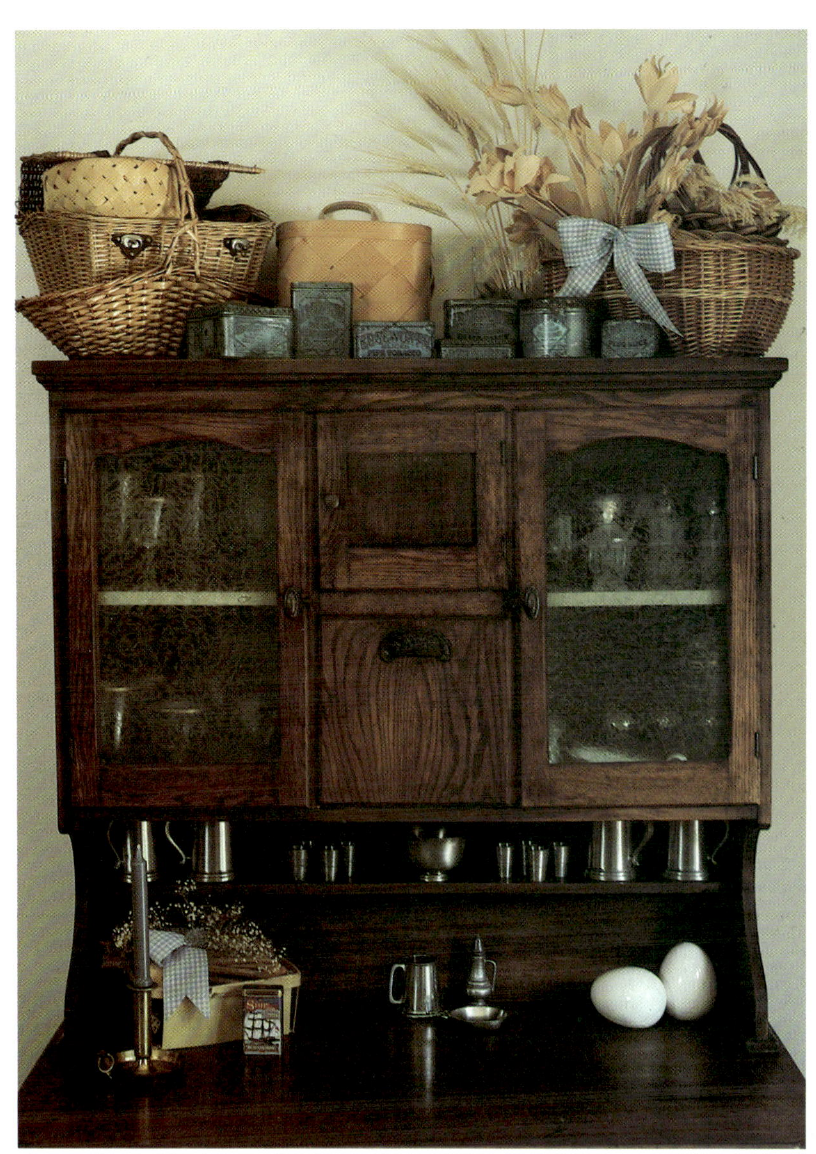

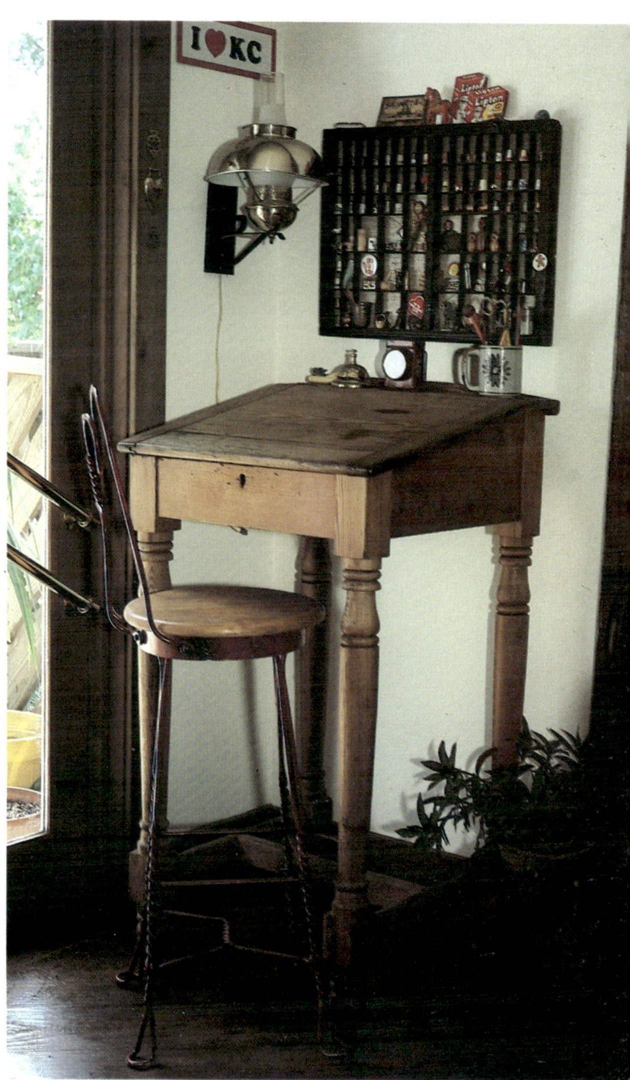
I ♥ KC

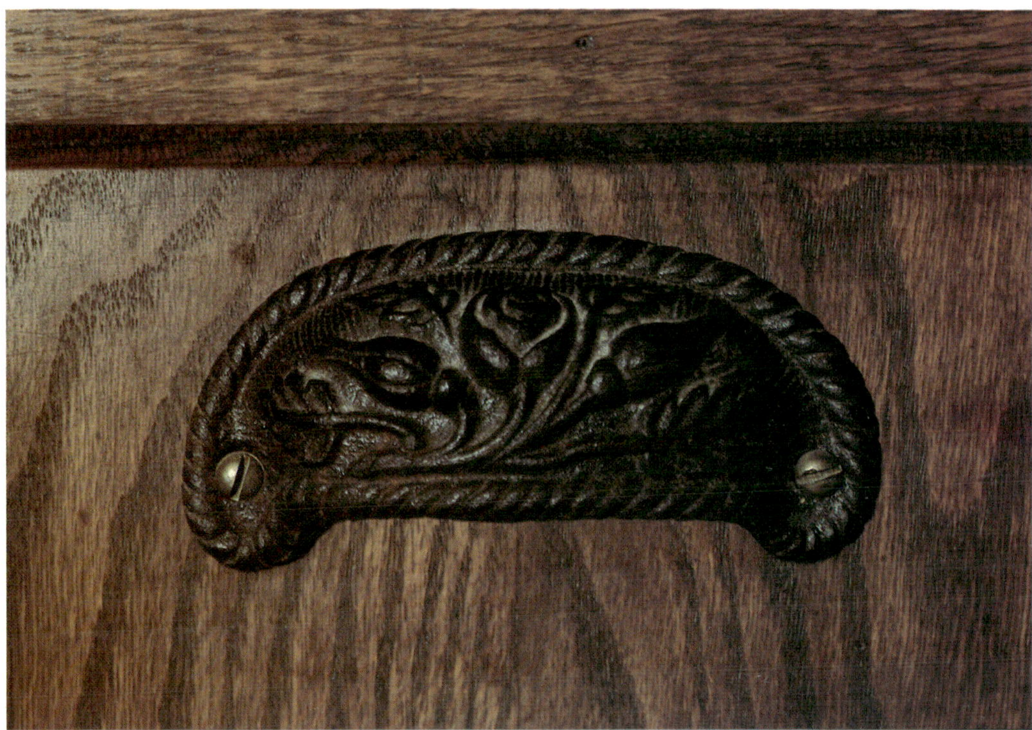

Climax Fruit Jar Filler.

No. 23R5098 Made with standard thread to fit any ordinary screw top jar, Mason's included. Cut represents filler in position, attached to a fruit jar. By using this the cook can take the jar right to the kettle, filling the fruit in **HOT,** so that it will **KEEP** perfectly. The thread of jar is covered; this prevents juice getting on same and cementing the cap so it can't be unscrewed. If jar is too full, it is easy to empty some back into kettle. **Price, each..........8c**

. . . . $2-6

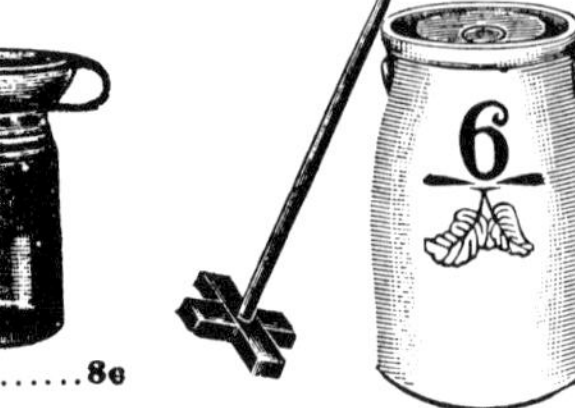

No. 2R635 Butter Churns with covers and best white maple wood dashers, white glaze, in seven sizes:

2-gallon, each	**$0.40**
3-gallon, each	**.50**
4-gallon, each	**.65**
5-gallon, each	**.75**
6-gallon, each	**.90**
8-gallon, each	**1.15**
10-gallon, each	**1.50**

. . . . $15-25

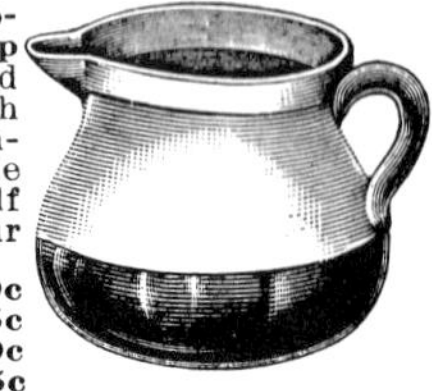

No. 2R640 Fancy Pipkins, Cream or Syrup Pitchers; can also be used for cooking purposes; with covers and stoneware handles; upper half and inside white glaze, lower half cherry brown glaze. Four sizes.

1-pint, each	**10c**
2-pint, each	**15c**
3-pint, each	**20c**
4-pint, each	**25c**

. . . . $8-15

Tin Colanders, IC.

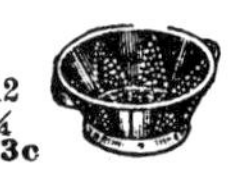

No. 23R5032 Eastern pattern.

Inches	10	12
Weight, each, pound	⅝	¾
Price, each,	**9c**	**13c**

. . . . $4-6

Water Dippers.

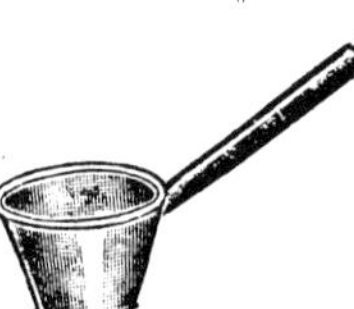

No. 23R5090
Tin Bottoms, IC.

Quarts	1	2
Holds quarts	¾	1⅛
Inches	5½x3	6¼x3⅞
Weight each, oz.,	4	6
Price, each	**6c**	**7c**

No. 23R5092 Copper Bottoms, IX. Two quarts; holds 1⅛ quarts; weight, 8 ounces; size, 6¼x3⅞ inches. Price, each..........**13c**

. . . . $3-6

Tin Wash Boilers, IX.

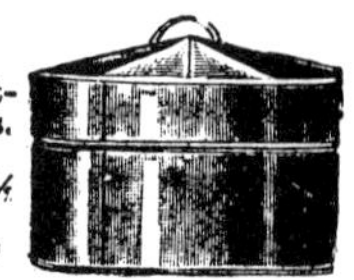

No. 23R5000 Flat copper bottoms, full sizes. Drop handles.

Nos.	7	8	9
Inches	9½x18½	10⅜x20¼	11⅝x22¼
Weight, lbs.	5	6	6½
Price, each,	**75c**	**85c**	**98c**

. . . . $25-40

Tin Coffee Boilers, IX.

No. 23R5030 Flat copper bottoms.

Nos.	7	8	9
Holds qts.	5	7	8¼
Inches	9x8½	9½x9	10½x9½
Wt., each, lb.	1	1⅜	1⅞
Price, each	**36c**	**42c**	**50c**

. . . . $6-8

Retinned Solid Ladles.

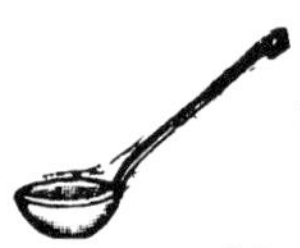

No. 23R5365

Inches	3¾	3⅞	4¼
Weight, each, ozs.	4	5	6
Price, each	**6c**	**6c**	**7c**
Per dozen	**61c**	**66c**	**73c**

. . . . $2-4

True Blue Enameled Ware Chambers.

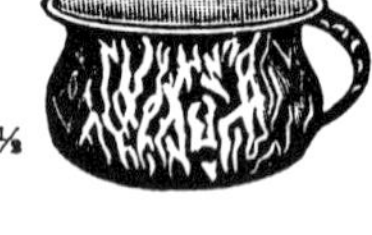

No. 23R4485

No.	1	1½	2
Inches	7x4⅛	8½x4⅞	9¾x5⅛
Price, each,	**41c**	**52c**	**62c**

. . . . $10-15

Apple Corers, IC.

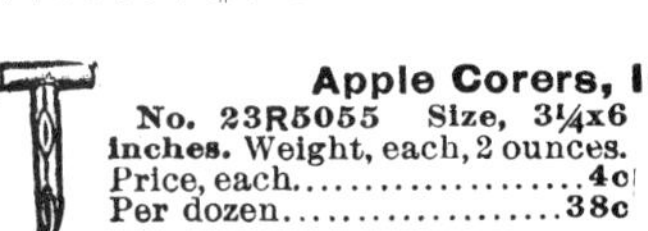

No. 23R5055 Size, 3¼x6 inches. Weight, each, 2 ounces.
Price, each..........**4c**
Per dozen..........**38c**

. . . . $2-4

New Idea Kettles.

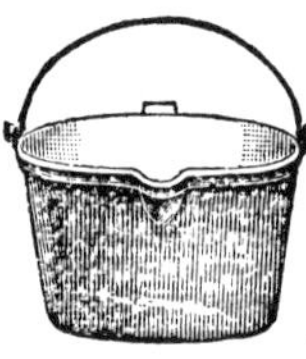

No. 23R3577 New Idea Cast Iron Kettles. White porcelain lined and enameled on outside with mottled blue porcelain. Smooth as glass and as easy to clean as a china dish. An ideal kettle for preserving fruits, etc., as it is not affected by acids, does not stain and will not discolor anything cooked in it.

Capacity, qts.	3	4	6	8	10	12	14	16	20	24
Weight, lbs.	4	4¼	6¼	7½	8⅞	11¼	12¼	15	17½	19¼
Price, each	**32c**	**36c**	**44c**	**52c**	**56c**	**60c**	**70c**	**80c**	**$1.00**	**$1.20**

. . . . $15-20

Retinned Wash Bowls, IC.

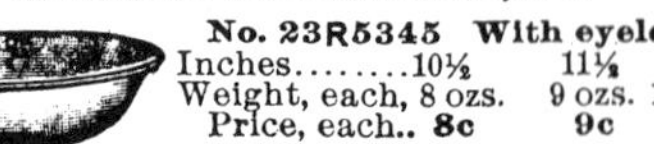

No. 23R5345 With eyelets.

Inches	10½	11⅛	13
Weight, each,	8 ozs.	9 ozs.	10 ozs.
Price, each..	**8c**	**9c**	**11c**

. . . . $15-20

Retinned Preserve Kettles.

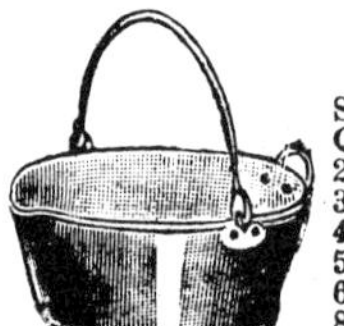

No. 23R5359

Size Qts	Holds	Inches	Weight	Price Each
2½	2 qts.	7¾x3¼	⅛ lb.	**10c**
3	2¾ qts.	8⅝x3⅞	⅝ lb.	**12c**
4	3½ qts.	9¼x4	¾ lb.	**13c**
5	4 qts.	9¾x4⅛	¾ lb.	**15c**
6	5 qts.	10½x4¼	⅞ lb.	**17c**
8	6¾ qts.	11¼x4¾	1 lb.	**18c**

. . . . $18-25

Ham Boilers.

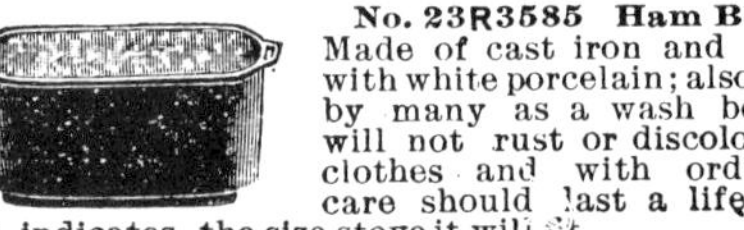

No. 23R3585 Ham Boiler. Made of cast iron and lined with white porcelain; also used by many as a wash boiler; will not rust or discolor the clothes and with ordinary care should last a lifetime. Size indicates the size stove it will fit.

No. 23R3585

Size	7	8	9
Length, inches	19	21¼	24
Width, inches	9⅜	11¼	13
Weight, pounds	20	22½	31
Price, each	**$1.20**	**$1.40**	**$1.58**

. . . . $18-35

Oblong Chopping Tray.

No. 23R8142 Hardwood Patent Oblong Chopping Trays.

Size	12 x 22	11 x 21	10½ x 19½
Weight, each, lbs.	3½	2½	2¼
Price, each	**35c**	**25c**	**20c**

. . . . $25-45

Sieve.

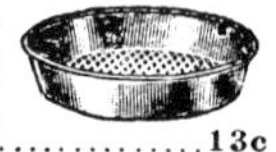

No. 23R5536 Tin Rim Sieve, plated wire bottom, 18 meshes to the inch, 12½ inches diameter, well put together; made of heavy tin. Weight, each, 6 ounces. Price, each..........**13c**

. . . . $2-6

DEPARTMENT OF COMBINATION OUTFITS AND HOUSE FURNISHINGS.

ABOUT THE QUALITY. **Different from many department and novelty stores** who sell assortments of inferior goods, our assortments are all made up from **regular stock merchandise of the highest grade,** every article that goes into every combination we offer is strictly a high standard quality **and so guaranteed,** and if not found to be such in every instance you are at liberty to return goods to us and we will cheerfully refund your money. **We are able to make this extraordinary offer** on combination outfits by reason of buying up **immense quantities** of the different articles during the dull seasons, when the manufacturers have little to do and are willing to make **very close prices;** at the same time when it is quiet with us we can assemble the outfits, pack them, get them ready for shipment. As it costs no more to handle **the complete outfit** once ready for shipment than one single item in the lot, we can afford to figure our profit **even lower** than on a general line. All this you get the benefit of in our prices.

PEERLESS STEEL ENAMELED WARE OUTFITS.

We have made up a combination of Peerless Steel Enameled Ware in three different sizes which we are able to offer in the complete assortment as listed below at $4.25, $4.93 and $5.47, in competition with anything you can buy anywhere at double the price. This Peerless Enameled Steel Ware is the highest grade, strictly firsts, not seconds, made by the best makers in America. These outfits consist of the following articles:

1 Peerless Enameled Steel Tea Kettle.
1 Peerless Enameled Steel Coffee Pot.
1 Peerless Enameled Steel Tea Pot.
2 Peerless Enameled Steel Preserving Kettles.
1 Peerless Enameled Steel Saucepan.
2 Peerless Enameled Steel Pudding Pans.
1 Peerless Enameled Steel Wash Basin.
1 Peerless Enameled Steel Windsor Pattern Dipper.
4 Peerless Enameled Steel Pie Plates, 9 inches in diameter.
1 Peerless Enameled Steel Soap Dish to hang on the wall.
1 Peerless Enameled Steel Dish Pan.
1 Peerless Enameled Steel Soup Ladle.

No. 23R3007 Our Peerless Enameled Steel Outfit for No. 7 Stove. Weight, 45 pounds. Price, complete..........**$4.25**

No. 23R3008 Our Peerless Enameled Steel Outfit for No. 8 Stove. Weight, 50 pounds. Price, complete..........**$4.93**

No. 23R3009 Our Peerless Enameled Steel Outfit for No. 9 Stove. Weight, 60 pounds. Price, complete..........**$5.47**

No. 23R3007	**$4.25**
No. 23R3008	**4.93**
No. 23R3009	**5.47**

ORDER BY NUMBER.

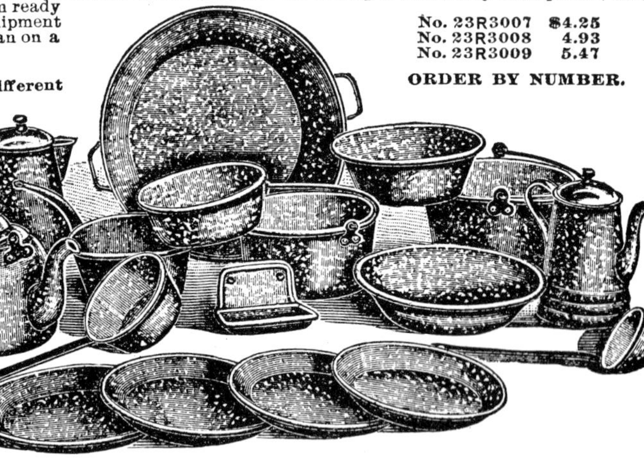

. . . . $20-60

OUR $1.75 40-PIECE GLASS OUTFIT.

No. 2R655 Imitation cut glass design. The pattern is the newest produced this year and exceedingly beautiful. We feel confident that you never heard of such a wonderful assortment of glassware for so little money.

SET CONSISTS OF 40 PIECES AS FOLLOWS:

6 Water Tumblers
6 Goblets
6 Salt and Pepper Shakers
12 Berry Saucers
1 Large Berry Bowl
1 Large ½-gallon Water Pitcher
1 Butter Dish
1 Sugar Bowl
1 Cream Pitcher
1 Spoon Holder
1 Pickle Dish
1 Tall Celery Glass

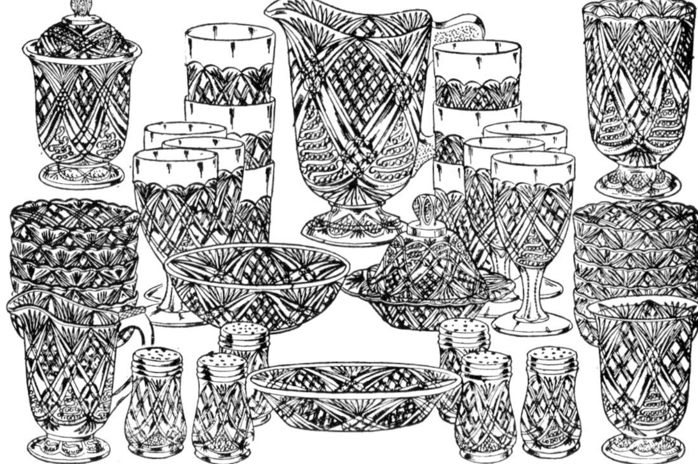

No. 2R655 Price, Complete Outfit................ **$1.75**

.... $150-300

No. 22R594 Step Stove, No. 425. Two burners on top and one burner on step. Size of top, 22x15 inches; size of step, 11½x15 inches; height to top of stove, 24 inches. **Weight, crated, 60 pounds.** Price, **$9.10**

See next page for price of our special drop door ovens.

Remember that the steel burner shells on all of our Acme Wickless Stoves give the largest and hottest blue flame of any oil stove made.

.... $250-600

PRICES OF OUR HIGH FRAME ACME WICKLESS BLUE FLAME CABINET OIL STOVE.

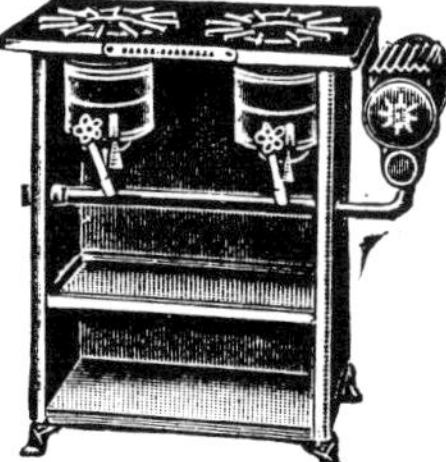

No. 22R592 High Stove, No. 422. Two burners. Size of top, 22x15 inches; height, 24 inches. Price............**$6.00** **Weight, crated, 50 pounds.**

No. 22R593 High Stove, No. 433. Three burners. Size of top, 33x15 inches; height, 24 inches. Price............**$7.70** **Weight, crated, 55 pounds.**

No. 22R592

.... $150-300

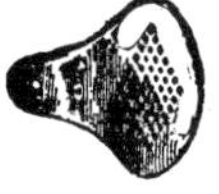

Pierced Milk Skimmers.

No. 23R5434 No handles.
Inches.................... 5¾x6¼
Weight, each, ounces.......... 2
Price, each................ 2c

.... $6-8

Retinned Milk Skimmers.

No. 23R5436 Pierced, handled.
Weight, each, ounces.......... 3
Inches.................... 4⅝
Price, each.................. 5c

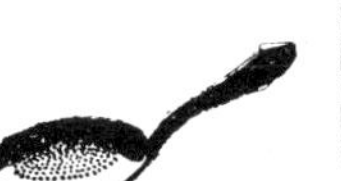

.... $6-8

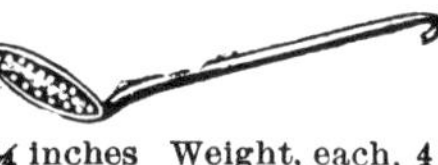

Retinned Flat Skimmers.

No. 23R5438 Fl handles.
4¼ inches Weight, each, 4 ounces. Each.......... 5c
5¾ inches Weight, each, 6 ounces. Each.......... 7c

Cake Turners.

No. 23R5445 Enameled wood handles. 2⅞x3¾ inches. Weight, each, 2 ounces. Price, each........ 3c

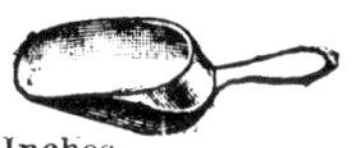

Retinned Covered Scoops.

No. 23R5450

Inches	6¾x4¾	9¾x6¾
Weight, each, ounces	5	8
Price, each	13c	21c

Shallow Pie Plates.

No. 23R5465 Full size.

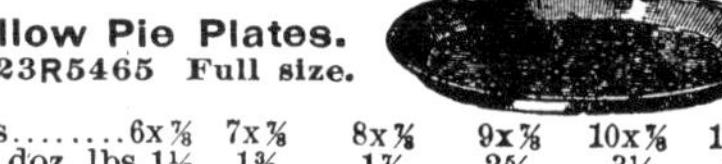

Inches	6x⅞	7x⅞	8x⅞	9x⅞	10x⅞	11x⅞
Wght., doz., lbs	1⅛	1⅜	1⅞	2⅝	3⅛	3⅝
Price, each	2c	3c	3c	3c	4c	5c
Per dozen	19c	25c	30c	36c	44c	54c

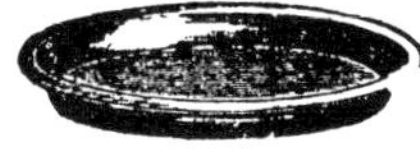

Deep Pie Plates.

No. 23R5467

Inches	9x1¼	10x1¼
Wt. doz. lbs.	2¼	3⅛
Price, each	4c	5c
Per dozen	41c	49c

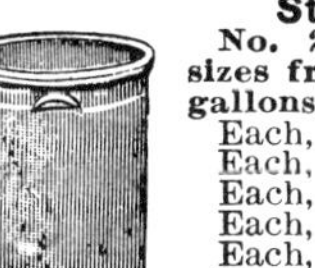

Stone Jars.

No. 2R610 Stone Jars in all sizes from ⅛ of a gallon up to 40 gallons. Bristol white glaze.

Each, ⅛-gallon	**$ 0.05**
Each, ¼-gallon	**.05**
Each, ½-gallon	**.06**
Each, 1-gallon	**.10**
Each, 2-gallon	**.18**
Each, 3-gallon	**.28**
Each, 4-gallon	**.40**

.... $10-40

Surprise Egg Beater.

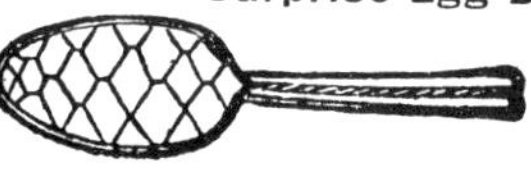

No. 23R6632
Weight, 1 ounce.
Price, each..... 2c
Per dozen....... 14c

.... $6-8

Dover Egg Beaters.

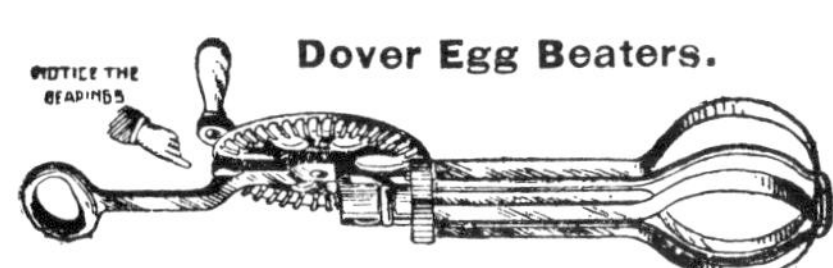

No. 23R6633 Dover Egg Beater. Length, 9 inches. Weight, 5 ounces. Wheels and handle are Tuscan bronzed; beater and frame heavily tinned and retinned. The kind and size commonly sold for 10 to 15 cents. Price, each.................. 5c

.... $4-6

Plain Gravy Strainers.

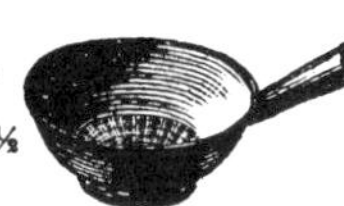

No. 23R5429 Tin handles.
Inches.................. 4¼x2½
Weight, each, ounces..... 3
Price, each.............. 4c

.... $2-4

Shallow Jelly Cake Pans.

No. 23R5470

Inches	9x⅛	10x⅛
Wt. per doz., lbs.	2¾	3¼
Price, each	4c	4c
Price, per dozen	38c	46c

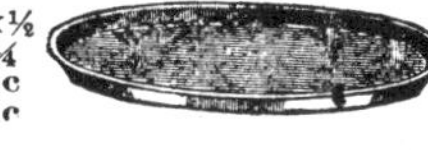

.... $4-8

Deep Jelly Cake Pans.

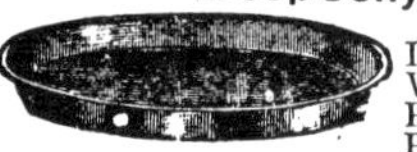

No. 23R5471

Inches	9x1	10x1
Wt. per doz., lbs.	2⅞	3¾
Price, each	4c	5c
Price, per dozen	44c	52c

.... $4-8

Mountain Cake Pans.

No. 23R5473

Inches	9x1⅜	10x1⅜
Wt. per doz., lbs.	3¼	4¼
Price, each	4c	5c
Price, per doz.	46c	57c

.... $4-8

Lettered Plates.

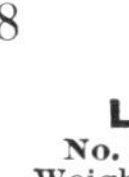

No. 23R5478 Size, 6 inches.
Weight per dozen, pounds... 1⅛
Price, each.......... 2c
Price, per dozen....... 19c

.... $10-15

Plain Round Patty Pans.

No. 23R5485

Inches	3	4
Weight per doz., oz	6	9
Price, per dozen	6c	10c

.... $4-6

Star Patty Pans.

No. 23R5486 Size, 3 inches.
Weight, per dozen, 6 ounces.
Price, per dozen.................. 8c

.... $2-4

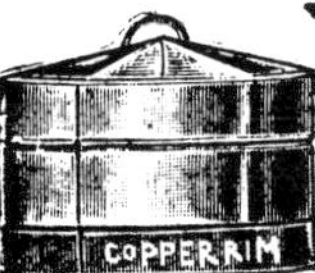

Copper Rim Wash Boilers, IX.

No. 23R5002 Copper rim, flat copper bottoms, full sizes. Drop handles.

Nos.	7	8	9
Inches	9¼x18¼	10⅜x20¼	11⅝x22¼
Weight, lbs.	5¼	6¼	6¾
Price, each	96c	$1.06	$1.24

.... $45-100

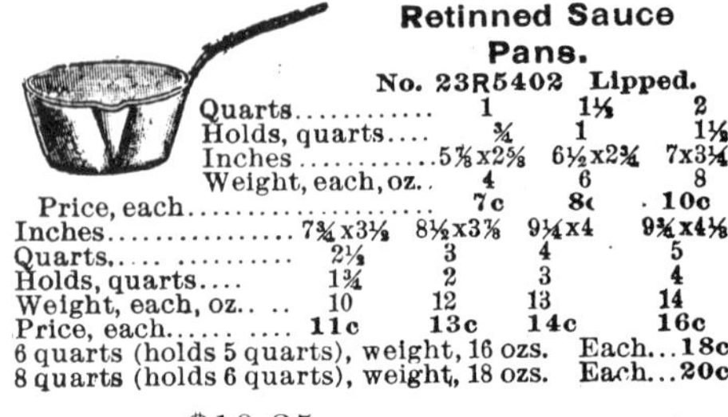

Retinned Sauce Pans.

No. 23R5402 Lipped.

Quarts	1	1½	2	
Holds, quarts	¾	1	1½	
Inches	5⅞x2⅝	6½x2¾	7x3¼	
Weight, each, oz.	4	6	8	
Price, each	7c	8c	10c	
Inches	7¾x3½	8½x3⅞	9¼x4	9¾x4⅛
Quarts	2½	3	4	5
Holds, quarts	1¾	2	3	4
Weight, each, oz.	10	12	13	14
Price, each	**11c**	**13c**	**14c**	**16c**

6 quarts (holds 5 quarts), weight, 16 ozs. Each...**18c**
8 quarts (holds 6 quarts), weight, 18 ozs. Each...**20c**

.... $10-25

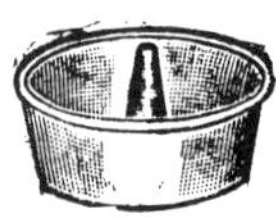

Retinned Round Cake Pans.

No. 23R5382 Deep, with tubes.

Quarts	3	6
Holds quarts	2½	4½
Inches	9¼x3½	11½x3½
Weight, each, ozs.	6	12
Price, each	**11c**	**15c**

.... $3-9

Retinned Bread Raisers.

No. 23R5420 Sizes are actual capacity. Extra heavy.

Quarts	10	14	17	21
Inches	14½	16¼	17¾	19½
Weight, each, lbs.	2¼	2¾	3	4½
Each	**49c**	**57c**	**68c**	**79c**

.... $28-40

No. 23R5396 Plain Muffin Pans.

Inches..............7¼x14¼
Cups.................8
Size of cups.......3¼x1
Weight, each......½ lb.
Price, each.......**12c**
Inches, 10¾x14¼; cups, 12; size of cups, 3¼x1. Weight, each, ¾ lb. Price....**17c**

.... $2-6

No. 23R5398 Corn Cake Pans, plain.

Inches	Cups	Size of Cups	Weight, each	Price
37¼x14¼	8	¼x1½	⅝ pound	**13c**
10¾x14¼	12	3¼x1¼	⅞ pound	**18c**

.... $2-6

Turk Head Pans.

No. 23R5400 Plain. Size, 7¼x14 inches; No. of cups, 8; size of cups, 3¼x1½ inches. Weight, each, ½ pound.
Price, each.........**13c**
Size, 10¾x14¼ inches; number of cups, 12; size of cups, 3¼x1½ inches. Weight, ¾ pound. Each....**18c**

.... $2-6

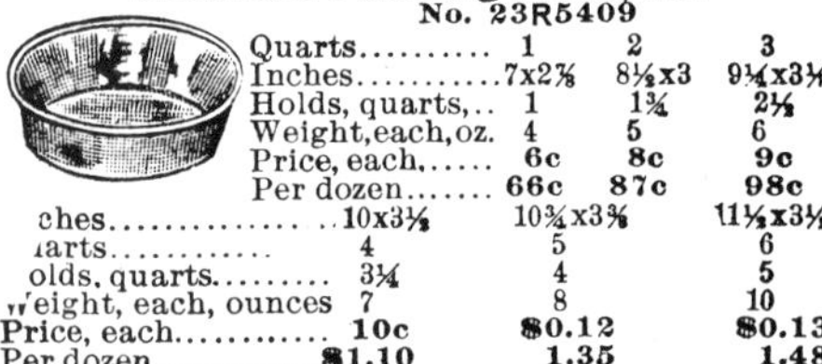

Retinned Pudding Pans, IC.

No. 23R5409

Quarts	1	2	3
Inches	7x2⅞	8½x3	9¼x3⅛
Holds, quarts	1	1¾	2½
Weight, each, oz.	4	5	6
Price, each	**6c**	**8c**	**9c**
Per dozen	**66c**	**87c**	**98c**
ches	10x3½	10¾x3⅜	11½x3½
arts	4	5	6
olds, quarts	3¼	4	5
eight, each, ounces	7	8	10
Price, each	**10c**	**$0.12**	**$0.13**
Per dozen	**$1.10**	**1.35**	**1.48**

.... $5-8

Retinned Angel Cake Pans, IC.

No. 23R5387 With tubes. Size, 9⅝x4 inches. Weight, each, 12 oz.
Price, each....................**18c**

.... $4-6

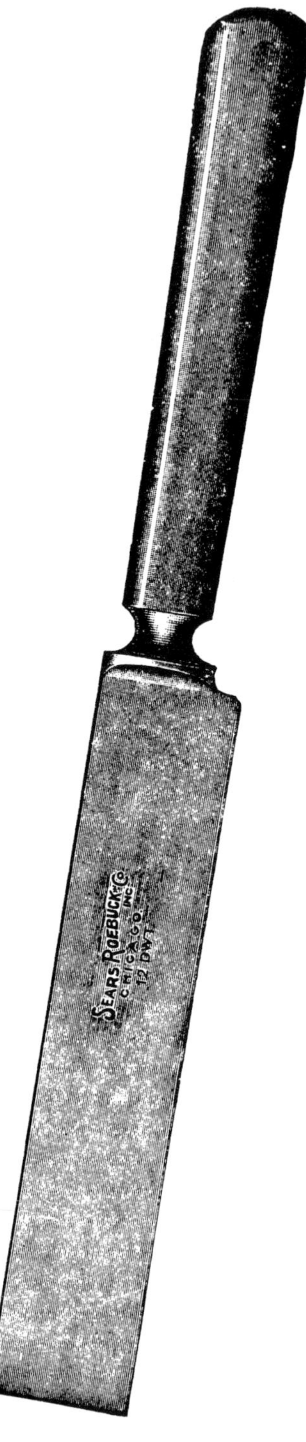

No. 5R6649 Plain Medium Knives, per dozen **$2.60**

Hardwood Bread Board.

No. 23R8200 Hardwood Bread Board, hand carved and well finished. No family should be without one. Diameter, **11** inches. Weight, 1¼ pounds.
Price, each......................**23c**

.... $15-40

Retinned Dish Pans, IX.

No. 23R5415 Qts.	Inch,	Holds, quarts	Wgt. each, lbs.	Price, each
10	14½x5⅛	9	1¼	**25c**
14	16¼x5½	12	1¾	**30c**
17	17¾x5⅝	15	2	**36c**
21	19½x6	18	2½	**41c**

.... $8-12

Potato Mashers.

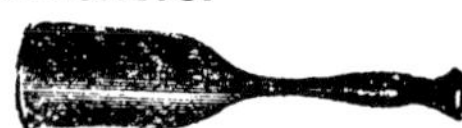

No. 23R8160 Potato Mashers, with driven handles. Weight, 6 oz.
Price, each.........**3c**

No. 23R8161 Potato Mashers, made complete with handle, all from one piece of wood. Weight, each, 10 ounces. Price, each..........................**4c**

.... $5-7

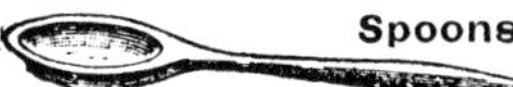

Spoons. **No. 23R8165 Wood Kitchen Spoons,** 14 inches long. Weight, each, 3 ounces. Price, each...............................**2c**

.... $3

Retinned Round Cake Pans.

No. 23R5380 Shallow, with tubes.

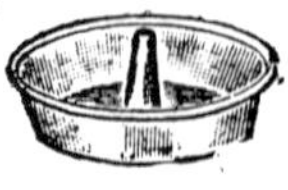

Quarts	3	5
Holds quarts	2	3½
Inches	9¾x2¾	11¾x2⅝
Weight, each, ozs.	6	10
Price, each	**10c**	**13c**

.... $5-8

Turk Head Cake Molds.

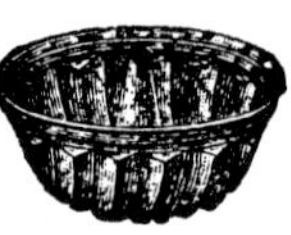

No. 23R5385 Retinned, with tubes.

Size, quarts,	3	5
Holds quarts	1¾	3
Inches	8x3½	9½x4
Weight, each, ounces	8	12
Price, each	**12c**	**17c**

.... $6-8

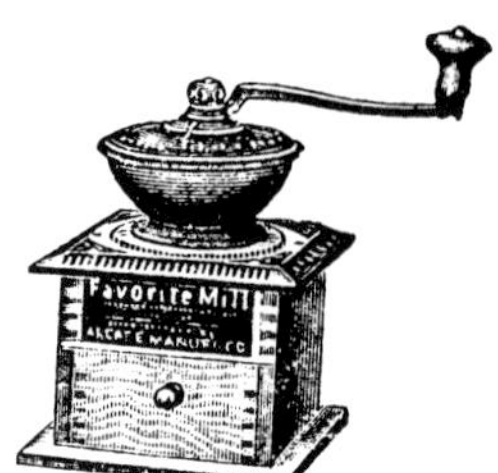

No. 23R904 Raised Hopper Mill with hinged cover, hardwood box and dovetailed corners, highly polished and covered with best copal varnish, **bronzed irons, patent regulator** and improved grinder burr that will **thoroughly pulverize coffee** when desired. This mill has an ornamental top to the box, which makes it strong and durable. Price, **38c**

.... $15-22

Salt Box.

No. 23R8261 Salt Box, made of nice clear wood, is 4½x5 inches square and will hold two small bags of salt. Weight, each, 14 ounces. Each..............**8c**

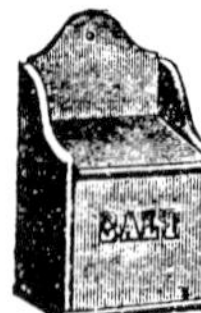

.... $15-20

Hardwood Salt Box.

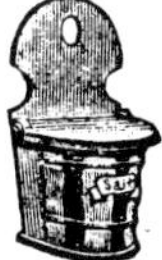

No. 23R8263 Hardwood Salt Box. The front is made of alternating strips of dark and light wood, varnished and highly polished to bring out the beautiful grain of the wood. Has fancy metal plate, engraved with the word Salt. An artistic kitchen necessity. Will hold a small pack of salt. Is 10 inches high and 5¼ inches wide. Weight, each, 1 pound.
Price, each..**17c**

.... $15-20

Folding Ironing Boards.

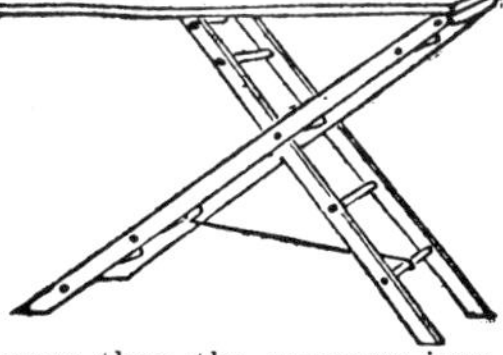

No. 23R8414 This convenient household article is in great favor wherever shown. It has basswood top. The legs are of hardwood, and the table may be easily and quickly adjusted to three different heights. When not in use occupies but little more space than the common ironing board. Weight, 14 pounds. Price, each......**45c**

.... $25-45

Stoneware Jugs.

No. 2R620 Jugs in all sizes from ¼ of a gallon to 5 gallons, white glaze, best quality stoneware and full measure.

¼-gallon..........................**6c**
½-gallon..........................**8c**
1-gallon..........................**12c**
2-gallon..........................**25c**
3-gallon..........................**35c**
4-gallon..........................**45c**
5-gallon..........................**55c**

Also 5-gallon jugs for cider and other beverages with faucet hole.

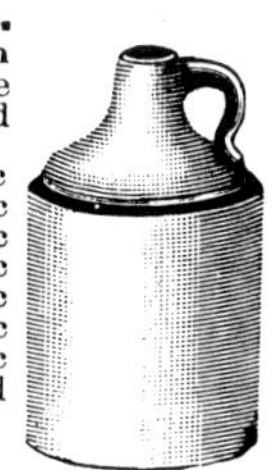

.... $15-20

Bean Pots.

No. 2R615 Genuine Boston Bean Pots, for baking beans; in four sizes; walnut brown glaze.

1-quart, with cover, each.. **9c**
2-quart, with cover, each..**12c**
4-quart, with cover, each..**15c**
8-quart, with cover, each..**25c**

.... $18-22

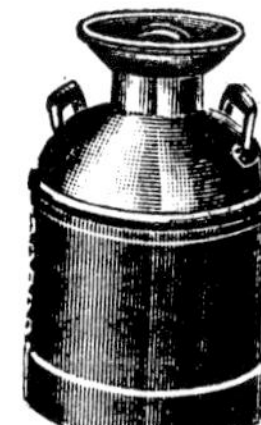

No. 23R9003 The Iowa Pattern Railroad Stiff Steel Milk Shipping Can. This is the most popular of the many styles of cans and is used in every state in the Union. While medium priced, it is constructed to give great service; has seamless neck and cover with non-pull-off handle, improved round handles to prevent cut hands, stamped seamless breast with ⅝-inch half oval steel bumping band to protect can from getting jammed in. Heavy stiff steel body, will not dent, **riveted and soldered,** drawn steel bottom, heavy tinned steel bottom hoop 2¼ inches wide; bottom is flanged and riveted through hoop and body. Realizing the hard usage to which these milk cans will be subjected, we use an extra amount of best pure solder, making them leak proof and durable. The seams are loaded by floating into them the best pure solder, making every part of the inside of the can as smooth as glass, leaving no little spaces or rough seams to collect sour milk. We have critically examined cans of this pattern from the leading can makers and have no hesitancy in claiming a better can of this pattern is not made. **Many of our customers tell us they have seen non so good. We guarantee actual capacity.**

Capacity, gallons.	5	8	10
Average weight, pounds	12½	17	18
Price, each............	**$1.50**	**$1.70**	**$1.80**

.... $40-60

Heart Patty Pans.

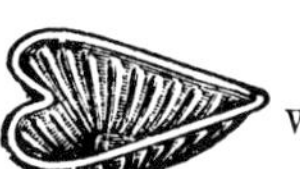

No. 23R5490 Size, 3 inches. Weight, per dozen, 6 ounces.
Price, per dozen..................**8c**

.... $6-8

Scalloped Round Patty Pans.

No. 23R5488 Deep.

Inches..................	3	4
Weight, per doz., ounces	7	9
Price, per dozen.........	**6c**	**10c**

.... $4-6

Retinned Milk Strainers.

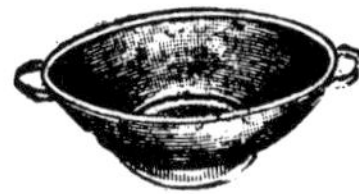

No. 23R5424 Feet fast.

Inches............	10¼	11
Weight, each, oz.	8	10¼
Price, each.......	**13c**	**15c**

.... $4-6

$9.54 Buys the NEW MODEL COAL AND WOOD PRINCESS RESERVOIR COOK STOVE.

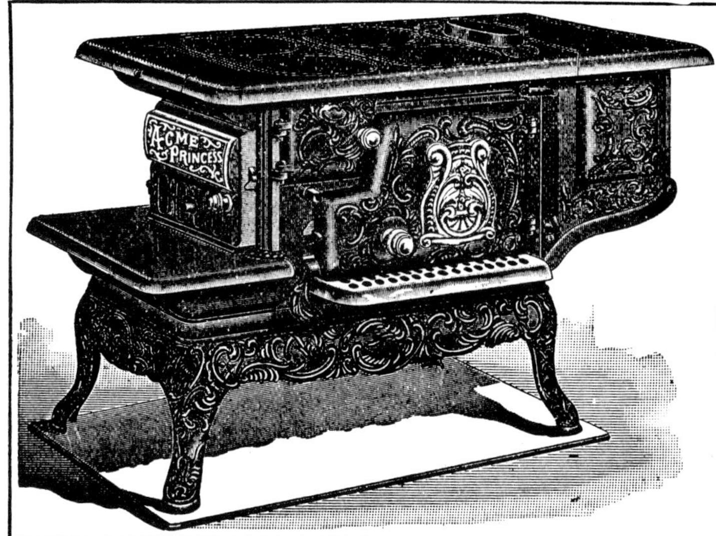

AT $9.54 in the smallest size and $10.98 in the popular 8-18 size (a big reduction from all previous quotations), we will dispose of our surplus stock of high grade Princess cook stoves. When our surplus stock is disposed of no more of these stoves can be had at the price. We would, therefore, advise you to place your order at once.

UNDERSTAND, we guarantee the stove to reach you in perfect condition and please you or we will immediately return your money, and in the years to come you can always get castings from us for repairs and at a very low cost to you.

THIS STOVE is made in our own foundry in Northern Ohio from the best material that can be procured. From the illustration, engraved from a photograph, you can form some idea of the appearance of this handsome reservoir cook stove.

THE ACME PRINCESS burns hard coal, soft coal, coke, wood or anything for fuel. It is made with very large flues, cut tops, heavy cut centers supported by post, heavy covers, heavy linings with very heavy sectional fire back; large bailed ash pan, slide hearth plate, nickeled outside oven shelf, pouch feed, oven door kicker, nickel plated panel on oven door, nickel plated door knobs, heavy tin lined oven door. When ashes are removed from under oven they are scraped into the hearth, avoiding all possibility of spilling ashes on the floor when cleaning the stove.

THE ACME PRINCESS is furnished with a lifter, shaker and scraper for removing the ashes from under the oven. It is fitted with a large porcelain lined reservoir, as shown in the illustration, and is furnished on a large handsome rococo pattern base. It has every up to date feature of every high grade reservoir cook stove, every improvement up to 1902, and is one of the best reservoir cook stoves on the market.

Until our surplus stock is disposed of we will furnish the Acme Princess in the following sizes at the special cut prices named:

PRICE LIST OF ACME PRINCESS WITH PORCELAIN LINED RESERVOIR.

Catalogue Number	Size	Size of Lids	Size of Oven, Inches	Size of Top Including Reservoir, Inches	Height, Inches	Pipe to Fit Collar, Inches	Length of Fire Box, Inches	Weight, Pounds	Price
96R1138	7-16	No. 7	16x14½x10	22x40	26½	6	16½	265	**$ 9.54**
96R1140	8-16	No. 8	16x14½x10	22x40	26½	6	16½	265	**9.59**
96R1142	8-18	No. 8	18x17 x11	24x44	28½	7	18	310	**10.98**
96R1144	9-18	No. 9	18x17 x11	24x44	28½	7	18	310	**11.05**

.... $300-900